CCCC STUDIES IN WRITING & RHETORIC
Edited by Steve Parks, University of Virginia

The aim of the CCCC Studies in Writing & Rhetoric (SWR) Series is to influence how we think about language in action and especially how writing gets taught at the college level. The methods of studies vary from the critical to historical to linguistic to ethnographic, and their authors draw on work in various fields that inform composition—including rhetoric, communication, education, discourse analysis, psychology, cultural studies, and literature. Their focuses are similarly diverse—ranging from individual writers and teachers, to work on classrooms and communities and curricula, to analyses of the social, political, and material contexts of writing and its teaching.

SWR was one of the first scholarly book series to focus on the teaching of writing. It was established in 1980 by the Conference on College Composition and Communication (CCCC) in order to promote research in the emerging field of writing studies. As our field has grown, the research sponsored by SWR has continued to articulate the commitment of CCCC to supporting the work of writing teachers as reflective practitioners and intellectuals.

We are eager to identify influential work in writing and rhetoric as it emerges. We thus ask authors to send us project proposals that clearly situate their work in the field and show how they aim to redirect our ongoing conversations about writing and its teaching. Proposals should include an overview of the project, a brief annotated table of contents, and a sample chapter. They should not exceed 10,000 words.

To submit a proposal, please register as an author at www.editorial manager.com/nctebp. Once registered, follow the steps to submit a proposal (be sure to choose SWR Book Proposal from the drop-down list of article submission types).

Recollections from an Uncommon Time

4C20 Documentarian Tales

Edited by Julie Lindquist, Bree
Straayer, and Bump Halbritter

Michigan State University

Conference on College
Composition and
Communication

National Council of
Teachers of English
www.ncte.org

The WAC
Clearinghouse
wac.colostate.edu

Staff Editor: Kurt Austin
Manuscript Editor: Don Donahue
Series Editor: Steve Parks
Interior Design: Mary Rohrer
Layout: Mike Palmquist
Cover Design: Pat Mayer
Cover Image: "Migration" by Cera (Instagram: cera_streetart) and Katie Batten (Instagram: katie__batten)

Print ISBN: 978-0-8141-3952-3; epub ISBN: 978-0-8141-0067-7; PDF ISBN: 978-0-8141-3953-0

It is the policy of NCTE in its journals and other publications to provide a forum for the open discussion of ideas concerning the content and the teaching of English and the language arts. Publicity accorded to any particular point of view does not imply endorsement by the Executive Committee, the Board of Directors, or the membership at large, except in announcements of policy, where such endorsement is clearly specified.

NCTE provides equal employment opportunity (EEO) to all staff members and applicants for employment without regard to race, color, religion, sex, national origin, age, physical, mental or perceived handicap/disability, sexual orientation including gender identity or expression, ancestry, genetic information, marital status, military status, unfavorable discharge from military service, pregnancy, citizenship status, personal appearance, matriculation or political affiliation, or any other protected status under applicable federal, state, and local laws.

Every effort has been made to provide current URLs and email addresses, but because of the rapidly changing nature of the web, some sites and addresses may no longer be accessible.

This book is copublished with the WAC Clearinghouse. It is available in open-access digital formats at wac.colostate.edu.

Library of Congress Cataloging-in-Publication Data

A catalog record of this book has been requested.

Contents

Introduction

Julie Lindquist, Bree Straayer, Bump Halbritter

CCCC 2020 AND THE DOCUMENTARIAN PROJECT

What has become this particular collection of tales was occasioned first by the 2020 CCCC Convention, and then, later, by the cancellation of it. In its original conception, it was intended to document a conference experience; in its current expression, it has become a means for Documentarians to share a common experience in this uncommon time of the COVID-19 pandemic.

The idea for the Documentarian project first came about as an expression of the CCCC 2020 theme, "Considering Our Commonplaces," which invited conference attendees to participate in conversations about the implicit values, core beliefs, and normalized practices at work in our professional community. The new role of conference Documentarian came about, specifically, as a means by which CCCC, as a professional community, might learn more about the needs and experiences of its members. We knew that the conference served a diverse array of professional people and purposes, but we wondered about how we might surface particular experiences of the conference through the stories Cs-goers might tell, if given the opportunity to articulate their plans, document their activities at the conference, and then reflect on these expectations and experiences. We suspected that everyone has an *idea* of the CCCC conference, and that everyone seems to want something from it, but— even given the post-conference surveys typically administered by CCCC staff—we didn't have a nuanced understanding of what those ideas, experiences and desires are. We wondered: what IS a CCCC conference?

If you're reading this, you probably know—or are learning—that the Conference on College Composition and Communication is the largest and most influential professional organization (among a cadre of organizations with similar disciplinary orientations) for those who work in the field of composition and rhetoric studies and who work as scholars and practitioners across institutional types in higher education.

1

Accordingly, the CCCC Annual Convention is the most well attended and most highly visible professional meeting for the field of composition and rhetoric studies and has been running, since its inaugural meeting in 1949, for over 70 years. The CCCC Wikipedia page will tell you that the annual conference typically has over 3,000 CCCC participants each year (presenters and attendees). It specifies, as well, that the conference is an itinerant affair: every year, a new city hosts the conference. The 2020 Convention was to be held in Milwaukee; the 2021 meeting—before it, too, was moved to a virtual platform—was to be in Spokane, Washington. The 2022 conference, scheduled to be held in Chicago, was also moved to a virtual platform. Conferencegoers can choose from a repertoire of activities that includes traditional panels, workshops, keynote speakers, and interest-group meetings. There are awards ceremonies for outstanding scholarly work and exemplary contributors to the profession.

From what we heard in listening sessions with our colleagues at MSU, we found, even via conversations with our students and colleagues in one institution, that our suspicion that CCCC represents a diverse professional community was affirmed. We could only imagine what kind of diversity existed on a national scale, to further complicate commonplaces about what the conference is and does, and for whom. Bump, in particular, had had some experience with the potential stakes of our commonplaces about CCCC. He recalled that the question, "What is a conference?" emerged in a particularly dramatic way for CCCC 2018 in the wake of travel advisories for people of color in Kansas City. If the conference were to be relocated or moved into virtual spaces, what all would need to be recreated? If there were no conference, what would be lost? What most needed to be preserved for the good of the Cs community? What did the conference *do* for people? What kinds of conference experiences could we imagine? It occurred to us that having a non-space-bound way of addressing problems of space and participation for CCCC could offer a benefit: each year, there were more people who wanted to participate in the conference—and get support for their participation from their home institutions—than there was space at the conference location. What if we could imagine a role that could be of service to the community that was NOT so inflexibly contingent on considerations of space, and thereby change the terms of participation in the event?

Our goal all along with the Documentarians project has been to surface a story of our field of practice via the stories of individuals working within it. Originally, when we conceived the project entitled

Recollections of a Common Place, the experience of the conference itself was the means for this larger view of who we are as a community of professional practitioners, and how we do our work.

ENTER COVID-19; EXIT CCCC 2020.

When the 2020 conference was canceled, one of the things we felt as a loss was the new Documentarian piece. How would we document an experience that . . . wasn't? When the three of us (Julie, Bree, and Bump) met for our planning meeting immediately following the decision to cancel CCCC 2020, we began commiserating about the loss of the Documentarian opportunity, as we'd had such faith in the potential of these collected stories to teach us more about common (and uncommon) experiences of our professional community. But we quickly realized that the project did not *have* to be lost—that it could be just as relevant, in some of the same ways, but also, perhaps, in different ones, in this time of COVID-19 and the profound, wide-scale disruptions to our everyday working lives. We saw that these narratives documenting a week of the pandemic—the week during which CCCC would have taken place—could not only document a period of time, but could also tell stories of learning, inclusion/exclusion, access, and professional participation—just as with the original version of the project.

Our goal in reconceiving this project has not changed; we want to make available a story of our field of practice via the experiences of its diverse practitioners. In the case of *Recollections from an Uncommon Time,* however, we do so via accounts of the shared experience of disruption in our work lives—which, as it turns out, also teaches us how deeply the terms of our work are implicated in our experiences of home, family, and everyday routines. A conference is a public-facing event relevant to our work; a pandemic returns us, abruptly and often traumatically, to private spaces relevant to that work. In this returning, we are invited—compelled even—to confront many of the commonplaces of our professional lives.

THREE READERS READING

The three of us worked closely together throughout the process of conceiving the idea for the Documentarian project, and editing the manuscript for *Recollections.* The story of our collaboration is one story the collection tells, since it, too, is a story of work routines and professional lives during the onset of the US response to COVID-19. Even as we worked in consultation (and often, in direct conversation) with each other as we made decisions about what the book would be and how it would develop, we were very much aware—especially as we read the contributions, listened to the stories they were telling, and found moments of value and resonance in them—that we were three distinct humans, each with a history, set of lived experiences, and ways of finding meaning in (and ascribing meaning to) the stories. Sometimes we were in agreement about the value of the work a piece would do for its readers and for the collection; sometimes one of us would find and be deeply compelled by resonances having to do with her or his own experiences (of home, family, work, etc.). Throughout the process, we were very much aware of reading as *these three readers;* even so, we were also aware that there are and will be readers with many other kinds of experiences very much outside the scope of our own—and these other, potential readers (so many potential readers!) were not represented by our small editorial team (a fact that one Documentarian, Shelagh Patterson, points to directly, writing: "It scares me that my thoughts through this form may become aggregated data that I have no control over: a difference between creative writing and comp-rhet narrative. I have decided we are allies, but we don't know each other well yet."). We deeply appreciate having the honor to work with the stories that Documentarians have entrusted to us, and we feel the weight of responsibility that comes with their goodwill and generosity. We come to this project with particular experiences and investments having to do with the work we do and our role in it.

In what follows, we reflect on how we came to the project and to the stories collected here.

Julie

My vision for CCCC 2020 was developed, from the very beginning, in dialogue with Bree as my student and conference assistant, and with Bump, as my long-term research partner and collaborator. As is the customary charge of program directors, I needed to define a conference theme, an idea that would frame the experience as a whole, and serve as a heuristic for the contributions of convention participants. Bump and I had often remarked on how, as WPAs, we were compelled, in managing the everyday predicaments addressed to us by our teaching colleagues, to confront the truth that often the most deeply held values and practice of teachers were both responsible for sustaining and thwarting their best efforts. From this observation—that enduring teaching principles and traditions of practice were not only responsible for thinking productively about teaching and learning, but also that these commonplaces could be *unproductively* durable—came the idea for the conference theme, "Considering Our Commonplaces." This was to be not so much a topical theme as a kind of invitation for reflection.

Accordingly, one of my goals for the conference—the most important one, to my mind—was to create a learning experience: a pedagogical event. I was hoping that the learning would happen for conferencegoers in their interactions with others, but also that we could surface stories and experiences that may otherwise be unavailable to the organization itself, to help it learn how it might do a better job of supporting education-related professional activities. This would be one way, I thought, for us as a professional community to consider our commonplaces. Bump and I had written about an approach to story-based learning that was very much in alignment with life history approaches, one that put methods of documentation and reflection to work to scaffold occasions for discovery via narrative inquiry. In fact, our first-year writing curriculum at Michigan State was (and is) an expression of this model of teaching and learning; it asks students to "preflect" on their plans and expectations for learning: to collect not only the drafts they submit for grading, but all of the exploratory drafts, peer-review work (given and received), instructor feedback, and process reflections. This archive of their previous writing activities and products serves as the corpus by which, in their final reflections, they identify their strengths as writers, lessons they have learned, and goals to direct their ongoing development. Their *preflective* works help them *pre*pare to *re*flect (Halbritter and Lindquist, "Collecting and Coding," "It's Never about What It's About," "Witness Learning,"; Lindquist and Halbritter, "Documenting and Discovering Learning").

When we learned from Cheryl Caesar, our colleague at MSU, about the Community Writing Conference Documentarian, we imagined that the concept could have uses in making visible the multiple, varied stories of the CCCC experiences, and that the scene of the conference itself could be another scene of our curriculum of narrative inquiry. I was terrifically excited to see what stories this role would surface and to find out what we would learn about our colleagues across the field from them by way of their stories. In late February, the idea that the conference could be *cancelled* was remote, abstract, unthinkable. On March 1, alarmed by the news I was seeing about the virus and the conversations on social media that were developing in response to it, I wrote to my fellow CCCC officers with an alert and a question: the coronavirus situation seems to need our attention: should we talk? On March 2, we met with the NCTE executive director, reviewed what information we had about the situation so far, and approved a plan to go forward with the conference. By the second week of March, that possibility had morphed into a very different, much more ominous shape. And when, on March 11, we met as an Executive Committee to vote on whether to cancel the conference, that decision was inevitable, imperative, and unanimous. On March 12, members received notification that the conference had been cancelled. At that time, when the news had to be shared with the Cs community, the damages to the financial stability of the organization assessed, and plans for alternative means of sharing made, there was no time to indulge any experience, or to embark on any project, of grief. That particular agenda item could not, as it turned out, be permitted to rise to the level of priority. It was only later, when the most urgent business of following up on our decision to cancel 4C20 had been mostly accomplished, did I begin to confront what the loss of that event meant to me, the Program Chair. A moment of reckoning came with the first Documentarian survey on the morning of what would have been the first day of the conference, a day when we were to have met the members of the new Documentarian community at a reception that evening at the Milwaukee Hilton. I recall that the explicit invitation to reflect on the experience of that day the survey extended was a moment of turning to look that grief squarely in the face, and to begin the long, and ongoing, process of taking stock, feeling, healing. After the years of conceiving and thinking and planning that came to an abrupt halt on March 11, 2020, I should have been expecting that very thing. I'm pretty sure that it speaks to the level of enabling deferral I had been managing in the weeks prior.

Bree

As a PhD student on the job market, I was keenly aware of the sometimes disorienting project of navigating the CCCC conference; so in my role as assistant, I wanted to make visible those hidden stories of entering a new field and/or residing on its margins. The Documentarian project made space for those stories to emerge, and with the print and digital publications, those stories would also have a platform to be heard by the field more broadly. Then the whole world itself became disorienting with the onset of COVID-19. The same curiosity resided in us as a team: how do we as individuals, educators, researchers, and students navigate this new space in our worlds, particularly as work becomes more acutely intertwined with home? In many ways, we thought the new version of the project might end up being even more insightful as individuals not only reflected on the loss of the conference, but also documented the pivoting taking place as their professional lives were upended.

On a personal level (where many of the stories in this collection reside), home and place became a theme that had a profound impact on my experience, and on my subsequent investment in this collection of stories. With my three teenage children, I had to move to a temporary place to live because my former home had people at high risk. We were generously welcomed in this new place, but it was challenging to meet the needs of my family while moving our entire lives, vocations, and school experiences to a home that was not our home. We were guests in a place that was new, in a world that was new. In addition, the uncertainty of the job market made it unclear the length of this temporary displacement as weeks stretched into months. Completing my dissertation felt peripheral as the crisis unfolded all around us. Questions and uncertainty kept me awake at night. How will I make enough money to support four people if hiring is put on hold? Where will we live? And then the guilt of those questions surfaced, especially when weighed against other larger ones. Will people we love become sick? How many people will die?

I include this tiny excerpt from my personal experience to make clear the lens with which I approached the project and the stories in this collection. In my own way, I also hope to honor the vulnerability the participants offer by offering it myself. This collection and the Documentarian experience was at times a comfort for me. I appreciated the daily structured space for sensemaking in the surveys. When I read the daily survey excerpts from others, I found I was not alone with my personal and professional life blending together in ways that offered both hardship and opportunity. Others were scared and hopeful. Others were in new spaces and appreciating the home they had. People worried about their students and questioned our definitions of productivity. The project in many ways revealed that we cared about the work we do and how our lives move in meaningful and intentional ways in both our personal and professional lives.

Bump

Throughout the long process of 4C20 planning, I was pretty much *behind-the-scenes guy*. As Julie's long-term research partner, I had grown used to tackling most of each of our professional responsibilities and opportunities, to some extent, together. 4C20 was no different. I had just finished a 3-year term on the CCCC Executive Committee, and I was excited to leverage that experience to help brainstorm possibilities for the conference (and even happier to not have to do the heavy lifting of planning them!). However, the Documentarian project was truly a thing that, while suggested from something that happened at another conference, was reimagined by way of our work over the years: first by way of our LiteracyCorps Michigan documentary project (Halbritter and Lindquist, "Sleight of Ear" and "Time, Lives, and Videotape") and then by way of its pedagogical adaptation: Experiential-Learning Documentary (Halbritter and Lindquist, "It's Never about What It's About"; Lindquist and Halbritter, "Documenting and Discovering").

When we lost the conference, I remember sitting in Julie's office (now my office—where I sit writing this reflection) commiserating with Julie and Bree the consequent loss of the Documentarian project. I recall one of us saying how we wished we could still do it, and then Bree saying, "Well, why don't we?" We may have lost the conference, but we still had the infrastructure—that we had designed and built—to do it. We had a team of Documentarian volunteers. This was no pipe dream. This could happen. In quick succession, 1) we reimagined the role to document our shared experiences of the days that would have been spent at the conference—days that would also be the first days of the US response to COVID-19, 2) we revised our daily surveys to facilitate our documentation, 3) we resituated our common place(s) to be our homes as we sheltered in place, and 4) we reconnected with SWR to see if they may be willing to work with us to publish the reborn project.

They were!

It all re-happened so fast. "What *is* a conference experience?" became "What *is* a non-conference experience in the first days of the US response to COVID-19?" Little did we know, the global COVID-19 pandemic would be only the first of the shared crises to impact the lifecycle of our project and the emotional and social conditions of our reflecting on it.

In retrospect, we were lucky.

It seems wrong to say that given all that has happened since that day in March 2020. Nothing about this virus, the social unrest, or the economic crisis that has erupted in its wake has been lucky. The losses we have sustained world-wide, individually and collectively, have been terrible. Nothing about the conditions of the times could be construed as having to do with "luck."

However, *we*—Julie, Bree, and I—were lucky. We just happened to have a tool—an infrastructure that we had created—for documenting the experiences of our colleagues at a time when an unprecedented set of experiences were beginning to unfold. In documentary-speak, we just happened to have our cameras out and rolling as the new storms began to roll in. In that sense, we were lucky. We were lucky, too, to have each other—trusted partners and colleagues who had been working together for many years and who have, together, faced previous challenges and pursued previous opportunities. Together, this new crazy thing seemed possible for the three of us to pursue. We were especially lucky to have a diverse cohort of Documentarians who had the courage and the goodwill to document and share their experiences of this wholly uncommon time. We were lucky to have SWR—and series editor, Steve Parks, in particular—share our enthusiasm for both designs of the project.

We were lucky. I was lucky. I *am* lucky. This project has turned into some of the most rewarding work of my career. I ended my Documentarian Post-Reflection on Sunday, April 4, 2020, with these words:

> I hope that others have enjoyed and profited from this work as much as I have. I doubt that anyone could have had a more rewarding experience from it than I have.
>
> It has buoyed my leaden heart. It has kept me tethered in a time when I have felt unmoored. It has connected me during a time of isolation. It has helped me see productivity in disruption.
>
> It has helped me search for, discover, and name hope.
>
> Inquiry, Discovery, and Communication.
>
> That might could become a thing. :)

I am lucky. I hope that the Documentarian Tales in this collection and its larger electronic counterpart will help readers and researchers feel lucky to have access to these accounts of the experiences of their peers during these most unprecedented times.

THE WORLD AROUND US: A TIMELINE

Since we put out the call, and since the time during which 4C20 was scheduled to happen, much has happened—and continues to happen—in the world. When we put out the revised CFP in early spring 2020, the over-determining national event was the spread of the COVID-19 pandemic. By the beginning of summer 2020, we were witnessing a historic shift in the national conversation about race relations.

At the time of the final revising of this Introduction (the first weeks of February, 2021), it is already hard to remember how we got here—what we learned and when we learned it. So much happened in 2020, it can be difficult to remember versions of ourselves who did not, yet, know what we know now. Consequently, the Documentarian Tales in this collection may seem . . . *naive* . . . to readers who encounter them in 2021 or later. But neither these stories nor their authors are or were naive. We encourage readers to regard these tales as *nascent*, collected and recollected during the first months of the global CO-VID-19 pandemic, protests for racial justice in the US, and the 2020 US presidential campaign. As these tales were being drafted, the systematic dismantling of the US Postal Service was not yet being called into question, the election had not yet happened—or, rather, had not yet begun happening, the legal challenges to the election results had not yet ensued, the US Capitol had not yet been the scene of an act of domestic insurgency, and no president of the United States had yet been twice impeached. Nor can I imagine that any of us could have realistically expected that two months into the new year would find us with more than 27 million COVID-19 infections, nearly half-a-million COVID-19 deaths in the US, and daily COVID-19 death tolls that would surpass 4,000 US citizens. Back in the spring of 2020, few of us could foresee how dramatically 2021 would come in like a lion.

But, in, like a lion, it came.

Furthermore, the slew of things that will undoubtedly happen later this week, and next week, and the next, had not yet happened and were not yet informing the recollections and the voices of the Documentarians in this collection. However, they *are* informing us, now, as we read these stories. The former selves who wrote the tales in this collection were, as were all of our former selves during that time, *coming to know* what we now know. We were learning. The stories of *Recollections from an Uncommon Time: 4C20 Documentarian Tales* give us a window into that learning in progress. With hope, they will provide a window into yours, as well.

And yet, it can be hard to unknow what we now know. In Table 1, we provide an incomplete sketch of happenings during the window of time that Documentarians were carrying out the work that would become this collection. The left-hand column indicates early- or late-month markers. The center column contains relevant developments in Documentarian duties that correspond to the time markers in the left-hand column. The right-hand column contains a vastly incomplete record of world and national events (especially those related to the unfolding COVID-19 pandemic and demonstrations of racial unrest in the US) that coincided with the Documentarian duties listed in the center column. We have shaded the four rows from late April through early June to highlight the active drafting time for Documentarians. These events are compiled to help readers place events that may have been (or were not yet) informing the Documentarian Tales in this collection.

Table 1: Dates for national and world events pulled from public news records: COVID-19, George Floyd, and Breonna Taylor timelines

Month	Documentarian Timeline	World/US National Events
Late Dec. 2019	**Dec. 23:** Documentarians are invited to do introductory survey and instructional module.	**Dec. 31:** First Cases of COVID-19 in Wuhan, China, reported.
Early Jan. 2020	**Jan 6:** Training Module and introductory survey completed by those who would have a role as Documentarians at 4C20.	**Jan. 11:** First COVID-19 death reported from Wuhan, China.
Late Jan.		**Jan 30:** World Health Organization (W.H.O.) declares global health emergency. **Jan 31:** Travel from China to US suspended (by this date, 213 people had died and nearly 9,800 had been infected worldwide)

Month	Documentarian Timeline	World/US National Events
Early Feb.		**Feb 11:** W.H.O. names the disease COVID-19.
Late Feb.	**Feb 25:** CCCC 2020 online program published announcing names of Documentarians.	**Feb 23:** Italy becomes a CO-VID-19 hotspot. **Feb 29:** US reports its first CO-VID-19 death.
Early March	**March 2:** CCCC Officers meet with NCTE Executive Director to assess coronavirus threat for CCCC2020. **March 11:** CCCC Executive Committee meets, decides to cancel 2020 convention. **March 12:** Notification to CCCC community that 4C 20 would be cancelled.	**March 13:** Trump Administration declares national emergency. **March 13:** Breonna Taylor is killed in Louisville, Kentucky. **March 15:** C.DC recommends no gatherings of more than 50 people.
Late March	**March 20:** Notification to CCCC community about revised Documentarian opportunity and forthcoming CFP. **Tuesday, March 24–Saturday, March 28, 2020:** Five Days of 4C20. **Wednesday, March 25–Saturday, March 28:** 8 Conference Surveys	**March 26:** US becomes world leader in new cases. **March 30:** Stay-at-home directives become widespread in US
Early April	**Sunday, April 5:** Post-Conference Reflection due. **April 10:** Initial Survey Data released to Documentarians.	**April 2:** 6.6 million Americans apply for unemployment.
Late April	**April 20:** Call for Documentarian Tales.	**April 17:** Armed Protests against state restrictions in Michigan, Minnesota, and Ohio. **April 26:** Global death toll surpasses 200k; COVID-19 Task Force stops delivering daily briefings. **April 27:** Wrongful death suit filed in shooting death of Breonna Taylor. **April 30:** Airlines require facemasks.

Month	Documentarian Timeline	World/US National Events
Early May	Documentarians are drafting their Documentarian Tales.	
Late May	Documentarians are drafting their Documentarian Tales.	**Monday, May 25:** George Floyd is killed in Minneapolis, MN.
Late May	Documentarians are drafting their Documentarian Tales.	**May 26:** Protests erupt in Minneapolis and other cities. **May 27:** US COVID-19 deaths surpass 100k **May 28:** National Guard mobilized in Minneapolis. **May 31:** President sequesters in White House bunker as DC protests turn violent.
Early June	**Monday, June 8:** First drafts of Documentarian Tales are due.	**June 1:** Two autopsies rule George Floyd's death a homicide. **June 1:** Peaceful protesters teargassed for President's public statement at St. John's Church. **June 3:** Officers charged in George Floyd's death. **June 5:** #SayHerName campaign is launched in honor of what would have been Breonna Taylor's 26th birthday. **June 5:** DC mayor orders "Black Lives Matter" painted on 16th Street, adjacent to the White House. Mayor renames this section of 16th Street, "Black Lives Matter Plaza."
Late June		**June 19:** Juneteenth protests **May 26 - June 30:** *NY Times* reports tens of millions self-report protest participation in response to George Floyd's killing.
Early July	**Mid July:** Communication to Documentarians about decisions for this (print) volume.	**July 6:** Trump Administration withdraws from W.H.O. as US COVID-19 death toll surpasses 130k. **July 10:** New COVID-19 cases set record highs for 11 consecutive days.
Late July	**Saturday, August, 14th:** Revised drafts of Documentarian Tales are due.	

On a smaller scale (and yet, one that often can feel global, from the perspectives of academics), the world of higher education was in a time of unprecedented crisis management—triage—as colleges and universities struggled to make decisions about campus re-openings and instructional modes. This, too, was happening in the background as we worked through the stages of developing this manuscript. In the course of our work together on this project—developing the Documentarian concept, creating surveys, crafting the call(s) for papers, collecting submissions, reading and curating narratives, communicating with contributors, and writing the introductory material—we noticed a particular arc of production, productivity, interruption, and frustration. In spring 2020, when we were composing the revised CFP, building the surveys, reading the surveys, and making sense of what we were seeing and hearing, we met frequently—once or twice a week—to project, collect, and reflect on what was emerging in the work before us. Later in the summer, as we were pressed to plan for fall semester 2020 against the shifting landscape of the response of higher-ed (and our home institution) to the COVID-19 threat, our work routines shifted. It became more and more difficult to sustain the regular work routines we had established at the start of the lockdown (which, at first, promised to have very different affordances of time). By early fall, we found ourselves working in fits and starts, our project routines undercut by the persistent mundane interruptions of crisis management. We imagine that our experiences of crisis and time management during the fall of 2020 are not unfamiliar to you or to the authors in this collection.

In fact, a focus on lamenting professional "productivity" emerges across several of the Documentarian Tales of this collection. In the eight daily surveys that spanned Wednesday, March 25, through Saturday, March 28, Documentarians were asked in the mornings, "What do you hope to accomplish today?" and in the evenings, "What did you accomplish [today]?" It becomes clear that many Documentarians took these questions to be primarily asking for reports on professional productivity.

For example, Maggie Christensen, in Chapter 15, "Documenting Our Solastalgia: A New Landscape," wrestles with discussing accomplishments that would not be "quantifiable" on a CV:

> On Saturday evening during 4C's week, in response to the question "What did you accomplish?" I wrote:

For the fourth day in a row, this question nags at me—as if I must always be able to list my accomplishments, like a line on the cv. Earlier in the week I took great comfort in this question: it reminded me to take stock of all that I am doing amidst all the uncertainty and fretting. Today—perhaps because it's Saturday—the question feels more like a weight: what if my accomplishments today were not quantifiable? I curled my elderly mother's hair for her and rubbed lotion on her dry feet; I gave my daughter some respite from her busy 3-year-old; I reassured a student that she would be okay in her comp class.

In my fatigue from Saturday evening's writing, I wondered if I was doing enough.

In Chapter 14, "Growing up Again (and Again)," Shauna Chung reveals her shock at encountering a former version of herself in her responses to the daily surveys.

> Revisiting my answers to the survey questions—e.g., what do you hope to accomplish today, what emotions are invoked by your reflections, describe the scene around you, etc.—I read another unrecognizable version of myself. Who was this person calling a "walk in the sunlight" an "accomplishment"? She expressed feelings of gratitude for the opportunity to "tune my ears more intentionally to those around me." She even described and reveled in the sound of people snoring in the next room, the familiar scent of floral shampoo, the buzz of a light as she sat at a desk in her childhood room to write about the mundane moments of her day.

Across the Documentarian Tales in this collection, we can find and follow bread-crumb trails of authors' journeys to learn about the commonplaces of their work lives and their relationships to and understandings of those commonplaces. We imagine that readers of this collection will find and follow these and other bread-crumb trails of learning in progress. We are hopeful that these will help readers, too, find and follow bread-crumb trails of their own.

PROJECT DETAILS: BECOMING A DOCUMENTARIAN

Although we found ourselves in a position to capture an uncommon moment, a significant amount of planning and project development led up to that moment. When we initially recruited for the project through the conference CFP, contact with caucuses, and personal invitations, we had 323 people interested in participating. To indicate continued interest in inclusion on the program, participants needed to complete an online informational module, which 146 people completed. In addition, those individuals agreed to complete the following project components:

1. Attend the convention
2. Choose a path through the convention experience and record some observations about the things you see and hear
3. Complete morning and evening daily surveys during the conference about your intentions for each day and reflection on your experiences
4. Potentially attend a Documentarian reception during the conference
5. After the convention, compose a reflective narrative about your experiences (prompt given).

Once the conference was canceled and the Documentarian role was revised, we sent out a renewed call for participation to all who had expressed interest previously, and 171 people signed up. Figures 1 through 5 show charts indicating the self-identified demographics of those who expressed interest in the revised version of the project.

We asked participants to share their gender, disability status, race/ethnicity, professional status, and level of conference experience. The language of these demographic questions followed that of demographic inquiries from the CCCC organization itself. In looking at professional status and conference attendance, we see that the participants were predominantly graduate students and non-tenure-track faculty. In many ways, we had hoped to hear the more hidden stories of the conference, so we were encouraged to see so many community members from marginalized professional statuses sign up. We also noticed that a substantial number of the participants had either never attended the conference or had only attended one previous time (Figure 2). These fresh encounters with the conference were also what we hoped to hear.

We had hoped to hear from a broad diversity of voices from the field; however, we found that the majority of those who participated in the surveys were white women (Figures 3 and 4). In some ways, this body does represent the overall demographics in our field, but the gender and race/ethnicity demographics became especially important as we engaged in the editorial process. We found that we did not always have a diverse range (in the available set) from which to select.

Current Professional Status
109 responses

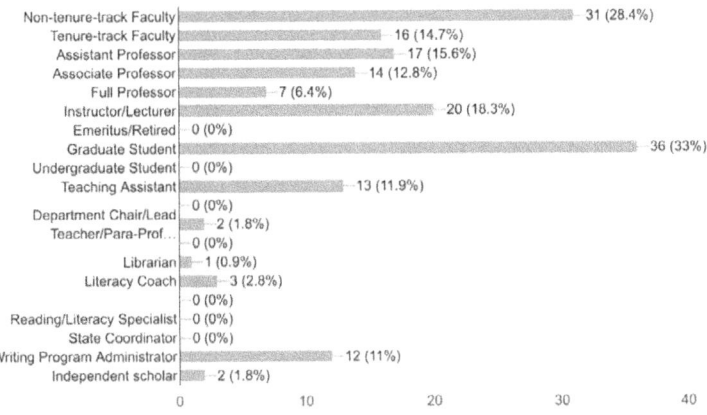

Figure 1. Current professional status

How many times have you attended CCCC?
108 responses

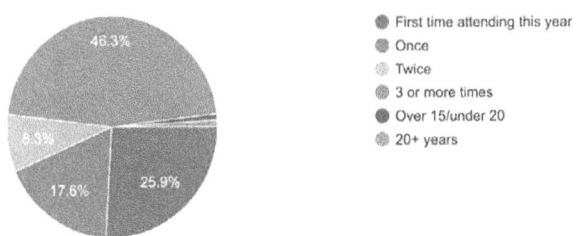

Figure 2. How many times have you attended CCCC?

Race/Ethnicity
108 responses

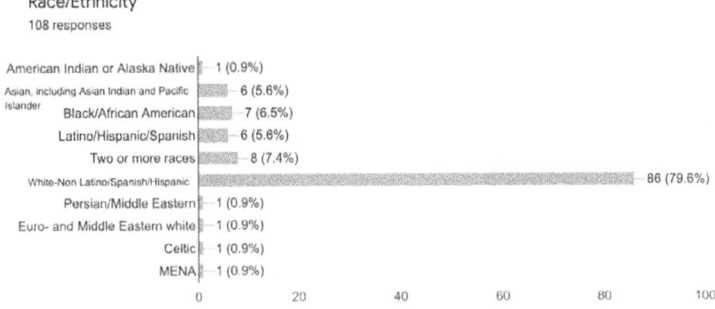

Figure 3. Race/ethnicity

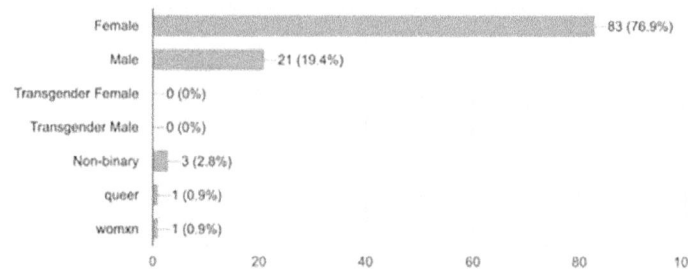

Figure 4. Gender identity

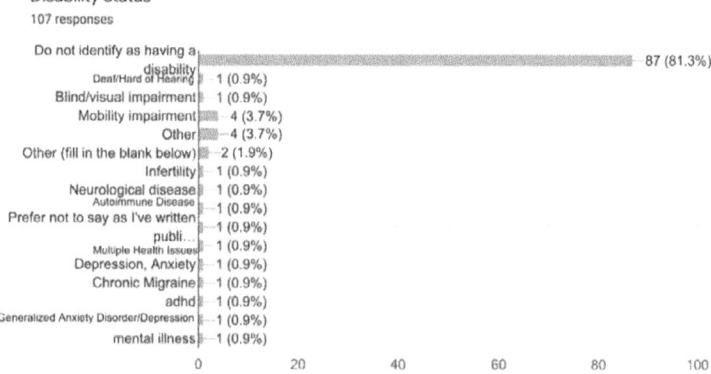

Figure 5. Disability status

In particular, we received few submissions from writers who identify as male, and especially few from R1 institutions. In fact, we did not have a single paper submitted from a tenure-line, male faculty member at an R1 institution. We are left to ask, why? We wonder if the idea of "serving" as a Documentarian was not particularly attractive, if the labor of the position and/or the investment in training seemed too demanding, if the newness of the role made it seem too risky, not legitimate enough, too hard to justify on a CV. We hope that, in future iterations of the Documentarian role, that more male-identified Documentarians from across the diverse reaches of our field will volunteer to serve in the role.

When we initially inquired about disability status (Figure 5), we considered the ways this might impact navigating conference and social spaces. When the conference was canceled, space and place took on a whole new dimension with people no longer navigating a new city or location, but instead navigating intensely familiar home spaces but with new work demands imposed upon those spaces. Some challenges gave way to others as those with underlying illnesses or disabilities expressed concern over the danger of the COVID-19 illness. Anxiety and depression took on new shades as isolation grew. Many expressed challenges within the narratives they wrote that did not necessarily show up in the demographic identification.

The overall demographics of the project provoked us to consider Documentarians' motivations for participation as well as how this group of people represented our field. Who was missing? Why? Was it the design of the project itself that appealed to particular people? Did this initial group offer some insight into labor conditions, participation, and voice in our field? Many of the Documentarians in the collection write about their professional roles and working conditions in a professionally diverse—and not always equitable—field. We believe that the matter of how the invitation was taken up, and by whom, surfaces this story, as well.

WRITING AS ARCHIVING, EDITING AS CURATION

The Documentarian Tales collected here began their lives as responses to four sets of daily (morning and evening) surveys sent out to all who wished to participate as Documentarians 2020 (pandemic version[1]). We designed the surveys that Documentarians would complete to serve three purposes: 1) to provide writing prompts for the authors themselves, 2) to amass an archive of each Documentarian's evolving experiences, and 3) to offer a means for Documentarians to share an experience during the days when CCCC 2020 would have taken place. In that they are records of a kind of shared experience and of a particular moment, the surveys *were* our convention. A foundational premise of the Documentarian project all along has been that when we each go to the same convention, we each come away from a common place with a unique (even uncommon) conference experience; similarly, we assume that we have each had a unique experience in writing individual responses to the same survey prompts.

We designed our surveys both to define a shared experience and to document one. And we were confident that those documents would have things to teach us, each and all. For these reasons, we have named

---

1   Actual Participants in daily surveys: Wednesday 110, Thursday 109, Friday 107, Saturday 85 (some did not plan to attend this day).

the particular sort of reflective writing that is produced by acts and archives of documentation *Experiential-Learning Documentary* (ELD), in keeping with a term Bump and Julie had created to describe the acts and resulting products of students' reflections on the archives of their learning experiences ("It's Never About What It's About: Audio-Visual Writing, Experiential-Learning Documentary, and the Forensic Art of Assessment"). As part of their writing processes, Documentarians returned, in late April through early June, to their experiences of the span of time from March 25 through 28 via their documented survey responses, in order for their current selves to learn from interactions with those documents created by their former selves. In fact, the title of this collection, *Recollections from an Uncommon Time,* arises from acts of documentation: collecting observations, and then re-collecting storyable information from that archive. We find, in reading these collected Documentarian Tales (ELDs), that there is a diverse range of ways acts of documentation show up in the finished narratives: some make specific reference to survey texts—jottings of the moment—and some are more mediated, operating at a greater remove from the original acts of documentation that informed them. We suspect that, were the authors collected here to return to the writing produced by the original surveys *now*, rather different stories would emerge from reflections on those same survey responses.

So it goes with documentation and reflection.

So it goes with present and former selves.

Our first step, after the surveys were completed, was to take stock and to reflect back to Documentarians what was showing up so far. We did some reading and reviewing around and across all the responses to observe common trends and themes. We collected a sample of responses to be shared with Documentarians (along with a list of the most frequently occurring words) so they could begin to see the kinds of topics, concerns, and experiences that were being expressed and taken up and so that they could begin to imagine what kinds of stories that "data" such as these may suggest. When we did a scan for the most frequently occurring words (as indicators of thematic threads) across all the survey responses, we found the most frequently occurring words to be *work, time,* and *students.* Among words for emotions, *hope* showed up most often.

One of our first editorial tasks, after reading each of the submissions we received in early June, was to make decisions about which would go into the print version and which would be included in the digital-only collection. We asked ourselves: what would inform these choices? Our first priority was to choose a set of narratives that we thought rendered diverse experiences of pandemic work lives. This diversity expressed differences in embodiment and identity (e.g., race, gender, and sexual orientation) and in institutional positions, labor conditions, and kinds of work. We are not, as a field represented by CCCC membership, overdetermined by positions of high prestige and visibility in Research 1 institutions. Most of us, in fact, are teachers working under rather more precarious labor positions; many of us are graduate students looking ahead to an unstable job market. We saw that the new Documentarian role for CCCC was taken up mostly by people who were not, or not yet, in positions of high prestige and visibility in our field; accordingly, the CFP for *Recollections* drew authors whose stories of work experience and professional lives were not likely to be those most available, in published accounts, to the Cs community.

We also found ourselves drawn, for the purposes of this collection, to narratives that demonstrated that reflection is ongoing. Reflection is no static noun; it is a progression that emerges, always, as the product of a present progressive verb. Similarly, we found that many of these tales, as narratives that began their lives as records of experiences documented in real time, often came to us without a clear destination (or "lesson") in evidence at the onset. We saw this quality of unfinished-ness—of becoming—to be a virtue in rendering the uncertainty and disorientation of life during the early days of the pandemic.

Some of the pieces describe what the authors would have done had the 2020 convention gone on as planned. These stories teach us not only what many of those in our community *do* at the conference, but also what the CCCC convention means to them in their lives—one of the things we most hoped to learn in the original Documentarian project. We learn what Cs goers (or Cs didn't-get-to-goers) feel they're missing from their professional lives in the absence of a F2F meeting, often via reflections on other mundane activities.

THEMATIC RESONANCES: WORK LIFE AND LIFE WORK

As you read through the collected Documentarian Tales, you will notice a pattern of themes: for example, labor, home, family, work routines, community identity, precarity, access, aspirations. Many of the authors in this collection reflect on the experience of documenting and reflecting on their experiences as a writing practice that can be (among other things) difficult, vexing, enlightening, sobering, and/ or therapeutic. These thematic resonances are not surprising given the nature of the writing task and authors' everyday concerns, but they are also products, and expressions, of a particular historic moment. In our CFP, we wrote:

> Of course, we recognize that this is not just any uncommon time. It's a time of a dangerous pandemic that is unprecedented in our lifetimes. By the time this is published—possibly by the time you get this—some of us may be sick. Many of us will know somebody who is, or has been, sick. The stakes will have grown higher, the situation, more dire. To make sense of that (future) moment, we will likely return to the stories of this earlier moment. In sharing the experiences of having our practices and routines upended when COVID-19 hit, we may find that we are in different phases of this experience, different positions in relationship to it. Each story is a radically generative partiality: our collective stories are a way to map that experience in time, as well as across place.

As we reread these tales, we see that they are, in fact, products of a very specific moment in pandemic time, in the lifespan of a lockdown (lock, unlock, relock, rinse, repeat). As we finalize our preparations to release this collection, one year into the pandemic, these tales, grown from a set of inquiries in March 2020, speak to the novelty of the pandemic world—of a nascent new world, yet to be formed in its new set of expectations, reconciliations, hopes, and routines. At this moment, these would be different stories: they would surface new work routines, accommodations to a new relationship between home and work life.

In fact, another story these collected stories tell is one of a very particular moment in time and of the changes that have come with time elapsed.

ACCESSING THE ARCHIVE

Though *Recollections from an Uncommon Time* is an edited collection, the Documentarian Tales collected here are more curated than edited. And while the collection is published by an academic press (CCCC/ NCTE), the mission of this project is one that challenges (in the spirit of the 2020 conference theme) our commonplaces about scholarly editing. Even as the authors have contributed their ELDs, we, the editors, have curated them *as* ELDs. For example, an art museum may curate existing works of art from a sculptor (e.g., Rodin) or a group of sculptors (e.g., those from a specific period who worked in steel). Those artists (should they still be alive) would likely not present drafts of their sculptures. They would contribute finished sculptures. The curators of those works would not send the sculptures back with a list of requests for their revision that would make those works conform to their own ideas of the experience that they hope the exhibit would create for those who may attend the exhibit. They would work with the art as it was submitted/collected. They would curate these works—assemble them—not edit or modify them. In this way, our editing more closely resembles a form of curation. As individual Documentarian Tales, we have aimed to present these works, essentially, as is, working with each Documentarian in the print collection to adhere, primarily, to a maximum word count that would allow us to include as many individual Documentarian Tales as our finite number of paper pages would permit. As a collection, we have aimed to present not what we have determined *should* be the story of our work or perspective or sensibility or ethical commitment (those that get it, somehow, "right"), but rather the story/stories that the evidence they offer suggests. What *was* our work during the first weeks of the US response to the global pandemic? What did *we* experience?

The tales collected here might not reveal the learning until the end. Expect to have some of the tales resonate with your experiences and others to depict a process of sensemaking that might not align with your own. Some of the tales, and the learning they depict, are still in process—they're still happening. All of this is to say that this collection of Documentarian Tales might challenge your sensibilities . . . it might not fall together quite how you expect or even how you hope it may. But, really—given its mission, its diverse sites of origin and diverse authorship—how could it? We ask you to take a moment, read, and listen to each other.

In and across these tales, you'll discover many themes, many stories. If you're a student reading this book in order to learn about forms of work and professional lives in writing studies, you can read these Documentarian Tales in relation to a capacious landscape of ideas, with pathways defined by experiences of productivity, precarity, loss, grief, attentionality, reflection, anxiety, dread, disruption, trauma, hope, joy, crisis, resilience, connection, isolation, solitude, race, gender, reconciliation, participation, mundanity, curation, routines, mentorship, identity, self, observation, stress, process, community, perception, purpose, resilience, memory, access, space, learning, disjuncture, mindfulness, holism, time, work, students, privilege, risk, belonging, environment, dislocation, exile, faith, stasis, chaos, uncertainty, story, shame, home, patience, family, survival, inclusion, adaptation (to name a few). Insofar as these are tales of everyday life, you will see multiple planes of meaning, multiple threads and relevancies. We think that one of the lessons of the collection as a whole is just how much meaning, how much "aboutness" that extends into the project of understanding our work as writers and educators, is encoded in the mundane details of experience. Another is the value of reflective writing, something all the authors address implicitly, some of them directly.

In many ways, we struggled over how to create a story arc of these chapters as a collection. The collection seemed to resist that sort of linearity and neatness. We came to realize that a story of diversity is just that, and we came to realize that each reader of such a collection would interpret and prioritize the stories according to their own sensibilities and experiences. We encourage you, as a reader, to do just this—to feel free to chart a course through the collected tales that suits your inclinations, your present needs, and your habits of reading. That said, we understand that most readers are inclined to begin at the beginning of a collection, and to make their way through it in a more or less linear fashion. Because paper pages demand both priority and linearity, we've ordered the pieces in such a way to give attention to particular moments of encounter, or points of contact, as each reader makes their way through the collection: first, the experience of entering the world of these tales; next, that of moving from one Documentarian Tale to the next; and finally, that of concluding the reading journey. We begin, therefore, with Adrienne Jankens' piece as a point of departure; Jankens speaks directly to the fact of the cancellation of the 2020 conference, and the sudden shift in plans that this disruption occasioned. Accordingly, we end with Rachel Panton's call for reflection and mindfulness as an ongoing practice of learning, healing, and self-care. The pieces that lie between these two points are organized in what you might think of as a braided, or enchained fashion, each one treating the adjacent pieces as present interlocutors, proximity to which offers additional framing and context for what follows and precedes. You might think of the authors in this collection as seated around the table at a dinner party, at which each guest may be in most frequent conversation with those seated on either side, but which conversation across and around the table is also possible.

And with that, let's meet our dinner companions.

In "A Sweet Spot, a Safe Space," **Adrienne Jankens** writes, "I realized, as I took notes during the week that we didn't go to Milwaukee, that the conference had become part of an annual restorative pause for me, sometimes in the midst of deep personal pain. The work of conference preparation aside, the experience itself was a retreat into safe being." Jankens begins her tale looking at the ways CCCC has offered that safe pause. She then goes on to reveal a complicated set of conditions of relative safety in the spaces of her life during the pandemic—safe in that the spaces function as scenes for the acts they contain, not that they are in some way inherently safe spaces.

In "Other Disseminations," **Erika Luckert** invites reflections on what it means to relinquish attachments to the usual routines and desires for productivity and control and to embrace, instead, an ethic of patience. "Other Disseminations" considers the life-cycle of the pandemic and the thorny yet unpredictable effects it yields through the lens of the author's garden. Luckert wonders, "What is the mortality rate of tomatoes, collard greens, peppers, and kale? I can't find any projections, nobody online seems to know. I figure seven seeds, or maybe nine, should yield a healthy plant or two."

In "Seeking Shelter in the Eye: What We Can Get out of the Storm," international graduate student **Xiao Tan** chronicles her search for truths during the earliest days of the COVID-19 pandemic—from early reports coming out of China and through the reports in US media outlets (and the very real consequences these reports had for her in her daily interactions in the US). Tan writes, "Having access to both the Chinese and English media puts me at a unique nexus of opposing viewpoints and ideologies. It also gives me a jarring feeling to see the vicious accusation of China downplaying the severity of the disease when all I heard from the Chinese media in January and February was how dangerous it was." Tan finds that reflecting during this uncommon time offers clarity by way of exposing disrupted commonplaces. She writes, "I hesitate to see the pandemic as an 'opportunity' in the usually positive sense because I wish so badly that we would learn about ourselves and the world in a less traumatic and devastating way.

But a crisis of this scale forces us to detach ourselves from the daily messiness and to reassess the status quo."

Nancy Henaku, an international graduate student, shares the effects and affects of her experiences of sheltering in place in the US during the time that was to have offered access to her first-ever CCCC experiences. In "Navigating the Ph.D., and Everything Else, in a Pandemic: Reflections on my New and Not-So-New Experiences," Henaku writes, "The effects of routines, scheduling, mobility and engagements (with people and news for example) form 'an archive of feeling,' to cite Cvetkovich, that reflect my status as an international student trying to be resilient in a moment of crisis." Throughout Henaku's tale, we follow her as she physically engages with familiar places and paths, and documents the ways they are altered during this time with the reflections offering an outline to form an "archive of feeling."

Lynn M. Ishikawa, in "Risk and Refuge: The Role of the Commonplace in Navigating Crisis," reflects on COVID-19 through the lens of a past national crisis she had lived through in Japan during the 2011 earthquake, tsunami, and nuclear disaster in Fukushima. In comparing these two situations, she discusses the role of the "quotidian" and risk assessment as bringing both healing and harm. She draws upon the movie *Night of the Living Dead* to highlight that what we fear on the outside might not be as terrible as the social inequities and unjust systems we find on the inside. She notes, "For me, home has been a refuge, but it is clearly not so for everyone; indeed for many, inside is more dangerous than outside. In this and other ways, the pandemic has exposed the inequities in society and the ways in which the systems meant to protect are either broken or unjust. What is commonplace for some is fraught with risk for others."

Morgan Hanson, in "'Yes, and . . .': Confronting Work, Miscarriage, and Grief during a Pandemic," returns to her daily Documentarian writings to narrate the experience of documenting a period of loss and grief in her life at a moment of profound isolation, reflecting on the effects of that reflective practice in her life. She writes, "Even though the Documentarian reflections had me confront the harder parts of my isolation experience and how that affected my productivity and mental health . . . I think of the great relief I felt with each reflection. Through the power of writing, my stressors became more tangible; they were real, and they deserved my attention." In telling this story of the difficulties and benefits of reflective writing in a time of trauma, Hanson is motivated to consider her relationship to professional "productivity," a relationship further vexed by isolation and grief, and invites us all into a reflection on the meaning of productivity.

In her piece, "On Choosing," **Lindsey Albracht** wrestles with the decision to leave her home in the city and move to her family home. She notes, "The choice to leave or to stay is not the same one." She reflects on the dynamics and the privilege of being given the choice to leave or to stay and what it means for others in her local community, but also what it means for her scholarly work and the work of education. Her piece ends with a call of sorts asking educators to consider what it means to move beyond "empowerment" and to consider how the machinations of the university are made possible in order to shed light on both privilege and the colonial history in education.

In "Pondering the Quiddities," **Miriam Moore** takes up and extends the project that we (Julie, Bree, and Bump) began in an earlier moment of encountering the products of the Documentarian surveys, performing a content analysis of the words that appear most frequently in her daily survey responses. In so doing, she identifies the "quiddities," or distinctive qualities, of her quarantine experiences, leading to a reckoning with, as she writes, "the very difficult lessons of my privilege."

Cheryl Price-McKell, in "Scholarship Interrupted: How Unsettling Compartmentalized 'Normal' Can Inspire Wholehearted Insight," rediscovers and considers the artifacts of her writing life: a collection of notebooks in which she had kept alive her practice of imaginative writing. By way of these artifacts, Price-McKell reflects on commonplace expectations of academic roles, writing selves deferred, and professional identity. She asks: "What physical, mental, and emotional work does it take to separate, compartmentalize, and choreograph our individual selves? What possibilities reside in that overlooked, wholehearted liminal space where—as students of writing, creators of writing, instructors of writers, and artists—identities overlap?"

Xinquiang Li's tale, "Pandemic Life: Adventures in the Virtual World," describes the changes in routines of teaching and interactions with students against the background of everyday life in lockdown. His tale is a meditation on isolation—social, cultural, professional. He considers the affordances for connection within the new virtual social world, reflecting that "With the limits of travel and expense erased, I could actually enjoy accesses to more social gatherings online, sometimes hiding behind the screen listening to the school president's announcements, sometimes sitting before a background image of a tropical beach and planning summer activities with colleagues, sometimes even attending a virtual film festival held in a neighboring town or discussing a fantastic TV show with an international group in London." Implicitly, the narrative explores solitude, loneliness, and the difference between the two.

Isaac Ewuoso's, "Some Lessons and Tales: Moving Classes Online in the Advent of a Crisis for Which No One Signed Up," offers the author's perspectives on learning to identify his students' needs as their interactions moved online. Ewuoso reflects on working to meet those needs both in and out of the classroom, on the challenging work conditions of adjunct faculty, and on the powerful potential for reflective activities to be of value to both instructors and students. He finds that personal connection through phone calls and texts have been instrumental in reaching those students who are struggling with life's complexities: "I found out about one or more problems they were having that they did not feel comfortable discussing in an email or Zoom. In fact, most would not say anything unless I asked them." After making these personal connections and hearing students' stories, he found himself questioning his former classroom policies and how we tend to think about student success and participation.

In "Building Strength in an Uncommon Time," **Catherine Lamas** reflects on labor conditions for contingent faculty—both in terms of teaching duties, often carried out at multiple institutions, and in terms of service to their larger professional communities. Lamas writes, "My 'temporary' status puts me in a different category than those who have tenure. This faculty divide was evident in the demographics of this activity. As I reviewed the demographics of this activity, I was both disappointed yet not surprised by the contributors to this data collection. We need a well-rounded group of educators to keep this data from being biased. Over 70% of the Documentarians were part-time educators. I wonder why we did not get a greater contribution from the Tenured faculty. There is an unspoken divide that I often witness between 'Full Time' professors and 'Contingent' faculty in my teaching institutions, and this was also visible at the 2020 CCCC convention."

In "Feminist Mishmash: COVID-19 CCCC," **Heather McGovern** reflects on her everyday routines of caretaking at home and work—that is to say, with family and co-workers—to suggest what the collapsed space and of the pandemic may reveal about the experience of women's work. In reviewing her daily Documentarian survey responses, she writes, "The observations in my journals about what I planned, what I accomplished, and how I felt are a tangled hair knot, a scramble. They're likely not a mash up, because that would be more intentional; they are not a hodge-podge because the things in them matter: they are a mishmash."

Shauna Chung writes in "Growing up Again (and Again)," about returning to her family home during shelter-in-place protocols. This movement prompted her to question what is lost in performance and productivity. She composes dialogue with her mother as she faces returning to a life where productivity at times is demanded and her mother encourages her to hold on to her humanness. She reflects, "'Don't forget to be human?' Didn't I meet my 'being human' quota after giving up so much time to be with family? Wasn't I the *most* human in the family since I was dedicating my professional life to the *human*ities? Doesn't my scholastic striving for attuned, empathetic, civic-minded rhetoric speak for itself?" In answering those internal questions, she finds the need to "re-version" herself, leaving space for the human, instead of reverting to her former life and notions of productivity.

In "Documenting Our Solastalgia: A New Landscape," **Margarette (Maggie) Christensen** asks, "what will the university be like after all this? What if we cannot or do not return?" Christensen names the feeling of regarding the familiar as suddenly unfamiliar *solastalgia*, "Sheltering in place, I was 'homesick,' longing for my familiar worlds and routines which were replaced by a gnawing sense of uncertainty and fear. Like many of my colleagues and students, I was experiencing *solastalgia*." Christensen offers *solastalgia* as a reorienting tool and a "collective comfort" even when a sense of closure or normalcy is not possible.

Soha Youssef, in "Self-Reflexivity is/as Resistance," reflects on ways her Egyptian heritage has influenced her relationship with productivity in her academic career path: a history that adds complexity to her experiences with self-reflection (brought about by way of the Documentarian role) and her revised work pace (brought about by the shelter-in-place orders in the US). Youssef writes, "Being forced to actually sit down, take a deep breath, and watch my own life—for the first time—I got to experience my own life as a viewer, instead of an active agent; as an acted-upon, instead of an actor. It was like a curtain had been lifted to afford me clarity of vision."

In "'Tending to My Life': On Resilience and Academic Work," **Charlotte Asmuth** invites us to reflect on our often-invisible work routines and on how graduate students are (and are not) socialized into these. She begins with a meditation on what the scene of her own dissertation work—the details of time, space, and the artifacts of writing—during quarantine have taught her about what it means to mentor students into work habits that are grounded in needs of the fully-embodied self. She situates these observations within scholarship on academic work routines (in particular, that of Paul Prior and Jody Shipka) to call attention to commonplaces of work, productivity, learning, and embodiment. She asks: "How can faculty teach graduate students to take up useful work habits and care for themselves during times of collective crisis? How can faculty support graduate students' work practices when both their own and graduate students' working conditions are increasingly precarious and inconsistent?"

In "A Controlled Freak-Out: Mentoring, Writing, and Parenting during COVID-19," **Katrina Powell** reflects on her learning about her professional community, roles, attachments, and responsibilities occasioned by the cancellation of CCCC at the moment when the pandemic crisis mandated a transition to working from home. Powell considers the benefits of the Documentarian experience at such a time, wonders how the practice of participating as a Documentarian might be taken up among differently positioned members of our professional community, and asks what the fact of this participation might reveal about professional roles more generally. She writes: "A question that I thought about throughout this time was whether the role of Documentarian and the time to write/reflect in this way has something to do with privilege. I wondered if most of my fellow Documentarians were graduate students and junior colleagues, and, if so, what does it mean that the role falls to them? I wondered if it mirrors administrative, committee, and mentoring work in our field that is often taken up by junior colleagues and underrepresented groups?"

In "Harnessing the Magical Properties of Collaboration for Transforming the Neoliberal University," **Shelagh Patterson** considers a complicated jumble of experiences during the first days of the COVID-19 pandemic in the US and reconsiders and re-presents them as a sensible rendering of a jumbled life. Patterson reflects not only on her life and professional responsibilities during the days of the conference, but also on both the personal vulnerability and collaborative empowerment she has found in her work as a Documentarian. Patterson writes, "My writing as a Documentarian exponentially increased the quality of my health and wellbeing which grounds me for resisting and reshaping the neoliberal waves gathering in our universities."

Gabrielle Isabel Kalenyi's tale, "Hitting Pause on Productivity: Finding Mindful Labor in Quarantine," is a meditation on the meaning and perils of "productivity," especially for those who feel a sense of responsibility not only to achieve legitimacy and impact, but to do so on behalf of marginalized others. She writes, "I believed my efficiency training would continue to serve me well, despite the unprecedented circumstances. Without clear boundaries, professional productivity has come to mean progress and living my personal life has come to mean a pause in that productivity. As a result, productivity for professional progress has begun to take precedent over what seems like pausing for personal connection." As a scholar of color, Kalenyi considers the additional burden of the quest for productivity for persons of color who feel a sense of responsibility to their communities: "If I don't do it, who will?"

Rachel Panton, in "'You Good, Fam'?': Mindful Journaling, Africana Leadership, and Dialogic Compassionate Rhetorical Response Pedagogy During a Pandemic," explores the uses of compassion and mindfulness in a chaotic time, and from a perspective of Black Womanist care and holistic understanding. She describes the benefits of writing as a Documentarian, observing that "reflective and mindful journaling in a moment of actualized trauma, heightened my personal self-care practice, as well as my Africana womanist pedagogical outlook on care in the classroom." Panton recommends that mindful, reflective writing can be a therapeutic and pedagogical practice, an antidote to pathologies of compartmentalization and hyperproductivity.

CONCLUSION AND INTRODUCTION

As the record here suggests, during those few months in the spring of 2020, we experienced a lot. And while we can find common experiences, we are mostly overwhelmed by myriad differences: we were isolated with our families, we were isolated alone, we were isolated at home, we were isolated far from home, we did familiar work from home, we did uncommon work from home, we ventured out into the world, we were afraid to go out into the world, we were glued to news coverage, we avoided news coverage, we remained healthy, we did not remain healthy, we did not start out healthy, we joined protests, we assessed our privilege(s), we were grateful for job security, we lost our jobs, we witnessed others lose their jobs, we worried for our loved ones abroad, our loved ones abroad worried about us, we had successful exchanges with our students and colleagues, we struggled to stay connected to our students and colleagues, we found comfort in doing the daily Documentarian surveys during the week of the would-be conference, we struggled to make ourselves do those damned things with the world seemingly bursting into flames all around us.

Our recollection of assembling and introducing this archive of Documentarian Tales, thus, ends with a beginning: this small collection of voices from our field points to the need for more and more voices. We hope this collection will be a critical mass to attract more voices—your voices—and ever more diverse representation.

WORKS CITED

Carrega, Christina, and Sebina Ghebremhedim. "A Timeline: Inside the Investigation of Breonna Taylor's Killing and the Aftermath." *ABC News*, 17 November 2020, https://abcnews.go.com/US/timeline-inside-investigation-breonna-taylors-killing-%20%20%20%20%20 aftermath/story?id=71217247.

"The Conference on College Composition and Communication." *Wikipedia*. Wikimedia Foundation, February 2021, https://.en.wikipedia. org/wiki/Conference_on_College_Composition_and_Communication.

Halbritter, Bump, and Julie Lindquist. "Collecting and Coding Synecdochic Selves: Identifying Learning across Life Writing Texts." *How Stories Teach Us: Composition, Life Writing, and Blended Scholarship*, edited by Amy E. Robillard and D. Shane Combs, Peter Lang Press, 2019.

---. "It's Never about What It's About: Audio-Visual Writing, Experiential-Learning Documentary, and the Forensic Art of Assessment." *The Routledge Companion to Digital Writing and Rhetoric*, edited by Jonathan Alexander and Jacqueline Rhodes, Routledge, 2018, pp. 317–27.

---. "Sleight of Ear: Voice, Voices, and Ethics of Voicing." *Songwriting Pedagogies,* edited by Courtney S. Danforth, Kyle D. Stedman, & Michael J. Faris. Computers and Composition Digital Press, 2018. https://www.ccdigitalpress.org/book/soundwriting/halbritter-lindquist/index.html.

---. "Time, Lives, and Videotape: Operationalizing Discovery in Scenes of Literacy Sponsorship." *College English,* vol. 75, no. 2, 2012, pp. 171–98.

---. "Witness Learning: Building Relationships between Present, Future, and Former Selves." *Writing for Engagement: Responsive Practice for Social Action*, edited by Mary Sheridan et al., Lexington Press, 2018, pp. 43–59.

Lindquist, Julie, and Bump Halbritter. "Documenting and Discovering Learning: Reimagining the Work of the Literacy Narrative." *College Composition and Communication,* vol. 70, no. 3, 2019, pp. 413–45.

Taylor, Derrick Bryson. "George Floyd Protests: A Timeline." *New York Times*, 6 January 2021, https://www.nytimes.com/article/george-floyd-protests-timeline.html.

---. "A Timeline of the Coronavirus Pandemic." *New York Times,* 10 January 2021, https://www.nytimes.com/article/coronavirus-timeline.html.

1

A Sweet Spot, a Safe Space

Adrienne Jankens

I remember everyone flowing out of the City Museum in St. Louis. In the crowd, I found my new friends from Wayne State, some I had known in grad school, some I was only just beginning to connect with. We formed a group and started walking through town, looking for a place to land for drinks. It was the first time I felt part of something outside of my family in years.

Being part of a discipline, a program, a cohort, a class, a writing team, can do that—can make a home outside of home. It's nice to know other people who obsess over scheduling lesson plans, or get excited about coding, or can share a look with you across the table at a meeting. It's nice to know the five people who have actually read the same book you are geeked about. You talk about your home lives during a six- or eight-hour break from home. It's something many of us are missing right now, even if we get to be in a safe home. My people saw me through three pregnancies, my dissertation, the death of my mother, divorce, a tenure-track job interview process. My co-workers and I are learning parenting together: potty training, elementary school, this terrible long wading into being responsible for teenagers. Eventually, we will let our children go, or teach each other's children in our comp classes—there is a good chance tuition discounts will lead to that.

For my colleague and friend Nicole and me, Cs in Milwaukee was going to be both a planned vacation and an inspirational work session. It was going to be pause, reflection, play, thinking, connecting, eating, sleeping. We would have arrived Tuesday evening, checked into our hotel, and I don't know what Nic planned to eat, but I was going to get a huge hamburger. We'd have wine. We'd celebrate our time away from classes, and, even though we would be antsy to get back to them the whole time, we'd celebrate time to just be us, away from children.

I realized, as I took notes during the week that we didn't go to Milwaukee, that the conference had become part of an annual restorative pause for me, sometimes in the midst of deep personal pain. The work of conference preparation aside, the experience itself was a retreat into safe being.

There's a picture of me in the plaza in Kansas City (Figure 1.1). It was the first time I had truly smiled in months, I think. The sun was out and we took off our hoodies to soak it up. My friend Conor and I had planned to try to eat barbecue at every meal (he succeeded, I didn't). We watched *Hot Tub Time Machine* in the hotel room and slept a lot. I had a magical moment in the hallway of the convention center where I saw Gwen, my dissertation director, in passing; we hugged, hoped to see each other soon, and parted. These were moments of light when, at home, I had just moved my four children into my parents' house, away from the home that had been in turmoil for months, years, and that had finally, at the point of my announcing I would file for divorce, manifested in total breakdown. I wasn't sleeping or eating much. Somehow I was still working. The smile in the picture—caught during a surprise laugh—is maybe disbelief, partly, that I could be happy again, in the right place, with people who loved me.

I drove to Indianapolis for the 2014 conference the day after my dissertation defense. At home, my mom had recently been diagnosed with cancer (again) and my cat had just died. The defense itself was both joyful and anticlimactic, as they often seem to be. Someone I had hoped would be there didn't show, and never said why. That was just one more small, sad thing on top of what late winter had already given me. When Whitney and I got to the convention center, I ran into Gwen and told her I didn't know what I was going to go see yet. She looked at me, knowingly, and said, "Maybe you shouldn't do anything." I took her advice, left by way of the escalator, went outside, and walked across the bridge behind the convention center, to the zoo. I talked to bears for a moment. I went to the botanical garden, walked paths away from people, found a spot in the back of the just-awakening garden, and cried (Figure 1.2).

It's not always traumatic. In Portland, in 2017, I got a room by myself and enjoyed dinner at the hotel restaurant alone, listening to an older couple plan their drive north to Washington. I found some moments to walk in the city with friends. Several of my co-workers shared a room and got sick while I was healthy and well-rested. We did an awesome presentation on mentoring. I made a lasting professional connection. I came home energized.

Figure 1.1. The author smiling in Barney Allis Plaza, outside of the Kansas City Convention Center.

Figure 1.2. A shaded courtyard in the DeHaan Tiergarten in White River Gardens in the Indianapolis Zoo.

I thought Milwaukee would feel that way. Nic and Sarah and I were going to present on a learning community-focused project we are intensely excited about. Conor and Michael and I were going to talk about critical pedagogy in our panel presentation. It was going to be a collegial love fest. It was going to be restful. There would be long walks and food and watching graduate students present their work and plenty of smiling and maybe one or two new connections.

~~~

In the week we didn't go to Milwaukee, I wrote daily in my Documentarian notes about a new anxiety: telling my ex I didn't think the children should visit him during the stay-at-home order. He has roommates who share parts of the house. Were they still going out to work? Was the roommate's daughter still visiting her dad? There seemed to be too many unknowns in a time where our direction was to, simply, stay home to keep all families safe. I finally mentioned it to him and he said we could do what I thought was best. I was relieved for a day. The next week, he came to play outside and threatened to "invoke" the parenting time order we agreed to in mediation but had not followed since: the kids staying with me most of the time while he worked six- or seven-day weeks—their school lives calm, our home life relaxed, everyone fed and sleeping well. Then the verbal threats disappeared again, emerged again, disappeared again, re-emerged. It was, for weeks, the same eggshell-walking I had to leave after so many years, but now, I was, at least, in my own home. I could, eventually, shut the front door, and be safe inside.

Setting aside a maybe self-indulgent walk through the strange, sad, and intriguing way that mid-March always seems to line up with some need for me to be away, to be safe, either alone, or in the comforting presence of good friends, writing during the week we didn't go to Milwaukee helped me think about how composition is, I think, for many, including students, a safe space in a loud, busy world.

Sometimes, maybe that space is surprising. Maybe it comes out in a reflection where someone writes, "I actually got into writing this essay," or "I liked it because I actually got to choose what I was writing about," and the thing being written is not work, actually, it is a chance to be oneself in the writing, or to try to be a version of oneself one is experimenting with. Maybe sometimes it's a space to say something you haven't said before but there it is, your teacher is asking you to make an argument—to spend six weeks writing an argument—and so why not use now to make a point about something you never thought someone would listen to you write about so seriously?

When we couldn't leave home, I found my writing time (for the Documentarian work, for my research, for my remote class planning) to be moments where everything else went away:

I wrote a poem this morning, shortly after getting moving. I had half a cup of coffee in me and had done some email work and there it was, so I got it into my notes app and then re-read it twenty times today. I posted it to Instagram, where I sometimes share innocuous poems, labeling it, "not a quarantine poem" (Figure 1.3). It's for a friend of mine whom I love and miss dearly, who is going through something I don't know a lot about. It's hopeful and realistic, maybe.

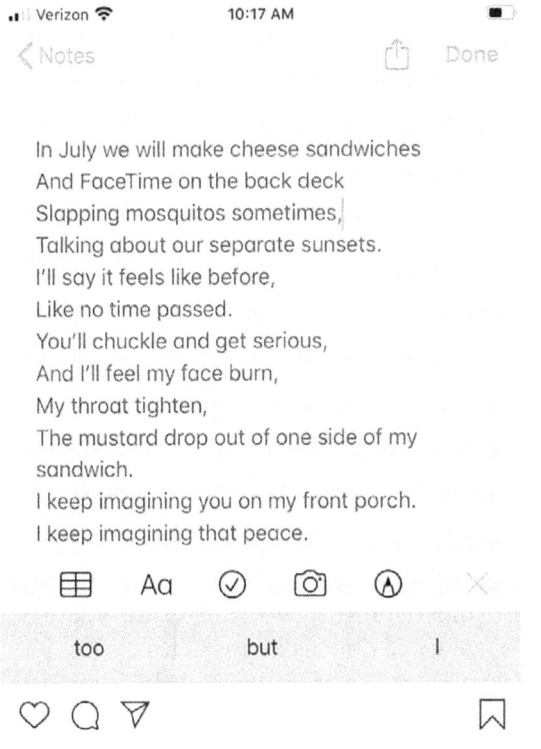

Figure 1.3. A screenshot of the author's poem, composed in the Notes app on her phone.

On the Wednesday of the week we did not go to Milwaukee, when I had planned to be with Nicole, eating lunch and getting hyped for our presentation, I wrote,

> This morning was a shitshow. I am a writing teacher. My seven-year-old spent seventy minutes complaining that he could not write his three sentences for his morning journal for school. He could not write one sentence. He would not write, "I don't know what to write." He would not write, "I see a blue jay outside." He would not write, "I ate a muffin." He tried writing in the kitchen, and then at the desk in the playroom, and then back in the kitchen. He tried one pencil, then another. None of the erasers were good enough. He erased the one sentence he did draft ("I will play with my sister.") so much that he could not write in that spot anymore. He wailed. He flopped. I gave in and let him move to the next thing. "No! I have to write my journal!" You're not writing your journal, though. So move on.

I wrote about how, in intentionally moving my office to my room to make a workspace for myself at the beginning of the stay-at-home order, I gifted myself with a restful space of my own, so that even hard work was peaceful. My desk in my bedroom is up against my window, facing the backyard. The blinds are mostly closed, with just a bit open. This is more for modesty when I am getting ready for bed than it is to limit distraction—it would be far more distracting to look at the rest of my bedroom and see laundry. Instead, through the bit of the blinds that are open, I can see the roof, mainly—some grass and leaves (Figure 1.4). When I am writing, I don't want distraction. I am not a procrastinator. Writing is happy work for me. During the week we didn't go to Milwaukee, I reclaimed writing in the morning, something I had not been able to do for years, when my home life was in turmoil. Writing in the morning over those four days helped me process my anxiety about the possible conflict with my children's father about visitation during quarantine. It gave me language for how to approach that conversation with him. Writing at the end of the day helped me put work to rest so I could spend time with my children.

Mental turmoil creeped in maybe more that week than any other during the whole time at home. I have tried to work through it in prayer and laundry and checking emails every five minutes. I know people are joking that we will all come out of this situation either really fit or with drinking problems. I am finding some disciplined balance between taking lots of walks and recognizing that one drink feels nice, but more than one has me up with indigestion in the middle of the night, so I better work through my stresses some other way. The midnight thinking becomes desperate. I'd rather be dreaming. I dreamed, that first night, that we were at Cs, and I was trying to find Gwen in the conference center. My subconscious was in Milwaukee, anyway.

Figure 1.4. The author's desk, with laptop, lamp, papers, pens, and the frame of her bedroom window.

Thursday morning of the week we didn't go to Milwaukee, I wrote, about the evening before,

> Hearing about the death toll rising was confirmation that we are doing the right thing by staying in, but it also made me think, as I washed dishes, that someone in my family will likely get sick or die from this, that the upper respiratory thing I have had for a week might be COVID-19 (though I am getting better), that the statistics don't keep anyone safe. It might be then that I decided to make a drink.

I have spent a lot of the last two months feeling like my home, once a safe space, and now cut through with my university life—a different kind of safe space—is, actually, no longer a retreat. It's constant movement, noise, wailing and gnashing of teeth. In the good moments, we recognize we are healthy and blessed with a nice home and good food to eat and at least one screen per person. In the not-good moments, I am an evil troll mom who forces her kids to remember they have homework and to actually do that homework, while I juggle lit torches, cackling and crying at the same time.

~~~

An octagonal package arrived for me in early May with a punching bag inside. Not the bag I wanted to buy for the last two years—I wanted one I could hang from a beam in my basement—but something less permanent, moveable, with a base to fill with so much water (Figure 1.5). It's living in my garage, so I can be outside with the kids this summer; they can play cars and soccer in the front yard, and I can punch and kick in the shade of the garage. I tried it out that first evening for a few minutes. The sound it made when I hit it was so much louder than it was in the gym. Or maybe it was the absence of any other bags being hit that caused the dissonant wave in my pocket of the neighborhood. "Hiiii!!!!" the little girl across the street called at me while I was one-two-hook-reverse-ing. I think her mother shushed her. "Hiiiiii!!!!" I called back.

Two months before I finally left my old house, with my children, I asked my sister to try kickboxing with me. We like trying things we are a little scared to do. Sometimes she picks them up with enthusiasm (paddle boarding), and sometimes I do (kickboxing), but we like trying. It was a rush to learn to do new things with my muscles. I kept going back to the gym. For a year, for two years. I signed up for individual training sessions.

I would not call the gym a safe space, necessarily. One time, a class-mate kicked me so hard through a kick shield I could barely move for two days. My rib was bruised, and I was glad it wasn't worse. Most often, the threat is just having to pair up for drills when I don't feel like being social, though. Sometimes, if I have stayed up too late the night before, or had drinks with friends, I am my own worst enemy, swearing through jumping jacks. But there is something very sweet about the routine of going, about climbing the stairs and saying hello to my teacher, about singing quietly while I put my wraps on, about the repetitive practice of the warm-up exercise. There is something very sweet about just being me—not mom me, not teacher me—a woman who is being reminded what sustained practice in something hard can do for her.

Figure 1.5. The author's Century-brand, blue standing punching bag, in her garage.

For a few weeks last summer, I imagined myself doing a spinning crescent kick. In my mind, I was in some interpersonal conflict with someone I was about to surprise with my martial arts skills. The conflict climaxed when the someone said something that implied I am a small, weak person. Fully composed, I spun and the top of my foot connected with the side of his face. I asked my teacher to show me how to do one. And then, I did it. Not perfectly—not close—but I did it.

In my one-on-one training sessions, we practice this combination where I throw a right, do a roundhouse, do a spinning hook kick, do a front kick, throw a left, do a roundhouse on the other side, do another spinning hook kick, and do a front kick again. I am a ballerina with gloves on. I travel so far across those twelve feet—I soar in a small space—and I can stop in an instant when I notice something is off—stop, in control, go back to my starting point.

Sometimes, in the midst of a training session, my teacher and I shift briefly to therapy. He makes a self-effacing joke. I reply with a serious solution to the cloaked problem. He acknowledges my contribution toward a solution. I respond by sharing how my solution comes from a related experience. We joke about how we are now playing therapists. I go back to practicing my combinations.

Nine weeks into the stay-at-home order, my teacher posts instructional videos that remind me of what I am supposed to be practicing. He shows us how to be invisible—how to not be where our opponent expects us to be, how to always be one step ahead. In the driveway, I teach my seven-year-old how to throw a one-two without being wild. I remind him to guard his head. We are not learning invisibility yet in these late May sessions. Our expectations are lower. I am learning how to successfully teach a jab. I am far more patient than when we are working on writing journals. We are all seeing different parts of ourselves emerge.

~~~

The swings between hope and anxiety that I wrote about during the week we didn't go to Milwaukee seem to have abated. I know that around 10 a.m. I will get stressed about my son's complaints about homework because I will struggle to imagine how I will get through my to-do list before dinner time, but I also know that every day, I have managed to get through it, and we have mostly happy evenings.

In two weeks, we will be left to flounder through the summer on our own. I have research to continue, but all of the deadlines are my own to create and to manage. I will not be flying to Portland for another conference. I will not be driving to Detroit for meetings. I will not be going to the gym for Saturday morning classes at 10:30. I will not be telling the kids, "It's 9:30! School is starting!" and popping my head in their rooms to make sure they're actually doing homework. My son and I will not be fighting about writing journals. We will not go to Vacation Bible School, we will not go to church on Sunday morning, we will not go to Thursday swim classes. We may choose to punch the bag in the garage. I may spend all day writing while everyone plays video games. I might make a fancy lunch. I might Zoom with Nicole and talk about all of the things we didn't get to talk about in Milwaukee. We have loads of possibilities; we have no demands. Somewhere in the middle of absolute summer and nowhere to go, we will find our sweet spot, our safe space.

2

Other Disseminations

Erika Luckert

The day the conference is cancelled, I take the money I would have spent on Wisconsin cheese curds and fries, and I use it to buy bags to grow potatoes in. I'd never imagined that potatoes could grow in bags, but an ad that keeps appearing in my Instagram feed fuels this dream. In the picture, potatoes spill out of a green felt bag—they tumble, abundant, from their sack of soil. I imagine my own hands, cutting open the bags at harvest time, pulling potatoes from the dirt. I dream of plants that could be more productive than I. More potatoes than space inside their seven-gallon bags, more potatoes than the volume of their soil.

As the dates of the cancelled conference approach, my university sends everyone away to their separate homes, and my dream of potatoes in bags grows into a plan for a garden. By the time the first day of the conference arrives, I've spent the refund of my first night's stay on the materials that I'll need to build two raised beds. By then, I've been researching specifications for a solid week, comparing plans from DIY blogs, checking over the tools that I have at home, scrolling through lumber yards online, cross-checking prices between Home Depot and Lowes, reading up on COVID precautions at each store, getting a curbside pickup order ready to place. Even my walks around the block are research trips, as I size up the construction methods of my neighbors' garden beds. The wood, I conclude, needs to be cedar so it doesn't rot. Fence pickets are the cheapest option, and they come ready-cut. The corners will need support from posts of some sort. Any solid piece of lumber should do—the standard eight-foot length, divided, will make four corners for two square beds. At the curbside pickup, I trade my conference room for eight fence boards, a pressure-treated 2x4, a box of wood screws.

I'm supposed to be in Milwaukee networking with fellow compositionists, but instead I'm on the phone with Jennifer the horticulturalist, who explains the ratio of topsoil and compost I'll need to make things grow. Instead of plotting out which panels to attend, I'm planning which plants I'll sow, calculating volumes of dirt. With the money I would have spent on accommodations for the next two nights, I buy a 100-foot garden hose, and 600 pounds of soil.

I'm supposed to be meeting leaders in my field, attending presentations, taking notes. I should be moving between the rooms of the convention center, halls crowded with thousands of other scholars, each of us gathering a whole bibliography of ideas. Instead, I walk a few quiet blocks to a colleague's house to borrow some seeds. She keeps the packets in a strawberry box, a little library to flip through. I pick a few—French radishes, collard greens, cherry tomatoes, hot peppers and kale. I make mental notes as she tells me which ones I should start as seedlings indoors—at night, it's still cold.

In this chilly spring, had I travelled to Wisconsin, I'd hoped to take a walk around a lake, maybe try out a trail or two. By the third day of the conference, I might have been ready for some time away, and, if the weather wasn't great, I'd heard the Milwaukee art museum was worth a visit, too. By the time the last day of the conference came around, I'd hoped to glean not only a sense of my scholarly field, its conversations and debates, but also a sense of the city, the state. I'd drive home through the still-unplanted fields of corn, back to my Lincoln, Nebraska, house, with one more day to prepare for the start of classes after spring break.

Instead, each day I take a walk around the block where I live, circle back to end in my backyard. In November, I planted bulbs there, nearly too late. Now the first daffodil has grown so tall that it has toppled over, its stem unable to support its weight. How could we have known then, forcing bulbs into winter soil, that spring would hold us here?

My students, too, have returned to their homes, to whatever gardens have or haven't been planted yet. Each day I struggle to imagine a way to split our classroom into tiny squares and scatter them across Nebraska's plains—to Seward, to Sarpy County, to Blair. The semester I'd planned for in winter is no longer there, and I haven't prepared my students for any of this. Every moment that I'd hoped to create in class feels too large, too strange for the space of our separate screens. I write ideas for online lessons out by hand on post-it notes, on index cards. My desk is covered with too many possibilities. What do they know already? What do they need to learn? I could have asked these questions at the conference too, might have returned to the remainder of this semester with freshly seeded ideas from across the composition field. As it is, I work from the things I have. I try to sift my syllabus down, and turn it over. As the weather warms, I rake the soil.

I've been counting out time in semesters for so long that I'd forgotten about seasons, about days. I try to conceive of how much sunlight can fit in a workday, how often it rains, or what that means for the garden I'm imagining.

When the time is right to plant the seeds inside, I pour the seed starter mix into trays. It isn't soil, but something lighter, made to give them the best chance at life. I level it, just a couple inches deep, and use the back end of a highlighter to make impressions for the seeds. I pinch them out of the packet and spread them over the palm of my hand. They're smaller even than I imagined they would be. When I count them, I plan for their deaths. What is the mortality rate of tomatoes, collard greens, peppers, and kale? I can't find any projections; nobody online seems to know. I figure seven seeds, or maybe nine, should yield a healthy plant or two.

A friend sends a link to the day's news. Some good, some bad, she says. The latest projections suggest that Nebraska won't run out of hospital beds. The latest projections, as April begins, suggest we'll have 424 deaths. We tell each other it isn't very many, all things considered. I don't know what "all things" we're considering, only that if I'm cautious, I might plan my way around my fear. I drop the seeds into their places, and cover them.

The herbs I planted in the fall remain the same. The thyme, timidly slow to grow. The basil, a bit too leggy, but still green. They've only ever lived indoors, under artificial light. But my seedlings need that incubation now, that place beneath the bars of UV bulbs. As each day lengthens, warms, my herbs will need to adjust, in their terra cotta pots, to the outside. I'm cautious with their lives, I've done my research, prepared a plan that will ready them for this new environment. I'm setting their pots in a sheltered place on the porch just a few hours every day. The gardeners call this hardening. It's not a metaphor; the plants need to form sturdier stems to withstand the elements. Otherwise, even under the generous light of a real sun, after all these months of UV bulbs, they'll die.

Is it softening we need to learn then, as we move our lives inside? I've been cross-stitching, rows and rows of exes in colored embroidery thread. When I reach the end of one shade of yellow, I move on to the next. The pattern is a sunflower, like the ones I plan to plant along the front of my house. Sometimes the thread snarls as I try to pull it through the cloth. If I'm careful and slow, I can untangle it and continue the row. More often, I pull it too quickly, too tight. The knot holds and I have to cut the thread. When the light in my living room grows too dim to stitch, I try to be still instead. I haven't learned how.

My most-Googled phrase: "how long will it take seeds to sprout?" Refining the search terms doesn't yield a better answer. The tomatoes I've planted may take anywhere from five to twelve days. Kale and collard greens take four to ten. Peppers, depending on the heat, might take seven to twenty-one. And some varietals still fall outside that range. Already I've checked the seeds I planted seven times today. My partner calls me a constant gardener. I call myself impatient, check on them again.

Nobody knows how long we'll wait inside, though we Google to find graphs that project a peak—a line we've come to associate with relief. I filter the data by country, by state, by month, by week. Here we are, waiting for the day when the very most people will die.

How long should we distance for? When will the toilet paper restock? How long can the virus live on plastic, on paper, on skin? How long will it be until everyone knows somebody who's died? The first sign that a seed is alive is not a leaf, but a looping thread, the folded stem that senses a bit of light, then lifts the great weight of two cotyledons above the earth. The word cotyledon comes from the Greek, meaning cup-shaped cavity, bowl, or dish. This suggests that the cotyledons are vessels, containers to gather light. Their new green tints purple as the UV spills over them. They tilt to catch it. A botanist might explain that a cotyledon is both embryo and leaf. After the cotyledons, the next leaves to unfurl are called "true."

The doctors check for a fever before they begin their work each day. From my home, I email each one of my students, subject line: checking in. I call my parents, text my friends. How are you doing? I hope you're well. I inspect my seedlings for signs of health. Are their leaves upright? Are their stems straight? Are they straining too hard towards the light? My peppers show no signs of sprouting, though the tomatoes, collard greens, and kale have each begun to grow. Online, I read about how quickly they could fail. Is the soil moist? Too wet? Too dry? I learn that even watering could disturb their tender roots.

For weeks I ferry my seedlings back and forth from beneath their UV lights to the afternoon sun of my porch. They grow stronger in their trays. When it's finally time to build the garden beds I've planned, I spread out the tools I'll need—a drill, a measuring tape, a pencil, a saw. I lay out the cedar fence pickets and mark their length—six feet. It's the distance we keep from each other now, the length I estimate when I pass neighbors on a walk, stepping off the sidewalk into the grass, the length of my father, lying down, for some unknown reason, on the ground. I cut the pickets in half, surprised at how easily I can divide them. My father taught me how to use a saw so many years ago. Did he know that now, with a border closed and 1,400 miles between us, I'd be measuring out three-foot lengths, forming right angles, driving the fasteners in?

At the scale of these three-foot-square garden beds, it isn't efficient to plant in rows. But the plants, like us, need to keep a particular distance. The tomatoes I've seeded require twelve inches. The radishes, only four. In 1981, the gardener Mel Bartholomew, an "efficiency expert" pioneered a method meant for gardens sized like mine. In square foot gardening, you mark out each block of soil in a grid, then seed each square as densely as the plants you've chosen can afford.

I've been missing my friends in New York, with their far-too-few-square feet apartments, their far-too-precarious jobs. It's hard to believe I lived there just a year ago, a place we call the epicenter now. When we talk each week, they tilt their computers to the window so that I can hear the sound—pots and pans banging, a vuvuzela, voices cheering, howling, the clamor of an entire city of squared-in people who spend what hope they have in a single synchronous 7 p.m. sound.

Everything else is asynchronous now, a word I hardly knew before. I plan lessons, reply to discussion posts, record videos that might be for tomorrow, for yesterday, for next year. What day is it? What tense is this? Perpetual present. Already history. Stasis. Slip. Only my garden happens slowly, growing at a speed that I have to believe is real time.

When the garden beds are built, before I fill them, I stand inside each one, where my plants will be. The space is small. The beds smell of fresh-cut cedar, and their edges are unsanded, rough. For the moment, the color of the wood is warm, though I know that rain and sun will silver it. I pour the dirt one forty-pound bag at a time, tipping it, unwieldy, into the wooden frame. I follow the ratio the horticulturalist described to me: two bags topsoil, one bag compost. I stir them together in the beds, then repeat. The boxes hold more earth than I'd ever imagined they might. When they're finally filled, and all the soil mixed, I mark out the square-foot-garden grid with twine.

I arrange my garden beds like I might a middle school seating plan—taking into consideration who will do well beside each other, who won't get along. My tomatoes will thrive beside onions, but they'll struggle next to beets. I consult a chart that calls those plants "antagonists," and I imagine them bickering, tossing pencils at each other in the back row. I account for height—for the view each plant will have of the sun, not the board. If I plan it all just right, I believe, my plants just might survive, even succeed.

My students are doing alright, as well as can be expected, at least. They turn their essays in, mostly on-time. They're tired, worried, sad. They tell me over Zoom how they miss their dorms. I confess I don't miss my office much, its windowless fluorescent light. Every afternoon now, as the sun rounds the corner past the shade of our neighbor's house, I carry myself outside.

Had I gone to the conference, it might have led to new collaborations, projects, research groups. Here in Nebraska, I've been investing in older relationships instead. The first friend I made here grew up in Wisconsin, and her family is still there. Her father keeps a garden, though she doesn't know when she'll be able to see him next—his health fits what we've learned to call "high-risk." She has one winter squash left in her pantry from the harvest that he gave her from his garden in the fall. The flesh will have spoiled by now, but we hope the seeds will be enough. We meet over Zoom, and I watch through the webcam as she splits the squash open, scoops the seeds from the center, and pulls the threads of flesh away. The seeds are flat, and firm, and pale. She spreads them out on paper towels across her kitchen table, which has become her office too.

Some days later, she shows up in my backyard with a baggie of now-dry seeds. We rake mounds of soil, squat six feet apart, press the seeds just one inch deep into the earth.

The root of dissemination might be the same as seed. Instead of looking it up, I walk around my garden, pull a couple weeds. My calendar tells me that the conference is long past; soon the semester will be too.

I still don't know when the disease will peak, or what that will really mean. My extensive research doesn't really explain how it is that potatoes grow, though by now I've planted dozens in their bags. There's a gap in the literature. A gardener might plant a seed in there. As a scholar, that gap is the place where I'm supposed to write.

When I check on my potato plants, I imagine those little animations that we watched as kids in science class, the ones of cells subdividing—I can see the soft seed potato splitting into two, then four, then eight, sixteen, thirty-two, until its wrinkled skin stretches tight and new.

Of course, I know by now that potato plants have leaves, and thick stems too. So my theory expands. I imagine the sun filtering down the stalk like those fiberoptic cables someone invented to bring sun into the subway system in New York, enough light for a green park underground. I imagine that potato plants might work that way, leaves like funnels to catch the sun, stems like fiberoptic cables full of condensed light, streaming live to the tubers below, so that they swell like small sun-balloons, pushing the dirt aside as they grow.

My research suggests that I should use that dirt to hill up my potatoes, which means that as they get taller, I'll keep burying their stems. Every inch of progress that they make toward the sun, every inch closer to escaping their bags, will plunge them, in slow motion, deeper underground.

These days, our bodies pass without a funeral six feet down into their graves. A friend texts to tell me that all of gardening is about loss. If this is true, then I'm planting my losses, tending them. Across the country, other gardens are planted, and some grow. People have taken to calling them victory gardens, as if this were a war. If I were at a conference, I'd point accusingly at the rhetoric, but at home, I think about our grief: each day we've lost or lived, the days ahead. Several years from now, with this pandemic past, will I call this my first garden, a beginning, or my last? For all the planting that I've done, I still don't know much about gardening, though I know the lengths that I will go to keep something alive.

On the last day of the semester, in a fit of screen fatigue, I flee outside. There, in my backyard, I find the first squash sprouts, where we planted them. The seedlings are huddled together, their cotyledon leaves already spread, a cluster of them, far too close. I've done the research and I know they won't survive that way. But I can't bring myself to thin them. I watch them, still as they are, and I imagine how they might grow.

3

Seeking Shelter in the Eye: What We Can Get out of the Storm

Xiao Tan

Another tranquil day at home, just like the other 60 days before it. I sit down on a mat on the patio, set the countdown for 35 minutes, and start to read for pleasure. The cat curls up at my feet, purring gently. The daily reading signifies the end of a working day. It's also the time of the day when I can observe the change of seasons, meditate, and connect to my inner self.

Two months into the outbreak of COVID-19 in the United States, I begin to appreciate, more and more, the fact that I have a safe place to live, a fridge stuffed with food, and above all, an orderly life in the midst of crumbling world orders. Having come a long way to combat anxiety and fear, I can finally set out to tell my COVID-19 story. But

Figure 3.1. The view from my patio.

I hope that this narrative can go beyond merely reconstructing a difficult experience. I hope to contribute to the discussion of rebuilding "normality" by bringing in my perspectives as a Chinese national, doctoral student, writing teacher, and member of the CCCC community.

The spring 2020 semester began with a looming presence of the coronavirus outbreak in Wuhan, China. In mid-January, I began to hear about a spreading disease, which was then considered local and regional, from major Chinese media and from friends and families in China. On January 19, while the number of confirmed cases was still small (around 170), many people started to wear masks to avoid contracting and spreading the virus. Four days later, on January 23, the epicenter, Wuhan, was locked down, and a nationwide "stay-at-home" order was issued and enforced with no exceptions. The drastic measures took me by surprise, as I did not fully understand the scale of the problem we were going to face.

Meanwhile, I was busy adjusting to a new schedule, new teachers, and new students as the spring semester unfolded. The sunshine in Arizona was just as bright and joyful as always. The outbreak of COVID-19 became a popular, gap-filling topic before each class session. My American classmates asked curiously about the situation, expressing empathy and condolences. Among the Chinese community, however, we talked with great concerns. One of my friends at Arizona State University (ASU), Emily (pseudonym), is from a city next to Wuhan. Both of her parents work at a local hospital. She shared with me first-hand information about the epidemic that involved not only statistics but also acute suffering and pain of the people in China.

In my first-year composition classrooms, however, I did not talk too much about COVID-19 with my students. The first time I addressed the issue was in late January when the first case at ASU was confirmed. I wanted to bring the potential risks to students' attention, but I did not want to make a fuss out of it, partially because I still considered the epidemic to be a regional problem. The Chinese community on campus, my students included, acted quickly and precautiously. Several of my students wore masks to class and even kept them on throughout the entire 75 minutes. At around the same time, a petition for closing down the school was launched and gained favor among the student population. The incident ended with a message from the ASU President on February 13, in which he assured us that the current risk level was low and that all school activities would continue as usual. Although I started to hear more and more conversations about the coronavirus on different occasions, the tone and attitude did not change much. The most frequent comment I heard was that, as you might imagine, "it's just a flu."

I remembered things started to go downhill on March 9, the last Friday before spring break. While I was looking forward to the upcoming CCCC conference, my mailbox was bombarded by countless new messages about travel restrictions, conference cancellations, and transition to online teaching. In less than a week, I witnessed with tremendous sadness that much of my hard work was drowned in the tectonic changes that have shaken the foundation of normality.

But it was not only my life that has been affected; it was millions of people who live in this country. While I tried to "build a fortress" around my little two-bedroom apartment by following the "stay-at-home" order, the world outside seemed to be falling apart and whirling up at the same time. For more than two months, the confirmed cases and death toll in the US have been on the rise with few signs of slowing down. Meanwhile, the tensions between different racial groups, social classes, and generations have built up through hashtagged coinages on social media (e.g., "#BoomerRemover" and "#KungFlu"), through hate-provoking tabloid articles based on hearsay, through armed protests in the name of freedom, and even through outright name-calling at the daily White House briefings.

What upset me most was the manipulated hate toward the Chinese community. On March 16, Donald Trump used the term "Chinese virus" for the first time in his tweet and kept doing so many times on different occasions. This has aroused intense emotional responses among Chinese communities, both in the US and in China. We felt disappointment, outrage, helplessness, and, above all, fear. In my daily log for the Documentarian project, I noted on March 17:

> I have great fear these days. Trump just openly used "Chinese virus" on Twitter, which is really hard to believe. I understand that the existence of nationalism and racialism is as long as human history. I just couldn't believe that the head of a nation (and supposedly the greatest nation of the planet) would openly support racism and xenophobia in such a conscious, unmistakable, and brazen way. My fear is that the American citizens might be instigated by such discourses and start to attack, verbally and

physically, the Chinese. I am, obviously, at the center of attack. We are already seeing such attacks happening all around the globe. The fear is so great that I had to avoid all people when I was jogging around the blocks.

As a student of rhetoric and composition, I understand that Trump's rhetorical move was politically intended to divert our attention away from the current turmoil; but as a Chinese national, I could not help but feel like living on the brink of collision. The feeling got augmented every time I had to step out of my little "comfort zone" for grocery shopping, especially in March and April when wearing masks was not yet mandatory (or even considered necessary). Buying shampoo at the CVS felt like shady business when you had to weigh the "side-effects" of wearing a mask against the risk of not wearing one. I did not remember how many times I had to storm in and out of a shop because I got too much unwanted attention from wearing a mask. Fortunately, I have never been openly assaulted or attacked in public, but stories of such were far from scarce. In a video filmed and published by one of my Chinese friends who lived and studied in Spain, she was called "Coronavirus" by total strangers on the street in Madrid. On Facebook, my Japanese American professor at ASU shared her story of being shunned in public spaces. Racial division, I felt almost for the first time, exists beyond sensational news headlines. It is real, and it is happening around me.

The feeling of anxiety and distress was exacerbated by the pressure of being a second-year doctoral student. My nonimmigrant F-1 visa puts me in a dire predicament. Going back home would be safer and better for my well-being since things in China were gradually returning to normal. But in doing so, I will have to face the risk of not being able to come back in fall. Weighing the losses and gains, I decided that staying put, for now, was probably my best bet; I decided to seek shelter in the eye of the storm.

Starting a quarantine life was not too hard at first, given that I have a place to stay and enough savings to get by. The challenging part, as I soon realized, was to deal with the amount of extra time that otherwise would have been spent on commuting, having lunch-break conversations, waiting in lines at the Starbucks, and hanging out with friends. In the absence of distractions, any negative thoughts, however trivial, were magnified and prolonged into a state of mind. This was aggravated by the fact that physical environment plays a vital part in managing cognitive load. Being constrained to a relatively small space for a long time is likely to result in fatigue and a short attention span. At times, I found myself picking up the phone more and more frequently. The act of checking news and updates became almost unconscious and impulsive. Counterintuitively, the extra time was not at all a blessing, but a lure to vicious circles that drained most of my energy.

To pull myself from the downward spiral, the first thing I did was to push social distancing even further. Instead of keeping pace with the fast-changing world, I chose to focus on my small universe. I believed what I needed most at that time was a tiny bit of control over my life, mind, and feelings. I have, therefore, set daily, weekly, and monthly goals to validate any accomplishment, taking into account even non-academic stuff, such as reading novels, doing water-color paintings and yoga, and trying out new dishes. I have also designed a detailed working schedule, of which I was not a big fan before the pandemic. I had always considered them restricting and inflexible to changes. But in a time of uncertainties, knowing that I need to do certain things at a certain time was a huge relief. Apart from telling myself what to do, I have also set rules of what not to do. On top of the list was spending too much time on social media, especially on reading comments that vent malevolence on Chinese people. The decision to keep myself away from social media sounded contradictory to the idea of staying connected online, but what if the virtual space is an even more split version of reality?

The next thing that I did to restore order was to begin reaching out to people that I know, especially my fellows at ASU. Their presence assured me that the world has not become a totally unfamiliar place after all. The English Department, to which I am affiliated, has done a fantastic job of bringing us together. Among its various efforts, I benefited most from the four weekly Zoom meetings: Coffee Hour on Mondays, Teacher Talk on Tuesdays, Happy Hour on Thursdays, and Flash Talks on Fridays. For me, joining these sessions had more to do with seeing old faces and exchanging greetings; the one-hour-long participation was a symbol of being part of a greater whole.

I also had great concerns for my students, as most of them are from China as well. In a way, I considered them more vulnerable because they are younger, newer to this country, and probably have few social connections. With the writing classes being moved online, I had no idea where they were, how they were doing, and whether they were able to cope with various difficulties. To understand their situation and emotional state, I conducted a quick survey on Canvas and held one-on-one conferences during the second week of online teaching. Quite to my surprise, most students said they were doing well in managing the workload and pressure and that they felt calm and motivated. To those who did experience hardship, I told them about my own situation and how I managed to survive. I could feel that students appreciated how I approached them as a friend and an equally troubled human being. Several of them even asked about my plan for the summer and sought advice on traveling back to China. Originally, the point of having one-on-one conferences was to send a message that we were in this together, but in the end, I was deeply touched by their courage and commitment, which, in turn, became a great source of power for me. Providing emotional support to students has reciprocal benefits for the teacher, and it is the crisis that has helped me to see such remedial effects.

At the time I put these words down in May, countries and states are struggling to go back to normal. There are signs of things turning for the better, although more in a sociological sense. In fact, the "stay-at-home" order in Arizona has recently expired, and businesses are planning to reopen gradually. I have also witnessed the initial panic fading into more conscious thinking about what we are dealing with. The pandemic, of course, is never just a highly contagious disease. As Peter Baker nicely summarized in a Guardian article, "disasters and emergencies do not just throw light on the world as it is. They also rip open the fabric of normality. Through the hole that opens up, we glimpse possibilities of other worlds" (para. 8). I hesitate to see the pandemic as an "opportunity" in the usually positive sense, because I wish that we would learn our lesson in a less traumatic and devastating way. But a crisis of this scale forces us to detach ourselves from the daily messiness and to reassess the status quo.

This was precisely what the CCCC community was trying to achieve collectively. In documenting their daily activities, chores, and feelings, many have taken the chance to reflect upon their roles as a teacher and/or administrator, the work-life balance, previous working experiences, routines, plans, and values. Several of us have revealed a shattered reality in the disguise of normality: PhD students paying too little attention to self-care, essential workers being undervalued for the important work they do, reflective practices being pushed to the corner by a heavy workload. As I skimmed through the survey responses, a sense of responsibility and pride emerged. I realized that I could indeed contribute to social development and make an impact through writing, publishing, joining the conversation, and making my voice heard. As much as I love my work and profession, I had never felt what I do was lifesaving or game-changing. Not being able to see the immediate impact made me question how useful and worthy my work really is. But the Documentarian project gave me a new perspective of looking at my role in the world. As I may continue to feel vulnerable as a foreigner and racial minority, I can now scoop up the courage to think about what makes me scared in the first place, apart from the disease itself. I am also in a better position to voice my concerns and complaints and to expect that, together, we could right the wrongs, as an anonymous respondent wrote: "Recording, documenting, and revisiting are critical to making sense of our work—so that when we return to 'normal,' it won't be the same old normal."

One of the fastest failing "normalities" that I see here is the way that public discourses are produced and received these days. Over the past two months, I was constantly overwhelmed by the amount of information that spewed with each swipe of the phone. Yet, amongst the sea of information, I wonder how much we can genuinely trust and share. Having access to both the Chinese and English media puts me at a unique nexus of opposing viewpoints and ideologies. It also gives me a jarring feeling to see the vicious accusation of China downplaying the severity of the disease when all I heard from the Chinese media in January and February was how dangerous it was. The point here is not to defend my country, but to urge caution against angry posts shouting, "blow China down to the ground." In a time of crisis, when accurate information and cooperation are most needed, we are unfortunately seeing disinformation and hate comments that aim to drive us apart. Alarmingly, today's political discourses are increasingly replete with post-truth rhetoric, to a degree where the public feel so vulnerable and powerless that they eventually give up their right to know. As Lee McIntyre, the author of *Post-Truth*, summarized, "the tricky part is not to explain ignorance, lying, cynicism, indifference, political spin, or even delusion. We have lived with these for centuries. Rather, what seems new in the post-truth era is a challenge not just to the idea of knowing reality but to the existence of reality itself" (10).

It is this nihilistic thinking about reality that we need to guard against. As a citizen and writing teacher, I wonder what I can do to fight against the sense of powerlessness. Now I have an easier time dealing with racist remarks and behaviors, ungrounded claims, and inciting languages, knowing that they are on the agenda of creating "different versions of realities." But understanding this is far from enough. Increasingly, I felt the responsibility of helping students to actively engage with public discourses has shifted to the shoulder of writing teachers.

In my classroom, one thing that falls short is the emphasis on fact-checking practices. Although I have urged students to use reliable sources, preferably those from academic journals, I did not give them a set of criteria to evaluate the validity of sources. In fact, I have noticed, every now and then, that some sources cited by the students looked suspicious. Regrettably, I did not go deeper into checking reliability or having a conversation with them. This is partly due to time constraints. But oftentimes, I question whether I know more about a specific topic than my students. Isn't the information that I receive on topics outside my field of study also from news and social media? Yes. Have I ever read an academic article on global warming? No. While the idea of becoming an expert by reading a couple of online articles is illusional, I do believe we can help students become more aware of how they collect, process, and produce knowledge. Although I have adopted a process-based approach in teaching first-year composition, the feedback that I give to each draft is still oriented toward the final product. I have never asked students to explain how they start a project, where they find the information, why they choose to cite a specific article, whether they would do it differently outside of the course, etc. There is, perhaps, a growing urgency to help our students understand how information is produced, distributed, and received in today's world, and the students' role in that cycle.

I remembered that two months ago, in a line at Fry's checkout counter, I overheard a woman behind me saying in a joking tone that "this (pandemic) is not an apocalypse." But I think it resembles an apocalypse in the sense that an apocalypse "is not a real end, but a rupture, a break, a divide that separates two different states" (Blanuša 228). The tearing down of an old state, covered with death and blood, is bluntly displayed before our eyes. As a member of the introspective Cs community, I am proud to see that we did not choose to look away but tried to build a new, better state out of reminiscences. As I write and rewrite this narrative, things keep changing rapidly. Recently, I have started to hear more discussions about a "post-COVID" era. In places where this word is used, there is a mix of anticipation and concern. Yet I remain positive and hopeful about a "post-COVID" world, because, as Rebecca Solnit pointed out, "When a storm subsides, the air is washed clean of whatever particulate matter has been obscuring the view, and you can often see farther and more sharply than at any other time. When this storm clears, we may, as do people who have survived a serious illness or accident, see where we were and where we should go in a new light" (para. 16).

WORKS CITED

Baker, Peter C. "'We Can't Go Back to Normal': How Will Coronavirus Change the World?" *The Guardian*, 31 Mar. 2020, https://www.theguardian.com/world/2020/mar/31/how-will-the-world-emerge-from-the-coronavirus-crisis.

Blanuša, Zrinka Božić. "Touched by Disaster: Writing and the Political." *Myth and Its Discontents: Memory and Trauma in Central European and East European Literature*, edited by Danijela Lugaric et al., Praesens, 2017, pp. 227–40.

McIntyre, Lee. *Post-Truth*. MIT Press, 2018.

Solnit, Rebecca. "'The Impossible has Already Happened': What Coronavirus Can Teach Us about Hope." *The Guardian*, 27 Apr. 2020, https://www.theguardian.com/world/2020/apr/07/what-coronavirus-can-teach-us-about-hope-rebecca-solnit.

4

Navigating the PhD, and Everything Else, in a Pandemic: A Storied Reflection on Precarity, Affect, and Resilience

Nancy Henaku

As late as March 7, 2020, I was still looking forward to attending the Conference on College Composition and Communication (CCCC) Convention. The cancellation of other conferences and the growing seriousness of the coronavirus pandemic in the United States, and elsewhere, hinted at a possible cancellation, but I continued to plan for my trip. This was going to be my first CCCC, so I was willing to take some chances. On March 12, 2020, a day after my university migrated online, I received an email about the cancellation of the conference. While I understood the rationale for the decision and anticipated it, I was still unprepared for the disappointment I felt. In 2018, I was supposed to co-present (with Stephen K. Dadugblor) a paper on the rhetoric of Mabel Dove, a pioneer West African feminist on a panel titled "Embodiment, Intercultural Meaning-Making, and Transformation." Unfortunately, I could not attend the conference due to pecuniary factors.

As an international student, there is always the possibility that I will return to my home country once I complete the PhD, which could affect the frequency with which I attend future conferences. Consequently, besides being excited about presenting my paper, "Chronotopes, Postcolonial Hybridity, and the West/Non-West Divide: Finding Commonplaces in Comparative Rhetorical Scholarship," I also planned to fully experience the conference since this was my final doctoral year. I believed the Documentarian role would not only make me accountable to my conference goals, it would also help me navigate my conference engagements as a first-time attendee. Post-conference, the role would provide a structure for reflecting on my first CCCC. Obviously, the cancellation of the conference drastically transformed the Documentarian role, and I ended up chronicling my experiences, over the three-day conference period, while stuck at home. I came to learn over those three days that while the pandemic had disrupted my routine, many of my experiences were familiar and, in fact, highlighted patterns in my doctoral journey regarding my work/life practices and their affective dimensions. The effects of routines, scheduling, mobility and engagements (with people and news, for example) form an "archive of feeling," to cite Cvetkovich, that reflect my status as an international student trying to be resilient in a moment of crisis.

ON (NOT) MANAGING EXPECTATIONS

I had defended my dissertation and was revising it for final submission by the end of the spring semester. I had also begun my optional practical training (OPT) and working as a consultant for twenty hours per week at the Michigan Tech Multiliteracies Center. I tutored for ten hours. The remaining ten hours were designated for writing center research. With the lock-down in place, coaching sessions were being held online. Because I tutored on Mondays and Tuesdays, I did not expect any engagements with students when I documented my experiences from Wednesday, March 25 to Saturday, March 28. I also provide content support services to my graduate school. This role has tended to be occasional, and because I had not received any assignments in the weeks prior to the documentation, I had no responsibilities for this role during this period. In addition to my work on the dissertation and my responsibilities as a writing center consultant, I was also applying for jobs, fellowships, and internships. But as the excerpt from March 25, 2020 indicates, these were not my only responsibilities. Activities such as filing taxes and cooking dinner—seemingly unrelated to my doctoral responsibilities—were a critical part of my routine.

> Prompt: What do you hope to accomplish today?
>
> Response: File my taxes; send feedback to a colleague . . . send a student feedback for a project submitted to the writing center; complete one or two applications; meet with a professor about a project we are collaborating on; do some work on my dissertation; spend one/two hours researching/preparing some content for a project; fill survey for CCCC Documentarian role; cook dinner. (Daily Entry—Morning, Wednesday, March 25, 2020)

Dinner is a crucial ritual in my house that took on new significance during the lockdown when we had minimal physical contact with people outside of our house. Our dinner conversations became centered on the coronavirus, often comparing statistics and responses from different countries. For international students, paperwork, including that related to taxes, is powerful enough to jeopardize one's status even in a pandemic. Besides managing the effects of COVID-19 changes, international students must also take the necessary steps to maintain their status.

Because there was so much to accomplish, I tended to be ambitious in my scheduling. Graduate students are always working on many projects simultaneously. The pandemic moved academic work online but that did not imply a reduction in responsibilities. Still, there were deadlines to meet. I did not always accomplish my daily plans, which was often a source of frustration. Surprisingly, I tended to measure my success and failures in relation to the amount of work done on my dissertation, which seems to take on a larger role, significantly shaping how I manage other dimensions of my life. Even in a pandemic, the stress of the dissertation becomes that which sucks much of my affective energy. While the dissertation was almost complete, the sheer length of the draft meant that my revision was taking longer than expected. There were also job/fellowship applications, another priority for me as I was at the final stages of my PhD I also had other responsibilities outside of academic work: to family, for instance. I remember feeling overwhelmed and worried the evening of March 25 as I could not shake off the thought that I may not complete my dissertation revisions on time, and yet, I looked forward to the opportunities of a new day.

> I am tired. I am worried that I could not work on my dissertation and complete my applications today, but tomorrow, these will be my priorities. I have mixed feelings right now, but I am looking forward to tomorrow. (Daily Entry—Evening, Wednesday, March 25, 2020)

On March 26, when "I spent most of the time working [on my dissertation]," I indicated:

> I feel a bit hopeful and confident. I think my work on the dissertation went very fast today, and I am looking forward to doing some more work in the coming days. (Daily Entry—Evening, Thursday, March 26, 2020)

When things went as planned on Saturday, I felt "satisfied with [my] work . . . on the dissertation [and . . . application] (Daily Entry—Evening, Saturday, March 28, 2020).

My days began very early, between 12:00 a.m. and 4:00 a.m., and often it was difficult to tell the days apart as my work flowed into other days. Working long hours meant that I became tired at some point in the day. For instance, because Wednesday started around 2:00 a.m., by 2:00 p.m., after a meeting, I just had to sleep, waking up at 4:00 p.m. to prepare dinner. My work on Thursday moved into Friday. I continued my work from 12:00 a.m. to 7:00 a.m., after which I slept and woke up around 11:30 a.m. to attend the virtual WPA-GO meeting and, later, a meeting for a Wikipedia program I was participating in. That evening, I indicated that "I feel like going back to sleep!" This peculiar scheduling characterized my PhD experience and was by no means limited to my work during the pandemic. As a doctoral student, you learn to work for long hours, sleep late and, depending on the day, wake up to more responsibilities. While the body reprograms itself in response to these transformations, it sometimes resists through feelings of tiredness that serve as embodied responses to the intensity of labor that the body experiences. To clarify these dispositions is to recognize, as Chaput argues, that "affect . . . functions as a fluctuating property that links energetic matter to forms of being-in-the-world" (92). Informed by Gill's observations on academic labor and its associated "psychic habitus," I observe that my dispositions were shaped by a notion of a model graduate student who, through hard-work and responsibility, fashions herself as a fitting subject within neoliberal academia (236).

Significantly, of all the days, it was only on Wednesday that I took an improvisational approach to my schedule. This also happens to be the day that I did not get much accomplished, causing me to experience negative pathos. The improvisational approach allowed me to make adjustments depending on my workflow. Besides the flexibility it provided in a week of chaotic activity, improvising gave me a kind of agency that was distinct from intentional planning. This balancing was my way of ensuring that the dissertation did not completely overwhelm me. The intentional scheduling often caused me to work with few breaks, mostly to visit the washroom and get some food/water. In some instances, my break was used to call family and a colleague. Even in the effort to intentionally schedule my plans, there were always distractions from unplanned activities, coronavirus news from home especially, colleagues who needed urgent feedback on write-ups and an unplanned viewing of a documentary (*Pandemic*). While intentional scheduling served as self-governing instruments, these distractions reinforced the ways in which the messiness of everyday life shapes my daily choices as a graduate student. On Friday, I could not complete an application partly because I was distracted by the news from my home country—Ghana. I later took a walk as it was sunny (the weather tends to be snowy in Houghton) and watched parts of the documentary, *Pandemic*, on Netflix, which was unplanned. With everything going on, I was drawn to watch this documentary, but slept in the process. Because I planned to work late on Friday, I felt guilty when I woke up at 1 a.m. on Saturday.

COMPOSING IN UNUSUAL TIMES

Much of the work I was doing during the period of documentation involved a significant amount of writing and reading, all of which occurred in my bedroom. Working from my bedroom was not necessarily a new development, as I had done so at various stages of my dissertation. Revising the dissertation requires that I consult several sources. Prior to the lockdown, whenever I was not working at the Multiliteracies Center, I divided my working time between the library and my bedroom. With the library closed, my bedroom became a space to access resources in one place. Significantly, there were hardly any changes in my bedroom during the period of documentation as scenic differences tended to be exterior rather than interior to my room. It was also almost always quiet.

> I am currently in my bedroom. The light seems dim. I don't know why (maybe it's just my min[d] playing tricks on me after being in the room for some days now), and I am currently sitting on my bed as I write this entry. There is another laptop (solely for the purposes of editing my dissertation) on the desk in the room. Papers and books are scattered on the floor, bed and desk, and the window seems to be slightly open. It seems a bit cloudy for 11:00 a.m. It is really quiet in the house, but there is a whirring noise probably from the heater, and, once in a while, I hear a car pass by. (Daily Entry—Morning, Wednesday, March 25, 2020)

> I am still in my bedroom working from my bed. The scene has not changed since I submitted the forms for Friday evening. The only difference is that I have the laptop on my lap right now

rather than on the bed. As always, there is a notebook here, a pen, and another book (now that I think about it, I am not sure why I moved this book to the bed as I don't need it now). I have not touched my desk since I filled in the Friday forms, so there is no change in the arrangement. I am typing on my laptop right now, and I am the only person. It is quiet, as most people are currently sleeping. There is no sound from outside. I can hear the buzzing from my own laptop. I can't smell anything. (Daily Entry— Morning, Saturday, March 28, 2020)

Working in other parts of the house meant moving material around, which was not advisable during the pandemic when there were concerns about the lifespan of viruses on surfaces. While I am used to working for long hours in one setting, the pandemic heightened my sense of confinement, because I no longer had the option of using other venues (like the library) for work. This confinement would sometimes interfere with my cognitive engagement, and in one instance, I indicated its possible impact on my spatial perception.

Completing graduate education is hard, but doing so during a pandemic, characterized by sharp changes and heightened isolation, is even harder and requires resilience, which is already considered as the most critical requirement for success in graduate school (see Cahn 5). What might resilience for a graduate student in such a moment look like? Resilience can be read as "attention to choices made in the face of difficult and even impossible challenges" (Flynn et al. 1), and among other actions, it includes "crafting normalcy" (Buzzanell 3). This was evident in my effort to break the monotony of my working space and "craft normalcy" for my composing process. I created two "workstations"—my desk and my bed—for different sorts of work. The desktop was for writing and reading that required "deep" attention. I always revised the dissertation or completed applications while using this arrangement. This helped me to focus in ways that I could not if I were to be working from the bed setup. I gravitated towards the bed set-up when I was tired of sitting and needed a break from cognitively-stressful work.

I always had books or papers (drafts of my dissertation and other work-in-progress chapters) around (on the floor, desk, or bed) for easy access (Figure 4.1). I often filled the Documentarian form or sent short emails while lying on my bed. For each set-up, I also had a notebook and pen for scribbling ideas before typing them (Figure 4.2).

Figure 4.1. Desktop setup.　　Figure 4.2. Bed setup.

MOBILITY, CONTACT(LESSNESS) AND AFFECT

My affective states during this period were somewhat linked to questions of mobility and contact. Besides Friday, March 27, I spent all the other days at home, working mostly from my bedroom. As Figure 4.3 shows, there was zero mobility outside of my house on March 25 for example.

However, on March 27, I took a 21-minute walk which helped me clear my head when I read news about the growing seriousness of the coronavirus situation in Ghana, my home country. I first went to the closest shop to my house where I have bought my groceries since the pandemic began. From there, I headed towards my university campus, which is right across from my house. I had not been to the campus since we migrated online.

The visual differences suggest an absence of activity and contact (Figure 4.3) as against movement and contact within other spaces (Figure 4.4). While I was physically isolated, I had significant virtual contact with others—for example, colleagues and family. As the images in

Figure 4.3. Google Maps timeline for March 25 (no mobility outside my house).

Figures 4.5–4.8 show, I hardly met people in my neighborhood or on my way to the shop and the Michigan Tech campus. The main street, which was usually busy at this time of the day, was empty. Most importantly, coronavirus-related signs were visible on campus and at the grocery shop.

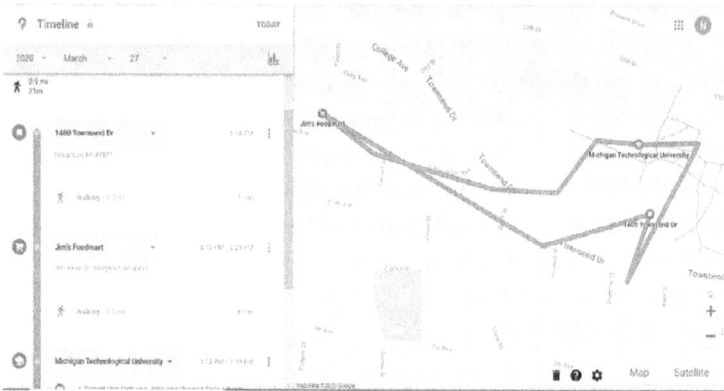

Figure 4.4. Google timeline for March 27 (mobility from my house to grocery shop and the Michigan Tech Campus).

Figure 4.5. "Stay at Home" sign in the window of an exterior door on the Michigan Tech campus.

Figure 4.6. An empty exterior corridor on the Michigan Tech campus.

Figure 4.7. Vacant roadways at the intersection of Townsend and Houghton on the Michigan Tech campus.

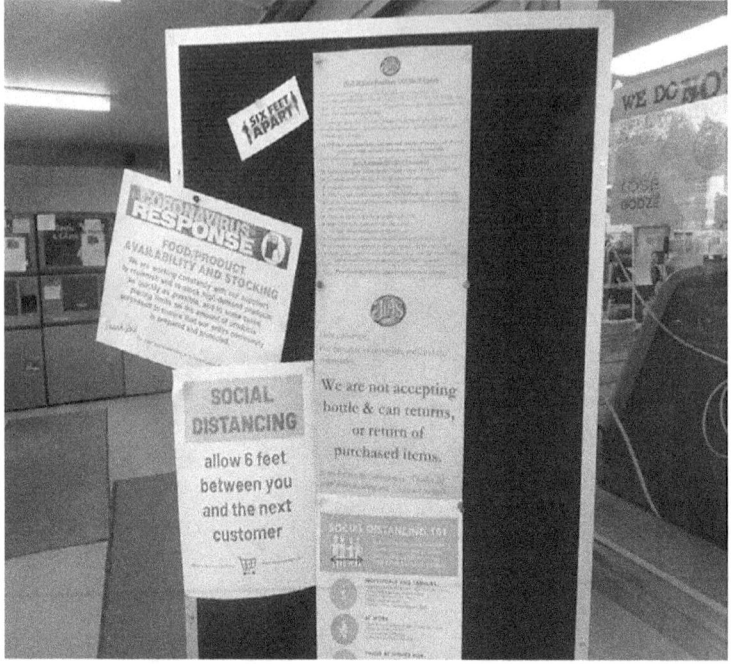

Figure 4.8. Signs regarding COVID-19-specific policies posted at the Foodmart near the Michigan Tech campus.

The images from around campus (Figures 4.5–4.8) highlight a crucial link between my personal isolation (Figure 4.3) and a social isolation engendered by the pandemic. If, as Ahmed argues, emotions "move" and that mobility "connects bodies to other bodies," then there is something to be said about the absence of socio-physical mobility and its impact on one's academic energy during a pandemic (11).

LIVING A TRANSNATIONAL LIFE

My CCCC presentation would have argued for how space-time entanglements of the transnational recalibrates our disciplinary commonplaces and complicates comparative rhetorical analysis—a point now supported by the transnational circulation of the coronavirus and its rhetorical manifestations across geopolitical contexts. Patterns in my narrative over the three-day period highlighted how my liminal state as an international student complicated my experiences and impacted my emotive state. When I began the Documentarian role on Wednesday, I was worried about not only the situation in the US, but also the increasing seriousness of the situation in Ghana where my family, including my husband, mother, siblings and many other members of my extended family reside.

While the pandemic is experienced on a global scale, its impacts are concretely experienced at local levels, and for those living at "borderlands" (Anzaldúa), such as international students, the sense of the local is itself complicated, for it includes not only the places we are physically located, however unwelcoming it might feel sometimes, but also our connections with the locations of those with whom we feel at home. If I was anxious about the coronavirus in Ghana, it was also because I missed the death and funeral of two relatives during my doctoral studies: my grandmother in 2016, and my father, last year. I have had to continue with my doctoral work as usual, even in these difficult times, by compartmentalizing—with my "unburied dead," to cite Busia, "follow[ing] behind through bedroom doors" (25). This affective residue flows into the new "psychic habitus," to borrow Gill's (236) term, engendered by the pandemic, heightening my sense of worry for my family in these moments and sometimes leading to distractions from work, which, in turn, increase my anxieties about not being able to complete revisions for my dissertation especially.

I was unable to file the dissertation in the spring, but an extension from the Michigan Tech Graduate School enabled me to complete my submission in early summer at no extra cost. I am still working as a content specialist in the meantime and searching for academic positions both in Ghana and the United States. I have received some rejections, but no response from others. I have also had interviews for some positions both in Ghana and the US, but I have not yet received any offers. I am currently in a state of uncertainty and waiting. As someone who is no longer a student, I do not have the same institutional support that students are able to receive, such as the recent effort to get the United States government to rescind its decision concerning international students. It is unclear how the economic impact of the pandemic affects the employment of international scholars. I had planned to return home depending on what happens in the first half of my OPT year, but a decision to go home is not an easy one. First, there are health issues to consider, and second, it has become even more expensive to return home. A mandatory fourteen-day quarantine for people entering Ghana implies that I would spend twice as much to return home. Not only am I unable to make future plans, I have also become practically immobile.

FINAL REFLECTIONS

Besides serving as an archive of my experiences, this documentation has provided a means to have honest conversation with myself about my experiences as a doctoral candidate completing a dissertation in these challenging times. It has allowed me to actually think, clarify, and ultimately articulate the range of emotions I was experiencing in these moments and their links with my constantly shifting affective states during the dissertating stage. While some of the emotions I am experiencing are not new, they have been aggravated by the pandemic and the precariousness of being an international student during a global crisis. Though I have completed my doctoral degree and do not have a permanent job, my routines have hardly changed. I am still doing more writing and reading—some of which are related to my part-time job as a content specialist, others are related to work-in-progress papers and job applications. I also have new responsibilities, like serving as a reviewer for an academic journal. I am not sure about the future, but I remain focused in spite of the uncertainties of my current situation. I draw much inspiration from Cavafy's poem "Ithaka," which literally motivated me through my doctorate. At some point, I even had it printed and pasted on my office wall to remind me that, though the PhD journey would be "full of adventures, full of knowledge," it would be a "long" road (Cavafy 37). As I look into the future, I know there will always be obstacles on this academic journey, but I continue to learn to not "carry them along within [my] soul," (37) but to be ready to pivot and be resilient in the face of unexpected changes.

WORKS CITED

Ahmed, Sara. *The Cultural Politics of Emotion*. Edinburgh University Press, 2004.

Anzaldúa, Gloria. *Borderlands/La Frontera: The New Mestiza*. Aunt Lute Books, 1987.

Busia, Abena P. A. "Exiles." *Testimonies of Exile*. Africa World Press, 1990, p. 25.

Buzzanell, Patrice M. "Resilience: Talking, Resisting, and Imagining New Normalcies into Being." *Journal of Communication*, vol. 60, no. 1, 2010, pp. 1–14.

Cahn, Steven M. *From Student to Scholar: A Candid Guide to Becoming a Professor*. Columbia University Press, 2008.

Cavafy, Constantine, P. "Ithaca." *The Collected Poems*, translated by Evangelos Sachperoglou, Oxford University Press, 2007, p. 37.

Chaput, Catherine. "The Body as a Site of Material-Symbolic Struggle: Toward a Marxist New Materialism." *Philosophy & Rhetoric*, vol. 53, no. 1, 2020, pp. 89–103.

Cvetkovich, Ann. *Archive of Feelings*. Duke University Press, 2003.

Flynn, Elizabeth, et al. "Feminist Rhetorical Resilience: Possibilities and Impossibilities." *Feminist Rhetorical Resilience*, edited by Elizabeth Flynn, et al. Utah State UP, 2012, pp. 1–29.

Gill, Rosalind. *Breaking the Silence: The Hidden Injuries of the Neoliberal University. Secrecy and Silence in the Research Process: Feminist Reflections.* Edited by Róisín Ryan-Flood and Rosalind Gill, Routledge, 2010, pp. 228–44.

Pandemic: How to Prevent an Outbreak. XG Productions (in association with) Netflix and Zero Point Zero Production, 2020.

5

Risk and Refuge: The Role of the Commonplace in Navigating Crisis

Lynn M. Ishikawa

March 25, 2020. I sit at the heavy oak table in the dining room, stacks of books, binders, and papers on three corners, my son's trumpet music and the US census form to my left, a bright bowl of oranges behind my laptop. Electric guitar notes echo from upstairs; water runs in the kitchen. Life goes on despite the fact that much of what we think of as "life" has stopped: going to work, seeing family and friends, traveling. It is both scary and surreal: already someone I know personally is suffering from COVID-19 (although, on March 25, he had not yet received his test results due to a backlog of unprocessed samples), and the Tokyo Olympics have been cancelled. A headline on the front page of *The New York Times* reads, "India Locks Down 1.3 Billion People for 3 Weeks." It seems hard to get more surreal than that, yet recently I often recall another strange day in March 2011—almost exactly nine years ago—when I took the train to the New Sanno Hotel in downtown Tokyo to get the potassium iodide pills that were being provided to American citizens living in the area, a precautionary response to the nuclear disaster that was unfolding in Fukushima. Then, too, reality seemed at odds with everyday expectations; it was surreal to be on such an errand on that lovely day. I stopped at an outdoor café on the way home, trying to enjoy the spring warmth despite the reality of Japan at that moment. Looking back, I don't know the point at which I became so acutely aware of life's tendency to veer. It may have been September 11; it may have been before. Most of my life I have been preoccupied with risk, and now here we are—the whole world—trying to assess the risk of stepping outside.

Looking back at my writing from that third week of March, when I should have been at the conference but was instead observing life through the window of my dining room, what stands out to me is my ability to proceed with the commonplace business of the everyday:

filling bird feeders, cleaning the house, planning lessons. My concentration lagged and my work felt less efficient at home, but I could get on with the typical tasks of life. I could move from room to room without feeling paralyzed, I could focus long enough to accomplish small things despite the chaos. Dread and anxiety are not unfamiliar to me; they wake me now and then in the middle of the night or seize my thoughts occasionally during the day, but they haven't incapacitated me in this current crisis the way they did in 2011. Then, even the most mundane household chore required thought and time; now, I got on with it, purposefully if awkwardly. The first time I went to the grocery store after the lockdown began, I wore a mask and a pair of magenta polyester fleece gloves. I was nervous and uncomfortable, my glasses fogging up with each breath, standing in the produce section trying in vain to find the opening of the slippery plastic vegetable bag. The trip itself was the result of risk calculation, timed to reduce the number of encounters with other people, and executed with the new accoutrements of daily life: wipes and hand sanitizer. But I managed. This was the new normal of engaging with the outside world, the new reality necessary to minimize risk. Of course, people made choices: some didn't wear masks or take the threat seriously; for whatever reason, the precautions were more than they were willing to change. I could judge them, but a part of me also understood. In Japan, in 2011, one of my friends carried a trowel in his backpack at all times in case he needed to dig himself or others out of debris. For me, it was too much. The idea that that was now the sane and recommended thing to do, that everywhere I went I should be prepared to find myself in a pile of rubble, felt like more than I could handle.

If you're looking for a film that captures our current moment, it's *Night of the Living Dead*, George A. Romero's classic horror film from 1968. The threat—"ghouls" that devour the living—seems to come from outside the house; yet in many ways, it is what happens inside the house—the bickering and the petty power struggles—that doom the residents. Because they are unable to work together and to see each other as connected—strangers, yes, but united by the same goal—the real threat ends up being the living people rather than the undead. The house is a refuge yet also a risk, and they can't stay inside forever. The characters in the film listen to radio and television reports describing a "national emergency" and a country in crisis from an "epidemic" (Romero). And then Ben, the main character and the only person of color in the film, survives the attack of the undead only to be shot by a militia-like figure acting on behalf of the sheriff. In the midst of the pandemic, we stay in to protect ourselves and others from the virus circulating outside, but increasingly it seems that our inability as a unified nation to agree on a productive way to manage our problems and our past is a bigger threat in many ways than the risks posed by the virus. Our home, itself, is the risk. For me, home has been a refuge, but it is clearly not so for everyone; indeed for many, inside is more dangerous than outside. In this and other ways, the pandemic has exposed the inequities in society and the ways in which the systems meant to protect are either broken or unjust. What is commonplace for some is fraught with risk for others.

How can one assess risk in daily life? This question has preoccupied me for decades, but it consumed me in the days after the 2011 disaster in Japan. I felt that if only I could determine a rational, objective sense of the risk we faced from the threat of another earthquake, I could make a clear-headed decision about what we should do. I looked at the reactions of both friends and strangers to see how they were coping and rationalized that if they could move on, then I should be able to as well.

Eventually, society started to return to normal. Shops opened; people went out to eat and drink. But by this time, I could see that something was different about how I was reacting to the aftermath of the disaster. On the occasions when we did go out, I scrutinized spaces for a place to take cover if necessary and mentally assessed the safety of every building we entered. I had to have the television on all the time at home in order to hear the early warning alerts. I was so distracted and on edge that it was difficult to accomplish even the smallest task. I was constantly worried about the radiation that my son, then four, was being exposed to. I read conflicting reports about air and soil safety and wondered whether it was okay for him to play in the park near our house. I watched as government officials explained efforts to contain the still unfolding disaster at the nuclear power plant in Fukushima. In those days and weeks following the disaster, everything seemed uncertain. I kept shoes at the foot of our bed in case we needed to flee in the middle of the night.

Quotidian routines require both calm and trust—the ability to escape the outside and a sense that the inside is safe. In the third week of March 2020, my dining room table became the center of this new inside world: office, conference room, break room, and cafeteria. In this case, "outside" did not necessarily mean outside my door—I left the house to take walks and go to the store—but rather closer to the Japanese sense of *soto*, or society outside the self (Bachnik 6). In my house, I felt an almost Zen-like sense of peace: my chief anxiety the knowledge that in a few days I would need to meet my students in an online space rather than around the large oval table in our campus classroom. I could stay in because I was being told to stay in, and theoretically I could manage the risk that my family and I faced by making choices about when, how, and how often I went out. In this sense, the danger seemed farther away and the risk less palpable than the March 11 earthquake-tsunami-nuclear disaster in Japan. I thought often of the similarities: the sense of loss and grief for those who had died as well as for everyday life—the way that both lent a sort of nostalgia to common daily routines, making the quotidian seem almost miraculous.

Spring is a turbulent time, March in particular. My father died on an unseasonably warm Michigan day in March; almost 10 years later, I met the man who would become my husband on the first day of spring. The fact that March is also my birth month makes it a time of commemorations and connections between past and present. Seen within the context of this dynamic significance, it's not surprising that at least two of the biggest unexpected disruptions in my life have occurred in March. On the day of the earthquake, my son had stayed home from daycare because we'd been invited to a friend's house. I was preparing for the beginning of the new academic year in April. It was a cloudy day, a little cool. As I was walking across the living room, I heard the tinkling of glasses in the kitchen cabinet; immediately after, the house began to shake and then to sway. When it finally slowed, I picked up the television remote with trembling hands, my son under the table, and turned on the public station. It was immediately clear that something major had happened. The emergency broadcast system played a continuous tsunami warning; on the map, almost the entire Japanese coast was blinking.

On March 11, 2020, I said goodbye to my students halfway through the semester without knowing when I would see them again in person. Like the disruption resulting from the triple disaster in Japan, the disruption caused by the pandemic has been enormous and difficult to fathom. For weeks now, life in parts of the world has stopped. I was told to leave my office and not return without first obtaining permission. Because I was not an essential worker, I took seriously the order to stay home, and when I did go out, I wore a mask and kept as much distance from others as possible. The sense of crisis, the questions of safety and whether the government was being transparent about what they knew reminded me daily of 2011. Both raised questions about preparation and what should have been done—but was not—in order to be ready for such a scenario. Both prompted discussions of life returning to "normal" and, like the other major crisis of my life, September 11, a thought in my own mind that things were forever changed in some way. And both, at least for me, involved almost obsessive checking of the news as a way of gauging behavior and decisions. Just as in *Night of the Living Dead*, the news was a source of both information and fear, deepening my understanding of the crisis but also my sense of panic. What is different about these experiences, however, is the role that the commonplace tasks of everyday life—the routines of making beds and meals and lists, the limited but purposeful movement from one room to another—played in each. Now the commonplace grounds me; then, it fractured my sense of self. Paradoxically, my obsession with risk nine years ago and my inability to fall back into the ordinary routines of daily life eventually made it impossible to go back outside and interact with society. Now, commonplace routines make it possible to endure a fractured society.

A week or two after the earthquake, in a conversation with my husband's grandmother, I commented, in halting, imperfect Japanese, on the fear I felt about both the current situation and what might happen in the future. At the time, I was obsessed with the concept of risk and trying to assess the chance of another large earthquake which might then trigger further unimaginable disasters. We sat at the dining room table together in the deep quiet of my mother-in-law's house near Nagoya, where my son and I had gone in an attempt to regain some stability. In a photo dated March 15, 2011, the day we arrived, she sits at the low kotatsu table with my son, their faces close, both smooth, her white hair against his brown. I didn't have the language skill to articulate my feelings well, but my deep preoccupation—the constant back-and-forth in my mind between the possibility of luck and the acknowledgement of risk—compelled me to attempt the conversation anyway, encouraged by her warmth and willingness to listen. I'm sure she could see and feel my anxiety. Earthquakes were frightening, I said.

Yes, she agreed, all of nature was frightening, capable of huge destruction. But, she added, humans were more dangerous. Then in her 90s, born just after World War I, she had seen the devastation humankind was capable of. She knew the pain of dislocation and loss. A natural storyteller, she was charming and popular with everyone who knew her, yet she had no illusions about human nature; she knew people well. Having lived her whole life in Japan, she also knew well the unsettling yet commonplace reality of the shifting earth in this land of typhoons, volcanos, tsunamis, and earthquakes. But ultimately, despite the overwhelming power of nature and the surreal disruption of our lives at that moment, she knew that the real risk was us.

WORKS CITED

Bachnik, Jane M., and Charles J. Quinn, editors. *Situated Meaning: Inside and Outside in Japanese Self, Society, and Language.* Princeton University Press, 1994. *JSTOR*, https://ww.jstor.org/stable/j.ctv8pzcdw.

Gettleman, Jeffrey, and Kai Schultz. "India Locks Down 1.3 Billion People for 3 Weeks." *The New York Times*, 25 Mar. 2020, p. A1.

Romero, George A., director. *Night of the Living Dead.* Image Ten, 1968.

6

"Yes, and . . .": Confronting Work, Miscarriage, and Grief during a Pandemic

Morgan Hanson

My quarantine officially began on March 6, 2020. I was six weeks pregnant, and I was terrified of experiencing yet another miscarriage. If I could have gone into hiding sooner, I would have, but I had to wait until spring break. The flu had been particularly bad on our campus and in our city for the month of February, and so I had been in mini isolation since February 25, traveling only between work and home. I was doing everything I could to prevent a miscarriage, and so I saw home as the safest place to be. I naively thought that viruses would greatly subside after spring break and that it would be safe to return to as normal of a life as possible. I'd also likely know the viability of my pregnancy at that point, and so I assumed that by mid-March, I would be able to relax a bit.

On March 11, we learned that the pregnancy had ended, a third consecutive miscarriage. I finally exhaled for the first time in three weeks. I no longer had to worry about a virus taking my baby; nature took care of that all on her own. I wasn't looking forward to the grieving process, but after five years of infertility, I wasn't new to grieving pregnancy loss or the loss of future dreams of children. I had spent so much time with infertility that pregnancy seemed scarier, but I know better. The real fear was another confirmation that I may never have children. I ended my spring break in the operating room on Friday the 13th.

When the lockdown officially began in Indiana on March 17, 2020, I was relieved. We had been granted a second spring break the week of March 16, but I knew that our university would likely shift to all online for the rest of the semester (and it did the following day), and so I naively thought that I would have the time and space to recover from the miscarriage. I rejoiced in my newfound freedom and purpose. I could work and grieve at my own pace in my home, and I could devote as much time as I wanted to heal and plan for the future. I imagined that developing online work would be creative, generative, and, most importantly, an escape. I've found that it's important to try to create after a miscarriage. When you discover your body can't create like it's designed to, you try to find as many places for creativity as possible to escape the harsh reality of loss. I could reap the benefits of escaping into work in the comfort of my home all while grieving at a pace I needed.

I took part in the CCCC Documentarian experience as another form of escape. Two reflective surveys a day for four days seemed like the perfect way to connect with others, create new ideas, and reflect on my time during a pandemic. In the days leading up to the reflection experience, I found myself looking forward to it. I couldn't wait to record my days in a space that seemed more public. My pandemic experience was about to be shared with someone else, and that made my experience seem more important. I couldn't wait to see how the days would unfold as I thought about an alternate reality (what CCCC could have been) and a present, seemingly idyllic reality (working from home) during a pandemic.

Little did I know that the CCCC Documentarian surveys would make me confront the harsh realities of isolation during an already isolating time in my life. Miscarriage and infertility are isolating on their own. Adding forced isolation made the beginning of quarantine a more difficult time for me. Through the Documentarian reflections, I saw the barren state of my current predicament during the COVID-19 stay-at-home orders. I was isolated, alone, and waiting for death to return. All of my grief escape routes were stripped from me by the pandemic, and so I had to encounter the effects of grief and death face-to-face for the first time since my first miscarriage in 2015.

ESCAPE ROUTES BLOCKED: CONFRONTING (RE)PRODUCTIVITY

I began the reflection period stressed, angry, and afraid. With the official lockdown, all of my grief escape routes were taken away from me. I couldn't go into work. I couldn't go ice skating or to yoga classes. I couldn't even go for mindless retail therapy. Initially, I thought that being at home would provide a space for me to grieve appropriately and plan the next steps for growing our family. But with the lockdown, those places for denial, healing, and planning were shut down.

I couldn't escape and thwart death like I had hoped. I had just experienced death, but here it was again. In isolation, I felt like I was sitting and waiting for death to return to me.

> Wednesday, March 25 (Morning): I'm stressed today. My husband is an essential worker. . . . We realized last night just how unsafe we are during this pandemic. One of his employees came in to work and announced that she had partied all week in Indianapolis, [and] while she was at it, she visited her brother who had tested positive for COVID-19. Even though I'm isolating (and have been since March 6), I feel like I'm just waiting for the virus to come to me. It's strange to know you're doing your part, but you're still at the mercy of others who aren't. . . . I felt like I was waiting for death to come rap on my door. . . . Also, I'm relieved I'm not pregnant anymore, which makes me feel guilty. I can't imagine dealing with a pandemic while pregnant, so I feel like that's one silver lining to an otherwise very sucky situation.

Before learning of my husband's renegade employee, I believed I was safe. I had not left my house in weeks, and my husband's company had taken great measures to increase social distancing at his pharmaceutical plant. With this news, though, I learned just how unsafe I was. COVID-19 could come into my home even though I was doing my part to control the virus's spread. I became paralyzed by fear and futility. I literally could not move away from the virus, and so I felt like I was sitting in my home not to escape death, but to wait for its arrival.

Social media amplified my apprehensions about the inescapability and inevitability of COVID-19 and death. A former sometimes-escape from the weariness of life, social media was now abuzz with COVID-19's rampage across the globe, New York and Italy in particular. My social media feeds were filled with retweets of terrifying news stories of the overwhelmed hospitals and morgues and scare-pieces about young adults dying from the disease. I understood the existence for these news articles: many young adults were not taking the virus seriously and were flouting stay-at-home orders. I also knew that my friends were reposting these articles because they wanted to feel like they had more control and power over the virus. I could not stop reading the news. If death was going to come to my door without my permission, then I needed to know everything I could about it to beat it. I became stressed and almost panicked by news and social media. One of the questions in the survey asked, "What was one news item, headline, or event that impacted you today? Why?" Almost all of my responses to these questions were about COVID-19. My response to the news in social media from Thursday evening captures my emotional response to social media throughout the pandemic:

> Thursday, March 26 (Evening): "What was one news item, headline, or event that impacted you today? Why?" THE SUPER STRESSFUL NYT ARTICLE ABOUT PEOPLE DYING FROM COVID19. . . . I know that this information is important. I know that there are people who are not taking this virus seriously. But I'm sitting at home, and I feel like I'm waiting for the virus to come to me because my husband has to go out in the world. It's terrifying. I have now banned myself from Twitter.

I don't know how many times I banned myself from social media and the news during the period of reflection and beyond, but it must have been at least a dozen times. In my Documentarian reflections, I addressed my avoidance or banning of social media five times. The more I read about the virus, the closer it felt. It was pressing on the walls of my home, my mind, and my heart. Everything I read was about death. Everything I thought about was death.

To top off the stress of the pandemic, the Documentarian reflections asked me to confront my productivity. I have always been embarrassed by my work ethic and productivity, so documenting my productivity daily and publicly made for a difficult week. When I realized that I was going to have to talk about work in every reflection, I was salty. I did not want to confront my struggling productivity during an already difficult time in my life. Even though I thought work would be a respite from grief and the pandemic, I quickly realized that working in the new conditions brought on by isolation in the middle of grief were not at all ideal. Furthermore, work, like the news of COVID-19, was ubiquitous because it was all online. I couldn't escape work. I felt like I had to be available to my students all of the time, and I felt like my course content had to be impeccable because of all the "free time" I had on my hands. Work further lost its appeal because all of its ego-boosting elements were stripped with the shift to digital and remote work. I couldn't see my students positively respond to my lessons and my jokes like I did every week. I couldn't hear what was working for them and what wasn't. I couldn't see my colleagues and laugh with them in the halls. All I could do was create sub-par content and respond to the many pieces of invention that I had assigned when I thought work would be a freeing space for my heart.

> Wednesday, April 25 (Evening): Today was not as productive as I had hoped. I was more introspective than I thought I would be. I oscillated between stressed and mopey, which I found strange. I assume it's both the stress of a pandemic and crashing hormones from a miscarriage.... I didn't live up to my expectations today, and I'm sad that I didn't even try. . . . I spent more time thinking about what could have been rather than what is right now in the present.

The miscarriage and infertility were obviously wrapped up in my conflicts with working during a pandemic. Throughout the Documentarian reflection period, I could not tell if my emotions stemmed from rapidly falling hormones, the stress of the pandemic, or both. I wished that my hormones were to blame for my lack of productivity because I felt silly for not being able to work very well during the pandemic. I could not extend any grace to myself on that front. I wanted to push through the hard things in life, just like I had pushed through pregnancy loss and infertility, and I found it embarrassing and pathetic that my work life was not stronger.

In response, I oscillated between extreme control and spiraling unproductivity and anxiety. The day that I thought was most productive (Thursday) was heavily planned out, largely in an effort to appear like I had it all together in the Documentarian reflections. I scheduled each hour of the working day with meetings, writing and research, creative endeavors, and play. By the end of the day, though, my newfound productivity was overshadowed by the seeming futility of my isolation efforts.

> Thursday, March 26 (Evening): I was feeling good about my productive day, but stupid Twitter ruined that. I'm proud of my productivity, but I feel like it's the calm before the storm, that I'm doing this for no real reason. If I get sick, then this is all upended. It feels like I'm just trying to avoid the inevitable.

By Friday, my stress, fear, and desire for control reached a crescendo. All I wanted was control and relief, but all of my efforts at control made for a disappointing day. I tried to be purposeful with my

Friday, controlling every detail and every feeling, but I had student feedback on a very low-stakes assignment looming over my head. I was so stressed by the feedback, that I avoided it until 3:30 p.m., and in the end, it only took me thirty minutes. I mindlessly scrolled social media to avoid work, which only fueled my anxiety and stalled my productivity.

> Friday, March 27 (Evening): How ridiculous to waste so much time dreading something so simple. That's the story of human life, though, isn't it?

Isolation and lack of escape routes made simple student feedback an onerous task. Through these reflections, I realized that it was time to try to let go of control and to let time and life be emergent. The more I stressed and obsessed about my current state of grief, stress, and isolation, the less I accomplished. By waiting for death, I had sealed my fate. I needed to shift directions.

TURNING POINTS: THE BENEFITS OF CONFRONTATION

Even though the Documentarian reflections had me confront the harder parts of my isolation experience and how that affected my productivity and mental health, the exercises in twice-daily reflection brought quite a bit of relief and even therapy to my days. In fact, whenever I reflect on the Documentarian experience, I think of the great relief I felt with each reflection. Through the power of writing, my stressors became more tangible; they were real, and they deserved my attention. I firmly believe that performing these reflections changed my outlook on both the pandemic and my infertility.

My first realization of a perspective shift came, from all places, a reflection on my miscarriage and infertility on Thursday night. A cohort-member from grad school texted me to let me know she was finally pregnant. In the exchange, she noted that she was worried that she'd be like me and just have miscarriage after miscarriage.

> Thursday, March 26 (Evening): Today, I heard from a former graduate school cohort member that she was finally pregnant. She noted that she was so worried that she'd be like me: that it would take her forever to get pregnant, and then, when she finally did, she'd just have a miscarriage. Unfortunately, this is not the first time a "friend" has said this to me. So many women

don't want to be me, and they have no problem letting me know it. I don't know why they feel like that's something they should tell me. . . . I have a feeling [the conversation] was precipitated both by insecurity and by fear. She's likely fearful about what this pandemic means for her and her baby. I will not lie; I was relieved to know I would not have to worry about being pregnant during a pandemic anymore. But that's not really a consolation in the end, is it? She gets her baby in a few months. I don't.

Her words stung, "I don't want to be like you . . ." After five years of infertility and three miscarriages, it wasn't the first time I had heard those words. Whenever I hear those words, I immediately yell inside my head, "I don't want this to be my life either, but I really have no control over it!" I hate to admit that when I first learned about recurrent pregnancy loss and infertility, I had those same thoughts. When I was 11, my fifth-grade teacher experienced a miscarriage, and through the parent rumor-mill, I learned it wasn't the first time that had happened to her. I sorted out what miscarriage must mean based on the sex-ed class we took that year, and I decided that I never wanted to go through that traumatic physical and emotional experience once, let alone multiple times. I remember clearly thinking that I didn't want to be like her or other women like her. But now, I am.

The purposeful confrontation of grief in these reflections changed this exchange for me. For the first time, I thought, "Wait. Who wouldn't want the life I have?" Just because I can't have children, it doesn't mean that I don't or can't have a fulfilling life. I am not less than because I am infertile. What could I have been missing because I had been loathing pregnancy loss and infertility for so long? How much of my life had I wasted hating something that had made me so strong? Through infertility, I've learned that I should put my happiness in eternal things. If something can be taken from me, then it can never make me happy. I can see goodness, joy, and blessings in the big and the little things in my life, and I can celebrate those things. How much had I lost by being self-consumed by hating one hard thing in my life?

This mental shift was a pivotal moment during my acceptance of infertility. Because I could not move or escape grief and because I was isolated for an unknown amount of time, I realized that it was time for me to look at myself and love me for who I am and for what I have in the present moment. If I couldn't do that, then this time of isolation would be unbearable. The lack of movement meant that I could not chase illusory things that could assuage my feelings of grief and being less-than everyone else.

After a disastrous Friday, I was determined to do better on Saturday, and so I declared that the day would be Self-Care Saturday. Throughout the day, my mentality toward the pandemic and infertility completely shifted away from death toward life.

Saturday, March 28 (Morning): I hope to accomplish self-care and relaxation today. I'm going to clean my house, and I'm going to shower and style my hair and paint my toes. I'm going to yoga. I have a FaceTime happy hour scheduled with a friend this afternoon, and I want to relax and do nothing after that. My hope is to love myself more than I did this week.

For the first time, I wrote about how I would care for myself. All of the previous reflections had futile hopes about productivity and escaping COVID-19. Saturday's hopes were purposeful and (relatively) achievable. I felt like I had been trying to perform all week. I wanted to be the perfect childless academic. So many tweets and hastily written articles were floating around at this time about how hard it was to be a parent in academe. Academic parents lamented that recent journals and edited collections would be comprised of pieces by childless academics. I felt a sinking feeling in my chest every time I saw a tweet or article that celebrated the childless professor. I don't have living children, but my time is filled with grieving the children I could have had and with the goals of beating infertility, either physically or through adoption. Work couldn't heal my pain, but reflection and changing my perspective could.

For Self-Care Saturday, I adopted the improv approach to a scene: "Yes, and . . ." I wanted my day to be filled with yesses, and I wanted to positively respond to any deviations from my "plans" or my preconceived notions of what Self-Care Saturday should look like. I took the day in stride, applauding the moments I had to care for myself through exercise, pampering, and relaxation. Even though I didn't record the moment in my reflections, I remember on my walk that I thought of Emily Dickinson's poem on stopping for death: "Because I could not stop for Death—/ He kindly stopped for me—." All week, I had stopped for death, but on my walk, I realized that I had decided not to stop for death. Death comes for us all, and death appears throughout our lives in many different ways. I met death directly at the beginning of March with my miscarriage. I met death again indirectly in isolation, and that death was far scarier. I stopped living over something I had no control over. It was time to go about business as usual and not waste my time waiting for something that may or may not show up.

Saturday evening's reflections are my favorite from the Documentarian reflections. In these reflections, the stressors and griefs I encountered throughout the experience appear, but I responded differently to them.

> Saturday, March 28 (Evening): I talked to my sister, a director of therapy at a hospital in Memphis. Memphis has the most cases of COVID-19 in the state of Tennessee (at the moment). I asked her about how stressed she was, since I know she's been in meetings about how her therapy spaces will be converted should there be a major medical crisis. She told me that she's been waking up every night for the past week scratching her face from the stress of it all. Scratching her face. She bought some melatonin today to try to find some help sleeping.

After talking to my sister, I realized how myopic my pandemic perspective was. Yes, the pandemic could come to my home, but there are people who are directly working with COVID-19, or who, like my sister, are preparing for COVID-19. I had wasted my week worrying about a possibility, when there are so many people dealing with the reality of the pandemic. I needed to think beyond the self. I desired to try to find some small ways of making the pandemic better for those around me. To do that, I needed to learn to accept the good and the bad in a day and to keep moving forward. In my final reflection on Saturday night, I moved closer to that acceptance.

> Saturday, March 28 (Evening): I was spending my evening in my window room. The last time I spent a Saturday night in my window room was three weeks ago, when I was fighting an intense bout of "morning" sickness in the evening. I had to come into this room because it was so cool. I just sat and reflected on how lucky I was to be pregnant. And now, I'm sitting here, not pregnant. I thought it would be relaxing to be in here alone tonight, and it's not. It's the first time I've actively missed being pregnant. It's the first time I've felt like I've grieved. It's strange when grief

hits you. And this is the first time I've ever felt guilty for mourning a lost pregnancy. The other two times felt justified. This one doesn't. I have a very good life, and I love my life. I feel sadness and relief. I don't need a baby to be happy, but it sure would be an extra bit of fun in this life. After a pandemic.

I had never written that I didn't need children to be happy. I know that I had thought it, one thinks a lot of things when going through infertility, especially after five years, but I had never put those words in print before. I felt so free in that moment. Even though I was sad, I felt almost freed from the depression that came with miscarriage and infertility. I finally felt that I had power over a very hard thing in my life. I could control this story by how I react to what it does in my life; I don't need to let it keep writing my narrative. I could say, "Yes, and . . ." to infertility.

TRANSFORMATIVE TAKEAWAYS

In the few months since the Documentarian reflections, I've found myself wondering how eight reflections over the span of four days could change my perspective on infertility. At this moment, I believe it was the power of writing and the invisible audience that helped me craft more purposeful reflections.

I'm ashamed to admit that I have avoided journaling for the past five years. Since the moment I realized that we were likely dealing with infertility, I've been afraid to document most of my experiences. I tried to write about miscarriage and infertility, but I was so afraid that by writing about it, I would be putting it into stone that I was infertile, that writing made it permanent. My identity would be infertility only and forever.

With these reflections, though, I had to face infertility. I made the decision at the outset of the reflections to confront these hard moments. I wanted to see what would happen when I finally put the hard things into words. Would I be defined by them? Would I work through the hard things? Or would I learn how to live with them, accepting them as they are in that moment? Could I say "yes" to them and still be happy?

I also think that the invisible audience changed my reflections because I felt that I was heard. Someone was reading these on the other side. Someone saw my joys and my sorrows. Someone knew that I was struggling and working through it. Someone was listening to me. But this someone wasn't responding, and because they weren't responding, I envisioned someone just sitting with my entries without passing any judgment on them. My reflections were acknowledged and valued, but they didn't make me perfect, and they didn't condemn me.

By forcing myself to be honest with the hard things and the good things during these reflections, I began to realize that these moments were simply moments. A day was not good or bad; it was just a day. My life is not defined by the day, but by how I respond to the day. If I could just say "Yes, and . . ." to each day, then I could move from one day to the next, attempting to live in the present moment. I'm not saying that I don't worry anymore, or that I don't over-obsess about being perfect, but I do try to not let the hard moments define me anymore. I do know one thing, though: I'm not sitting and waiting for death. Death is always close at hand. The more I try to avoid suffering and death, the more I suffer and die. I now try to turn my thoughts to those things that bring me eternal happiness, and I attempt to let the transitory joys and sorrows come and go. A day is just a day.

7

On Choosing

Lindsey Albracht

Across the street on the steps of the Catholic church, a couple watches me pack up our car. They're sharing a folded slice of pizza on a greasy paper plate.

I'm filing my dirty laundry, a bag of coffee, my work computer, and a suitcase full of sweatshirts into the back seat. Hours from now, we will drive away from New York City in the middle of a global pandemic. We will flee to my in-laws' house in suburban Pennsylvania: empty, because they are taking care of an older family member in Florida. We will be making a choice.

We keep telling ourselves that by taking another chronically ill person out of the equation, we're lessening the potential burden on the hospital system. We're one fewer vector in the grocery store line, one fewer fingerprint on the doorknob. We will say to ourselves that we're mitigating the risk by driving directly to our destination, stopping once, using gloves, staying inside. But we also know that we are leaving because we are scared, and because we can.

We must hold this knowledge in tension with the knowledge that we are handing off our monthly Metrocard at the bodega to someone who took the subway to work today: someone whose family member might also be unusually susceptible. We must hold the hundreds of years that are captured in this exchange: the imperialism, the racism. In the fact of our leaving, in the existence of our suburban Pennsylvanian destination, there is this history. In our choice to abandon our temporary city for temporary safety, leaving everyone less safe, there is this history.

When we arrive in the suburbs, we will order contactless delivery and stay inside for two weeks. And there will be a person on the other side of the door: one who might not be able to choose to opt out of the extra cash, one who we are sending into harm's way to pick up our food. Here, again, this exchange will appear. We will buy and eat the food that farmworkers harvested, and that a truck driver brought to the grocery store, and that the grocery store workers unpacked and shelved and scanned.

Our other choice is to stay in this city and to bear witness to constant sirens. In this alternate reality, we might hang our heads out of our window at 7 p.m. every night and bang on a pot and sing "Stand by Me" to show appreciation for the healthcare workers. We might deliver groceries to our neighbors. And we may feel that merely by the act of staying, we are "proving" our solidarity.

Staying has been posited as the less selfish choice: the one that is not an exercise of privilege. Of course, this is true while it is also untrue. Because in this reality, we would still be one more reason that subway ridership has decreased the most in wealthy neighborhoods and significantly less in poorer ones (Goldbaum and Rogers Cook). We would still endanger grocery store workers who have to bag our groceries behind the plexiglass wall and without the option of taking time off if we make them sick. So, we would still hold the knowledge that while none of us, individually, decided that Tony must keep the laundromat open, and that Lin must drive in from New Jersey and stand at the counter in front of the wall of baby photos and holiday cards waiting for us to bring in our heavy bags of dirty clothes, we have all made this possible. Those of us with the most power have collectively agreed that it is acceptable for us to expose Lin's older husband to this virus in exchange for clean laundry. We have agreed that there is no other choice, comforting ourselves with the thought that we are "supporting local businesses."

The choice to leave or to stay is not the same one. Leaving privileges our comfort over the safety of the gas station attendant in New Jersey, and the convenience store worker in Pennsylvania, and all of the many people who came into contact with them. We took precautions, but we could not eliminate the risk. So now, we have to sit with what it means that we might have killed someone, or more than one person, to secure the ability to go outside without needing to carefully measure six feet of distance with every step.

Still, the choice to stay does not change the fact that cafeteria workers were summoned to work at universities weeks after everyone else was allowed to go home, or that some security guards never got to leave. It does not change the conditions under which it has been made possible for people to sleep head to foot in a jail. It does not make social distancing possible in a shelter. Those facts remain.

The most glaring one of all is this: the labor of pontificating into my computer about disparate power dynamics in the middle of a global pandemic is made possible by the labor of people who we have collectively forced into shouldering incredible risk. The fact of whether or not my agreement is reluctant does not matter. Reluctant agreement paired with gross negligence will kill hundreds of thousands of people.

~~~

In these strange and uniform days, I will think, as I pretend to write my dissertation and to care about things that seem increasingly distant, of the Conference on College Composition and Communication. In 2016, Cs reminded us that language "empowers individuals to explore and change themselves and their worlds" ("Statement on Language").

I will wonder if part of the problem, all along, is that so many of us have continued to imagine that our job is to teach a good man, speaking well, to explore and change himself and his world.

When Black and Indigenous scholars and community leaders, when disability justice activists, told us about solidarity and care for all beings, decolonization, struggle, resilience, joy, transformative justice, persistence, two-way learning, freedom dreaming, and imagining otherwise, too many of us have continued to imagine the empowerment of individuals instead (Bambara, Cushman, Davis, Gilmore and Kilgore, Kynard, Love, Milbern and Berne, Mingus, Tuck, Tuck and Yang.).

Too many of us imagine that our work is "to [cultivate] thoughtful speakers and writers" rather than to cultivate interdependence and collective responsibility, interrelationality, resistance, antiracism, care, mutuality, and healing. We imagine that our job is to be of service to the students who happen to make it to our classroom. To conduct the research, to publish the essay that will advance our career. To join the taskforce that will ease our mind. To serve those who are able to stay, and to help them to achieve whatever serves their own purposes, even if those purposes are actively making the world a worse place to live.

Punctuated by refrigerated trucks parked outside of hospitals, by makeshift tents in a park only two blocks away from the apartment we abandoned, this moment will reiterate the consequences of individualism paired with disinvestment. It will be characterized by exhausted calls from our healthcare worker friends who had to use the same N-95 mask for three days in a row. And it will be forcefully marked by loss: of connection and routine, of future and life.

Amidst the loss, I will also find potent resiliency. I will meet New Yorkers on Slack channels and on Zoom calls, and we will strategize together about how to get groceries and medications and masks and money delivered to our neighbors. We will use new tools to perform old actions. I will watch people build incredible things to tell each other where to find toilet paper and hand sanitizer and how long the line is at Fairway.

We will freedom-dream—together, apart—in these new and old, distant and close communities, imagining a future without punitive justice and disposability. We will be reminded, again and again, in all of the times when we most need the reminder, that another world is possible. That it is both far away and already here, all at the same time.

And next to the trucks and the tents and the masks and the loss and the calls and the tools and the dreams, it will feel so small to think about the field's future, or my own place within it. The initial task of this essay—documenting our experiences at a conference—will seem so far away. But so will a lot of things. In the face of a coming eviction crisis, while watching my hometown refuse to abide by mask ordinances, while watching my family get sick, while witnessing an unending spectacle of daily cruelties, it will feel so insignificant to mourn the withering job market, and the loss of a kind of certainty. My moral dilemma about whether I can keep teaching students about how to belong to an institution that will love so few of them back will feel quaint. The contradiction between my outrage at the proliferation of the calls for papers about the COVID "moment"—this immediate need to intellectualize and document suffering—and the idea of being the kind of person who will respond to one will feel both consuming and silly.

And at first, worrying about the future of my public university, which educates such a large proportion of our city's essential workers and their children, might also feel small. But then, I will remember that the trucks and the tents and the schools form a more complete story. That the same reasons we require "heroism" from the working-class students of color in my classroom continues to starve their colleges of funding, to increase their enrollment caps, to hike up their tuition, to neglect the filling of their soap dispensers, to police their language and their bodies and their ways of knowing and being. It makes so many of their instructors tourists of their pain, deliverers of their "empowerment," rather than co-conspirators in their liberation. I will be reminded of the fact that countable deaths among our staff, and our students, and our faculty were higher than anywhere in the nation (Valbrun), and that none of this is disconnected from the other parts of it.

May this moment change it. May it be different this time.

May it convince more of us that we will not take apart this world with our individual choices, even though we must commit to making those, too.

May we move beyond "empowerment" as more of us begin to examine how our research, how our conferences, how our hiring processes, how our teaching loads, how our livelihoods, how our institutions are made possible.

Whenever we are in a year, or in ten, or in one hundred, may this moment finally move more of us beyond the "cultivation" of good men speaking well, and toward making inconvenient and uncomfortable and possible choices: individual ones, and ones that we cannot make alone. May more of us finally commit to imagining a world beyond the one where comfort and access for some are privileged over life for so many others.

May we commit to making choices that will bear fruit that we may never get to eat, as so many people have done before us.

And may we do it together, apart.

WORKS CITED

Cade, Toni. "The Children Who Get Cheated." *Redbook Magazine*, Jan. 1970, pp. 64–65, 156, 158–160, 162–163.

Conference on College Composition and Communication. "Statement on Language, Power and Action." National Council of Teachers of English, November 2016.

Cushman, Ellen. "Translingual and Decolonial Approaches to Meaning Making." *College English*, vol. 78, no. 3, 2016, pp. 234–42.

Davis, Angela. *Abolition Democracy*. Seven Stories, 2005.

Gilmore, Ruth Wilson, and James Kilgore. "The Case for Abolition." *The Marshall Project*, 2019, https://www.themarshallproject.org/2019/06/19/the-case-for-abolition.

Goldbaum, Christina, and Lindsey Rogers Cook. "They Can't Afford to Quarantine. So They Brave the Subway." *New York Times*, 30 Mar. 2020.

Kynard, Carmen. *Vernacular Insurrections: Race, Black Protest, and the New Century in Composition-Literacies Studies*. State University of New York P, 2013.

Love, Bettina L. *We Want to Do More than Survive: Abolitionist Teaching and the Pursuit of Educational Freedom.* Beacon P, 2019

Milbern, Stacey, and Patty Berne. "My Body Doesn't Oppress Me: Society Does." YouTube, uploaded by Barnard Center for Research on Women, 3 May 2017. https://www.youtube.com/watch?v=7r0MiGWQY2g.

Mingus, Mia. "Changing the Framework: Disability Justice." *Leaving Evidence.* 12 Feb. 2011, www.detroitdisabilitypower.org/post/mia-mingus-blog-leaving-evidence.

Tuck, Eve. "Suspending Damage: A Letter to Communities." *Harvard Educational Review*, vol. 79, no. 3, 2009, pp. 409–26.

Tuck, Eve, and K. Wayne Yang. "Decolonization Is Not a Metaphor." *Decolonization: Indigeneity, Education & Society*, vol. 1, no. 1, 2012, pp. 1–40.

Valbrun, Marjorie. "Lives and Livelihoods: CUNY System Suffers More Coronavirus Deaths than Any Other Higher Ed System in the US." *Inside Higher Education*, 23 June 2020.

8

Pondering the Quiddities: A Lexical Analysis of COVID-19 CCCC Documentarian Notes

Miriam Moore

Every semester, I assign a reflection essay at the end of the first-year composition course: students review their drafts, journals, feedback, and final portfolios. I ask them to observe this material, reflect on it, and then draft some "big ideas" about reading, writing, and language—a personal theory of literacy, if you will—that will stay with them in future courses. The paired practices of observation and reflection frustrate some students, who send me emails in hedged, uncertain language. "I hate to bother you, but could you tell me a little more about what you want?"

Over the four days that would have been the CCCC meeting in Milwaukee, I completed eight surveys, documenting my days at home—days I had planned to spend in sessions and conversations with colleagues. Now, a few weeks later, I am tasked with observing and reflecting on these entries to see what conclusions emerge about this experience—the time of the "un-convention." And like my students, I find myself ill at ease as I attempt this reflection, this pondering. To ponder in Biblical Greek is συμβάλλω (sumballo)—literally, to throw things together to see what patterns and insights emerge, to give consideration. I have looked at my survey answers, and I confess, I am flummoxed. What patterns could those four days possibly reveal, and why would they be of interest to anyone? What is there to discuss? I stayed home. I worked. It was spring break and the second week of a state-mandated stay-at-home order; the boundaries of my life got a lot smaller quickly. That's it.

When students find nothing to say, I tell them to look again, to ask questions. I must take my own advice: I read the prompts and all my entries yet again. They seem rehearsed, forced. What substance is in them? Over those four days, I got ready for the transition to online classes, and I worked on data analysis related to metalinguistic concept development. I refer to the data analysis in several entries; it must have been at the forefront of my thinking over the four days. The analysis required both concordancing software as well as manual coding. But what more can I say about it?

Making sense of a lexical analysis also requires pondering: a word list is produced, then frequencies and context of use are examined to find conceptual and syntactic patterns. It is an act of συμβάλλω yet again. I wonder: could my CCCC survey answers also be analyzed lexically? Would that reveal any insights, anything of value?

To explore this idea, I converted my answers from the eight surveys into a data file for analysis with the AntConc concordancing program (Anthony). I loaded the file and ran a simple word list: I had just 3,958 words to work with—far fewer than my research datasets (numbering in the tens or hundreds of thousands)—and fewer, too, than the output my students typically review in one semester. I had used 997 different words (252 unique words per 1,000). The student writers in my most recent study of journal entries averaged 124 unique words per 1,000. In other words, I employed a broader range of vocabulary than those students did. But surely that is expected—and not particularly helpful.

The highest frequency word in my dataset is *I*, which appears 238 times. The word *my* is also frequent, appearing 111 times across the entries. Of course, this makes sense; the entries are my own reflections. The prompts were questions directed to a second-person reader (*you*), so first-person responses are appropriate. And while I was writing for the editors, of course, and (potentially) members of our profession, there are no second-person pronouns in any of my entries: the focal point is myself. Even third-person personal pronouns are rare: only eighteen occurrences in the data. The first-person plural appears a bit more often—thirty instances across all entries. But still, nothing approaches the frequency of the first-person *I* (Figure 8.1).

That frequency fits my memory of those days: I felt I was alone most of the time. I articulated that thought—"I am alone"—five different times. But I am normally alone during early mornings and late afternoons; perhaps my perception of the un-convention was skewed in some way. I combed through the word list to find references to people. I was surprised by the results: across my surveys during the stay-at-home experience, I mention twenty different people (both individuals and groups), with 120 tokens (or thirty mentions per thousand words). My husband and son (also staying at home) appear most often. But the emphasis on people in my responses reminds me that I was not alone, neither physically nor virtually, despite changes to the rhythms of my usual interactions.

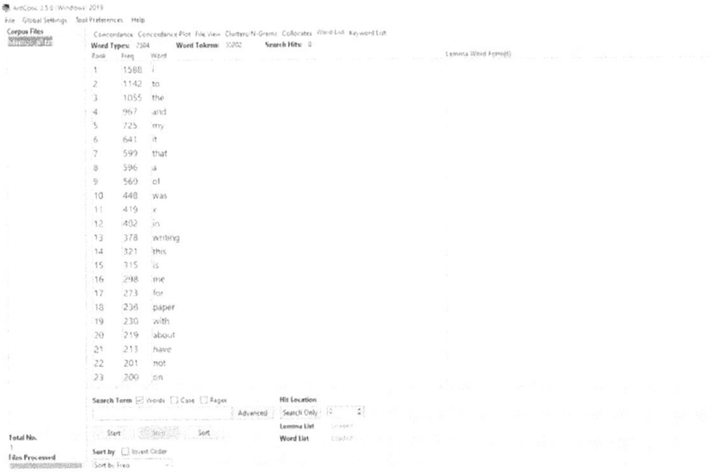

Figure 8.1. Screen capture of AntConc lexical analysis from the author's research project. The capture shows the frequency of the top 23 lexical items in the dataset.

Perhaps the sensation of being alone was augmented by my experience of time over the four days; cognitive psychologists tell us that the sense of time stretching out—time dilation—is powerful, just as the opposite sense (time compression) can be. Our perception of time may be tied to our understanding of space; looking back, I would say that time seemed protracted over the four days, while space, in contrast, felt constricted, given the limitations on my movements. I wanted to know what the surveys would show about my experience of space and time during those days.

The lexical analysis reveals a typical English-language reification of time: metaphorically speaking, it is a *thing* that I can *give myself*, I can *spend*, I can *redeem*, or I can *waste*. Time appears commodified in my entries; my responses read as minutes of a meeting, an accounting. But time is also metaphorically a container. We are *in* a time of isolation, and I got analysis work *in* before dinner. I worked *in* two-hour chunks, and I journaled and prayed *in* the mornings. We are *in* a season—and to be *in* a container suggests constraints, yes, but also secure boundaries. Such boundaries give shape to the fluid substance contained within. My days were not so much points on a line (punctuated by events *at* 2 or *at* 4), but a succession of open containers that I needed to fill and account for (Figure 8.2).

Figure 8.2. Time is a series of open boxes.

I did indeed fill the time-containers, dutifully and consistently. My survey responses mention more than thirty different activities, of which the most common include working (39), emailing (14), researching (10), planning (18), and walking (10). I also mention completing tasks or analysis, reading, playing badminton, grading, resting, teaching, writing, relaxing, shopping, reviewing, doing housework, journaling, packing, praying, cooking, editing, doing schoolwork, revising, reflecting, mentoring, doing yard work, revisiting . . .

And yet my initial reading of these responses led me to think my days lacked substance. Why would I have reacted that way? After twenty-five years of completing annual reviews and evaluations (only recently in hopes of tenure), I am accustomed to sorting activities into those which "count" and those that do not. We justify activities that count as *legitimate* instructional activities, *legitimate* institutional or professional service, and *legitimate* scholarship. Certainly some of my activities over the four-day period could be listed in a tenure-review portfolio; most could not. They are nonetheless valuable, and I am learning to check the inner critic who would rebuke me when I "alternate between things that had to be done (emails and shopping), things that energize me (research analysis), and things that calm my spirit and bring me joy (journaling, walking, spending time with my family)," as I noted in my survey on Thursday evening.

The most frequent activity, according to my data, was *work*—*variations* of this word appear thirty-nine times in the data (9.85 times every thousand words). *Work* appears as both noun and verb, entity and activity. As activity, I *do* it, *tackle* it, or *back off* from it; work dominated those four days. It is something I had to *get through* and *get done*. Also, work is an atelic process, one without a defined endpoint: I worked *on* research, I worked *on* emails, and I worked *through* the chunks of the day. But those instances of working do not contain a defined goal; I can say that I worked on a project *for an hour* (duration), but I cannot say that I worked on it *in an hour* (with the implication that something was finished or achieved). And perhaps the frequent repetition of this atelic verb in my data (in contrast to telic actions like *grading a paper, making leek and garlic soup*, or *buying toilet paper*) contributed to my sense that somehow these days lacked substance; much of my work did not lead to clearly defined products, despite meticulous planning. I am a planner: *plans* and *planning* show up eighteen times in my data, along with references to *schedules* and *chunks*. Even spontaneity during the stay-at-home period was, to some extent, planned: there were chunks of time set aside for *play* (which shows up only four times in my data, in contrast to the thirty-nine references to *work*). *Plans, schedules*, and *work*, like containers, gave shape to the un-convention days.

The surveys also asked us to consider the spaces we occupied between March 25 and March 28. The words in my data reflect descriptions of these spaces: *home* dominates the list (twenty-three mentions), as do spaces within and around my *home—den* (nine), *kitchen* (nine), *outside* (ten), *backyard* (six), *porch* (six). I do not have designated office space in my home, so I moved between the dining room and my den, where I sat on the *sofa* with a *lap-desk*. My words betray my preferences for how I engage in academic work—near bookshelves, with bright natural light. Three different times I noted that I was working near *bookshelves—writing*, if you will, in the company of other writers. Just prior to the closing of schools, my husband had floor-to-ceiling bookshelves built in our den (along with a library ladder, which I had coveted since the early days of our marriage). Throughout the stay-at-home mandates in March, April, and May, I found myself drawn to this space (Figure 8.3), despite the lack of a desk.

I have always found it easier to write, read, and think where words are prominent, in spaces that are beautifully designed, well-lit, and full of books. In my days at Baylor University, I was drawn to the sunny classrooms of the Carroll Science Building (now the English department) and the magnificent foyer and stained-glass windows of the Armstrong Browning Library.

In graduate school, I found respite in the Horseshoe at the University of South Carolina and nearby Trinity Cathedral, where concerts were held during lunch on Wednesdays. I remember stepping out of searing heat into the cool of the nave, adjusting my eyes, and finding an empty pew where I could read before the quintet or pianist or soloist began the day's performance.

Figure 8.3. The author's home library.

Figure 8.4. The author's open laptop displaying AntConc analysis data on its screen.

As I think about beauty in the sites of my academic work, I have to confront a difficult reality: my privileges. I looked again at my data for evidence of advantages in my staying-at-home that I might not have paid attention to before, beyond the comfort of the space in which I was working: I had freshly ground *coffee* (mentioned four different times), I had *internet* access, I had a reliable *laptop* (Figure 8.4), and I could stop when the work made my head spin and play a game of *badminton* with my 15-year old son, or take a long *evening walk* with my *husband*, or sit in the *sun on my porch* and watch the birds, chipmunks, and squirrels in our *backyard* (Figure 8.5). The objects mentioned in my data, from the *honeysuckle vine* (Figure 8.6) to the *tower fan* to the *Pandora* playlist, imply ease; despite difficulty in finding toilet paper, my time at home cannot qualify as hardship.

Figure 8.5. The author's back porch and laptop, where she both worked and relaxed during the stay-at-home period.

Figure 8.6. The author's honeysuckle vine.

Many of my first-year writing students do not share this privilege: some completed the semester without internet, without privacy, without quiet, without resources. The university tried to provide internet hotspots in campus parking lots, to reach out to struggling students, to ensure flexibility and accommodations. But my own words evoke privileges that my school and its well-meaning personnel cannot recreate or supply.

I am reminded again that we must not gloss over divides in educational access—and more importantly, educational experiences. I have taught in community college buildings and classrooms that are stark, utilitarian, plain. It was in such a classroom in New Jersey where I first encountered an educational experience that was utterly different from my own (and from the experiences of students at the state university and intensive English program where I had begun my teaching). In an early morning composition course at this New Jersey community college, where some students who were working full-time jobs attended class after finishing overnight shifts, we read an Oliver Sacks essay and talked about determinism in a space with cinder-block walls and no windows. At the end of one class, I encouraged the students to spend some time thinking about the assigned reading and what it might mean for the way they viewed the world. One of the students looked at me in exasperation: "When? I mean . . . when? I have three kids and a husband and a job. I'd love to sit and just think about all this—but I have a life."

The student was exhausted, and she was trying. I could not empathize, not fully; after all, I completed my undergraduate degree at a private liberal arts university on a full-tuition scholarship, and my parents had saved enough to pay my room and board. As an undergraduate, I selected classes because I wanted to, not because I needed them for a specific job after graduation (Greek sounded fun, as did a course on C.S. Lewis). I had an on-campus job as secretary to the Greek professor, not because of financial need, but because I could maneuver the Greek font on his manual typewriter (I had to change the letter ball to get all the accents in). I was—and am—privileged.

My survey responses hint at awareness of the divide created by privilege. There are references to both *gratitude* (five occurrences) and *guilt* (three times). I described my guilt as *nagging*, as it reminded me of those who could not enjoy the time at home. For example, I mentioned my brother, a truck driver who delivers milk across parts of Alabama and Georgia; he had to run some double routes during early days of the pandemic. And even now, as I am writing a few weeks later, the reality of diverging experiences dominates my newsfeed and my thinking: people of color have been disproportionately affected by this disease, and they have been killed for living *in* the spaces—the containers—of their lives. Nothing I know or have lived through compares. We have devalued the first-person *I* of Black men and women; my first-person pronoun connotes a different experience. When I say, "I can't breathe," people jump into action—an ambulance is called, a ventilator supplied. When George Floyd said, "I can't breathe," the knee pressed on his neck. Today, weeks after my CCCC journal entries, I see the privilege in my first-person pronoun, a privilege I must name as privilege. And I must name George Floyd. He mattered.

These thoughts point me to another privilege embedded in my survey responses: the ability to block news and distractions when I felt the need to do so. Five different times, I spoke of *turning off* or *avoiding* the news and other distractions. I played music; I went outside—I got away from reminders of COVID-19. I enjoyed stillness and the green of my backyard (Figure 8.7). To suggest that my choice to shut out the barrage of virus-talk came from willpower or determination would imply that anyone could do the same. But actions that I took to care for my spirit and my mind, though certainly deliberate, were made easier, made possible, by privileged circumstances of place, time, and resources. I could take a walk in a neighborhood under construction to relieve my stress. There are some in the state where I live who could not safely do so.

～～～

The tools of my work—my writing—during the stay-at-home period also connote privilege. I love the convenience of the laptop, to be certain, and the preparation for the transition to online work would have been all but impossible without it. Still, I delight in the feel of an ink-cartridge pen in my hand and smooth, empty page (Figure 8.8.). My survey data show that *journaling* by hand was part of the daily cycle for me; I began every morning with notes in the *journal*, and those notes provide a different perspective on my frame of mind over the four days that would have been spent in Milwaukee. My handwritten journal entries are both more fluid and more frenetic than my survey responses; in them, I did not try to restrain bouts of panic over the unknown. I did not revise or shape my words for an audience, nor did I digitize them to analyze lexical choices. They are a counterpoint to the surveys; the loops and angles of the cursive words fluctuate along with the emotions underlying my lexical choices, much as the pitch and speed of my speech might in conversation.

Figure 8.7. A corner of the author's backyard.

Even without concordancing data, I know the lexical range of my journal entries over those four days differs from the Documentarian survey responses: the words center on concern for my daughters (and their cats, quarantined with them in different states), anxiety for my husband, who was still working, the virus, PPE, the death toll in Italy, possible cures, laments and prayers. In the journal, I engage in soul-speak, the language of faith—words that are easy to quarantine, in a sense, away from the sphere of the academy.

And yet here again, my privilege is evident: I choose how to speak, and my choices are not condemned. But I have students whose

Englishes are judged defective, un-American, incapable of expressing logical thought—not even "real English." I have students whose
multilingualism may be viewed as a threat. They are told to keep the
cadences and accents and expressions of their languages and dialects
at home—or at least to mask them in public spaces. "Stay-at-home"
began, for some, long before the virus.

~~~

The downward pull of *weight* and *pressure* also appears in my responses:
*under the strain, under the circumstances, under stay-at-home orders, un-
der pressure*. But seeing myself *in* the situation, not *under* it, created
moments of joy and laughter, too. Once again, this simple act of framing the circumstance via a preposition may be a choice tied to privilege. To suggest otherwise would be cruel.

Figure 8.8. The author's journal.

In his autobiography, *Surprised by Joy*, C.S. Lewis described a friend who always demonstrated "a serious, yet gleeful, determination to rub one's nose in the very quiddity of each thing, to rejoice in its being (so magnificently) what it was" (199). In this συμβάλλω, I see my attempts—not always successful—to find the quiddities of quarantine and embrace them—including the uncomfortable lessons of my privilege.

As I write this now, I am still at home, back on my couch, laptop balanced on the lap-desk. *Back.* That word also appears in my CCCC survey data in reference to the *backyard*, but also in *looking back* or *looping back* or *coming back* (Figure 8.9). *Back* suggests repetition, return, movement towards what has already been, in cycles (if we conceive of time in a linear format, returning to a previous condition or location is going *backwards*). Cycles appear in my written data; I came *back* to my chair each morning, and *back* to the couch to work. It has been eleven weeks now, and I have cycled *back* to this space—literally—yet again.

I think coming *back* may be required to appreciate the quiddities fully, to name what we have learned, to recognize our privilege. I am not alone *in* this space, *in* this season. I have much to be grateful for. I hope that when I move *into* the next season and *come back* to the spaces I occupied before COVID-19—my office, my church, my neighborhood, and my classrooms—I will relish the quiddities of those spaces, as well as the perspectives and immense value of the people who share them with me.

Figure 8.9. Looping back.

WORKS CITED

Anthony, Laurence. AntConc (Version 3.5.8) [Computer Software]. Waseda University, 2019. https://www.laurenceanthony.net/software/antconc/.

Lewis, C. S. *Surprised by Joy: The Shape of My Early Life*. 1st American ed. Harcourt, Brace, 1956.

9

Scholarship Interrupted: How Unsettling Compartmentalized "Normal" Can Inspire Wholehearted Insight

Cheryl Price-McKell

I sit alone in my home office as the morning sun filters through the window and birds chatter in the trees. I watch a young family walk by, the mother and father lag while their toddler—head down and leaning in—pushes her empty stroller forward. Wind chimes sound in the distance. I "shush" my barking dog, face the computer screen, and settle into my writerly self.

My computer is arranged on a makeshift shallow desk against a back wall: a thick slab of recycled wood balanced on two IKEA file cabinets. Disheveled stacks of paper and books jostle for position around the base of the monitor. My real desk, the one tagged as a desk at the consignment shop, sits between me and the door. It holds potted succulents and a vase of colored pens. I swivel between the two workstations in an oversized black leather chair: a Mother's Day gift from my sons. All three pieces of furniture are too large for me. Signs of misfit are everywhere: a squatty stool for my feet, volumes of *Best American Short Stories* and old textbooks propping up the monitor, and a lumbar pillow declaring "Home" forced into the crook of my chair.

The work taking place within my home office has changed dramatically in the space of several weeks. It is no longer a private space where I retire to study, write, or prepare lesson plans. It has become more public and fluid. It is a space where I move my Comprehensive Exam notes out of the way in order to conference with students. It is where I meet with professors and committees while comforting my dog or speaking over video-game music emanating from the next room. It's where I document a non-conference experience while isolated in my home on the other side of the country.

As a graduate teaching assistant, I jumped at the chance to attend and document the 2020 Conference on College Composition and

Communication Convention in Milwaukee. I looked forward to connecting with the fellow Documentarians and experiencing the phenomenon of memory-making: an act of establishing story and identity through a rhetorical assemblage of diverse personal experience. I also recognized how occupying the conference space would contribute to my own identity-construction as a graduate student and novice scholar. How exploiting the badge of "Documentarian" would provide me the excuse and the courage to network, glean, and contribute: all performances necessary for fitting into the large space I am trying to occupy.

I was to present my research on a study I had conducted at my university exploring the level to which student roles, and thus identities, are constructed by the rhetorical nature of syllabi; and, how this commonplace and unacknowledged act of audience construction can conflict with instructor pedagogical principles. In other words, I was attending a conference as a means of academic identity-construction to present research that questions how we influence and perpetuate the construction of student academic identity. The irony is not lost on me.

However, as I sit in my misfit Arizona home office documenting my interrupted conference experience, I realize the story has become much more intimate and self-reflective than it would have been otherwise. I am no longer documenting a conference, but my feelings concerning a conference denied. I am no longer constructing an academic identity but negotiating an uncharted chaotic juncture where sorted identities have converged.

Not being able to step into different spaces and become that which I have learned is appropriate for that space lays bare my tendency to compartmentalize and prioritize identities. I suppose compartmentalization is my vain attempt to hide rough and unsightly insecurities behind a strategically constructed front of academic ethos. Of course, this shaky facade immediately cracked once my compartmentalized identities became sequestered to the same space. Since the home/personal and campus/professional dichotomy no longer applies, I am left feeling ungrounded and exposed.

I knew the role I was to play at 4Cs. I was acclimating to my role on campus as an instructor; and I was familiar with my roles as a writer, as a student, as a mother, and as a daughter and a friend. But, as I now swivel back and forth in my home office experiencing these roles simultaneously from within a common space, the lines separating my seemingly disparate identities dissolve. I am left feeling incomplete and insufficient no matter which direction I turn. It is an uncomfortable, yet familiar sensation, as if it has always hovered in the back of my mind or just under my skin but has now pushed to the surface. Perhaps the dissolution was only a matter of time: an inevitable crumble of cosmetic embankments against currents prone to shift, fluctuate, and deviate. Yet, perhaps this unsettling can also do more than shake my confidence. Periodic interruptions of normalized practices, spaces, and identity-construction can serve productive purposes. They can bring into relief the situations and expectations that necessitate such compartmentalized performative constructions. Because of this, compelled introspective documentation of these unsettled roles and practices end up being much more uncomfortable and riskier to write. Yet, it may also be the intimate level where authentic, full-bodied, and multidimensional stories and histories must begin.

I was to make my presentation at 4Cs at two o'clock, Saturday afternoon. Instead, I passed the afternoon sitting on the floor of my bedroom sifting through a cardboard box of decomposing creative-writing notebooks. At least an hour was spent exploring the thickest of the stack: its Mead cover stiff with Mod Podged words ripped from magazines and rearranged to form inspiring quotes and writing directives. As I leafed through its pages, I was surprised at my lapse of memory. While I had taken such artistic care to create a space worthy of them, I had thought of neither the stories, essays, and poems nor the person who compiled them in years. It was almost as if I was discovering them for the first time. Not fitting my current context of academia, this artist-writer had been shelved and left behind. Yet, this afternoon, I sat in a haze of filtered sunlight and read and remembered. I also began to wonder at the ways my concentrated academic performance had constrained my full-bodied authenticity and wholehearted engagement. When and why did I determine these different writerly identities could not co-exist? What fruits could inquiry and writing yield if both my creative and analytical selves were invited to the table and working in tandem?

It is easy to get lost contemplating the idea of wholeheartedness when it comes to intellectual inquiry and pedagogy. While the metaphor of the whole heart is commonly associated with emotion, it also suggests an optimal way of knowing that connects mind and emotion. After all, how common is the triumphant proclamation of knowing something "by heart?" Wholehearted knowing and acting is the opposite of compartmentalization. It acknowledges the different identities, perspectives, and interpretations available, and recognizes each as having the potential to contribute something valuable to the whole. Such wholeness in mind and body suggests not only authenticity but integrity. Compartmentalized parts working under the guise of separation can never lead to honest, accurate, and complete insight and inquiry.

The box of notebooks remained open in the corner of my bedroom for several days. Its presence seemed to fit my unsettled disposition. Even as I looked past it, it continued to serve as compelling evidence that this creative artist-writer may still exist and perhaps have something to contribute. It continued to resurrect long-forgotten thoughts, voices, and definitions of writerly success. It reminded me of a portion of myself that had been misplaced: an identity stored away because I was conditioned to believe it no longer fit, an identity whose loss was significant. And, like a young girl frantically pedaling a two-wheeled tricycle, handle-bar streamers whipping in the air, I began to wonder if momentum alone had kept me upright and moving forward. Since my trajectory had now been interrupted, the quotidian muscular strain and fatigue of overcompensation could no longer be denied.

I know my thoughts on wholeheartedness didn't originate with me. While I couldn't immediately name the source, I knew they were traces of something that I had earlier encountered. It took several days before I remembered bell hooks's *Teaching to Transgress*. Returning to the book and leafing through the heavily annotated pages, I was surprised to see how my academic situation and partitioned identities were playing out a very narrow sliver of hooks's rich inquiry of compartmentalization and wholeness: "Educational structures," hooks suggests, "seem to denigrate notions of wholeness and uphold the idea of a mind/body split, one that promotes and supports compartmentalization" (16). At some point, I had determined my creative writer identity to be academically detrimental or at least too immature or philistine to risk within the academic structure in which I was hoping to fit.

What physical, mental, and emotional work does it take to separate, compartmentalize, and choreograph our individual selves? What possibilities reside in that overlooked, wholehearted liminal space where—as students of writing, creators of writing, instructors of writers, and artists—identities overlap? What energy can be produced and applied with all cylinders firing in coordinated effort rather than in measured bursts and guarded application? Can we draw insight, empathy, and knowledge from recognizing and inviting nonacademic identities into our work without apology or rationale? Do we encourage this compartmentalization of identities within our students thus limiting their creative potential in order to fit the narrow academic norms to which we have conformed?

After shifting to remote instruction, I spent a good portion of my time Zooming with students. It was an odd sensation to glimpse into their private world and invite them into mine as we spoke from our relative living spaces. One student in particular seemed aware of the influence of space on her student-identity. She had returned home after the transition and sat on her unmade bed as we discussed the importance of credible sources. Rows of white teardrop lights covered the wall behind her, interrupted here and there with intricate charcoal sketches of cacti, birds, and flowers. Yes, she was the artist. No, she didn't have much time for art these days. After stumbling over the language of her academic research and writing, the student half-laughed and proclaimed her need to be in a classroom to "think like a student." "My brain works different when I'm home," she explained. I smiled, told her she was doing great, and we moved on.

What part of her whole self does this student leave behind when she travels to the university? What makes her consider her home identity as competing or at odds with her academic identity? What can be induced about wholehearted pedagogy from the commonalities between her experience as a student and mine as an instructor as acted out from our respective homes and private spaces? How can this nontraditional use of space and interaction invite a recognition of complex wholeness and how we may be influencing students or even requiring them to compartmentalize their separate ways of knowing? What would a class environment look like that questions partitioning constructs of traditional pedagogy and "allows us to be whole in the classroom, and as a consequence wholehearted" (hooks 193)?

Taking the time to pause, reflect, and document these types of personal experiences within the shared societal phenomenon of COVID-19 offers a rare glimpse of shared norms being unsettled in real time. As a writer, a student of writing and a teacher of writing, a mother, a daughter, and a creative person, being called on to act out compartmentalized identities all within a single space is forcing a reconciliation of estranged identities of academic, student, teacher, and artist. My struggle to negotiate, conform, and perform my traditional academic identity in an untraditional space brings into relief the uncompromising rigidity of those spaces that do not value the artistic or creative language I once prized. No matter how hard I have worked to compartmentalize, build up, and establish a persona fitting of academia, the efficacy of such fragile, half-hearted constructions become apparent as soon as the ivory structures within which they were enacted are physically off-limits. Perhaps the common sensation of misfitting suggests something deficient in the construction of traditional academic spaces and practices rather than in our inability as teachers and students to comfortably fit and productively employ all our "parts" from within those spaces.

What can be done with this fresh perspective? Traditional academic paths and identities have become so ingrained that other ways of doing and being are often considered impossible, illogical, or at best immature imaginations of an unlearned mind. Seeing beyond entrenched practices is difficult for those of us who have worked hard to successfully navigate them. Do we scramble back to our familiar and well-worn paths at the first sight of any semblance of normalcy, or do we take the chance to pause, look, and consider landscapes previously hidden from our view? Circumstances have changed. Perspectives have changed. The self-protective, elitist, clinical relationship between me and my students has been shaken, and I am left feeling exposed and vulnerable yet also curious and hopeful. This may be the perfect opportunity to reconcile the separation of my past writerly self and my present writerly self to more fully engage a wholehearted writerly self. This may also be a perfect opportunity to invite students to utilize all their creative identities in exploring and writing a more full-bodied truth of their lived experience and their unique ways of knowing.

As I sit in my home-office, I realize I have more questions than answers. Yet, documenting my experience has produced a desire to question and to explore the latent possibilities of wholehearted, multidimensional scholarship and pedagogy where complex identities are fully present, valued, and contributing. It has kindled a curiosity in the potential of inviting our whole selves and the whole selves of others—including students—around the table to contribute. Based on my personal experience of documenting an unsettled conference and its unsettling effects, I am excited to see what can be gained from an archived collection of the diverse perspectives of scholars and students concerning this shared exigence. I am eager to see how archiving our stories can create a new type of collaborative reflection and inquiry; and, how these insights can lead to more complex and wholehearted pedagogies that not only allow for but celebrate our multidimensional identities as instructors, students, and artists.

WORK CITED

hooks, bell. *Teaching to Transgress: Education as the Practice of Freedom.* Routledge, 1994.

10

Pandemic Life: Adventures in the Virtual World

Xinqiang Li

TEACHING

On the first day of my online teaching, I decided to wear my grey Uniqlo V-neck sweater for a decent look before the screen, and pajama pants and slippers to put me at secret ease during the class. I cleaned my room which had been a mess for weeks, tested the background light for the computer camera, hid all my diaries and shopping lists from the computer desktop, and then clicked "start meeting" on Zoom.

"Okay class," I managed a strangely gentle voice and spoke to a group of white names on black screens: "Why not free write about your life during the pandemic for ten minutes?" Then, turning off my camera and microphone, I quickly sneaked my way into the bathroom. Ten minutes later, I was back before the computer, tea in hand and enjoying the students' stories. Smiling and applauding, I was trying to deliver the same care and encouragement as I did in a classroom. The difference was there were fewer and slower responses online. I began to worry about what was going on behind the black screens. Might they be chatting with their friends on cellphones, or falling asleep, or walking away to play a video game? Still, I tried not to request for them to turn on their cameras, just to make themselves at home. "Making oneself at home," I believe, is one of the greatest advantages of the work-at-home mode. Rarely could students enjoy such home comfort to improve their learning in a traditional classroom. Realizing this, I felt fine with students who attended the online class in pajamas or eating dumplings, only if this enabled them to listen to me better. Besides, when facing computer screens, we often suffer a shorter attention span, and it will be very helpful to give them the choice to turn on or off the camera. I even suggested that they close their eyes from time to time to concentrate on the lecture. Such freedom, though it might be easily abused, could accommodate students' learning with more flexibility and enhance the effectiveness of lecture and communication. This is what could hardly be achieved by traditional class.

The self-paced learning with the recorded class video adds even more of such home comfort to learning. Actually, it turned out there were few students drifting away during the class, and I could almost always hear their voices when asking them questions. Gradually I got used to the silent but still attentive online audience. At the end of the class, I asked them to turn on their camera as a fun way to take attendance. I was glad to see their smiling faces eventually and many "thank yous" left in the Zoom chat box.

At night, however, when I watched the recorded class video, I sadly noticed my uneven teeth mirrored in the camera, the countless "you knows" in my speech, and my wrong pronunciation of the word "quarantine." It seems that the Zoom video has exposed and enlarged all the obscure defects unsympathetically before students' eyes. Now I have to speak and perform more carefully before the camera. Besides, I saw some students sharing the screenshot class photos on social media, which made me click "like" for the fun moments, but in the meantime worried about the privacy of the class. Despite these problems, to teach online is still fascinating to me. I felt like stepping into the wonderland of virtual space and having the whole world in my hands without a single step out of my apartment.

This is my first work-at-home experience in the COVID-19 pandemic, saving me all the errands to school and immersing me more in the comfort of home. There is, however, the unromantic side. I sadly found it is equally time consuming to prepare for the online class, and, once again, I ended up having instant noodles for lunch due to a busy schedule. To adapt to the new online environment, I still need time to reimagine and evaluate the practicability and effectiveness of all the class tasks online—lectures, discussions and activities, and goodbye, those warm-up short videos and fun activities. As a result, some of the original lectures have been transformed into online group meetings, and some short presentations have been changed into document sharing in the chat box. It seems the new online environment has set new rules on what works and what does not, and I still need to keep testing, verifying and developing new strategies for teaching.

On top of that, most of my students were international students, some of them heading toward airports, some staying in a hotel in China for a fourteen-day quarantine, some already getting back home in Saudi Arabia, and some still staying here in the US. Because of the time difference, I had to teach both synchronously and asynchronously, inviting those who were still in the US to attend the online class and recording the video for those who were not. Such complexity posed many challenges to my teaching. A student got stranded at an Ethiopian airport and asked for an extension on homework, and another disappeared without a trace during his fourteen days of quarantine. Because of these unexpected incidents, I was trying to personalize my teaching, offering more online office hours, being more flexible with homework deadlines, trying to figure out and follow a "rhythm" of the class, and knowing better when to give intensive lectures and when to relieve students' burdens.

In spite of these challenges, online teaching could easily fly beyond the limit of travel, time and expense, and such increased mobility helps to break different borders in different ways. Now that my students were located in different parts of the world, I was trying to make good use of this special situation and ask them to observe their local environment and write weekly photo blogs. Their contributions, ranging from the delicious barbecue served at the unknown street corner in Xian, to the gasping view of the Avatar mountains in Zhangjiajie, or the long-time-no-see plum juice and pineapple bun found in their quarantine hotel, all enriched the diverse culture of the class. Specifically, I felt the world in my hand when students from different parts of the world attempted to attend the same class despite the time difference, and one student from China even played the background music for a video I was showing here in the US.

SOCIAL LIFE

The stay-at-home rule in the pandemic did not come totally as a shock to me, as I have been living like a recluse for years: alone, confined in my apartment, most of the time preparing for teaching or contemplating at the window. Still, the missing social life did have an impact on me. There was no CCCC conference, no department lounge chatting, no end-of-semester party, and this struck me even more as I have been living alone. However, before long, people realized the power of online social gatherings. As one remote access tutor in my school said: we are "socially distant but virtually connected." Gradually there appeared more online school talks, departmental meetings, academic webinars and even virtual parties. With the limits of travel and expense erased, I could actually enjoy access to more social gatherings online, sometimes hiding behind the screen listening to the school president's announcements, sometimes sitting before a background image of a tropical beach and planning summer activities with colleagues, sometimes even attending a virtual film festival held in a neighboring town or discussing a fantastic TV show with an international group in London. Through these meetings, I could gain almost all the things physical meetings have to offer: meeting different interesting people and learning various new ideas, even though the physical intimacy could hardly be totally replaced. Watching and listening before the computer screen with more attention and composure, I could now know and understand my interlocutors much better: I finally understood Nathan's complex but wonderful ideas for scaffolding students' learning, noticed Brooke's silent but faithful presence in each meeting, and enjoyed the linguistic talent behind some New York City grassroots comedians' foreign accents.

Gradually I realize the online activities are reconstructing a microcosm of virtual society which I have missed in the real world. Now I could not only participate in various online academic webinars from home and abroad, but also enjoy free online TV shows, plays, museum tours and other various online events. If I want to take a class, Coursera provides tons of self-paced course videos; if I need to buy groceries, Instacart and Chowbus offer me a variety of choices ranging from whole-wheat bread to Lee Kum Kee soy sauce. All of these have fundamentally changed the pattern of my daily life.

Actually, the virtual world could also bring me a sense of real life in many ways. With convenient online technology, my mom video chats with me from China more often than before, specifically to make sure I am doing well in the pandemic. Every time she worried about me, I turned my camera to the beautiful trees outside the window, or the kitchen cabinet full of rice and flour which I have stocked up during the pandemic, to assure her my life here in America is still safe and beautiful, still remote from the statistics of coronavirus reports.

RETURN TO NATURE

However, there are drawbacks of online surfing. Before the pandemic, I had quit the internet for a while to improve my time management. Now, I had to reconnect it due to the work-at-home requirement. Then, the old bad habits bounced back, finding me again crazily browsing news on COVID-19 cases, and the ten minutes of after-dinner rest helplessly expanding into a four-hour indulgence in

Netflix movies. The long-time addiction to the internet racked my nerves and gave me a headache. Eventually, I decided the computer world is also poisonous and could harm both my mental and physical health. Until one day, fed up with news on coronavirus and finding little gained from online surfing, I unplugged the internet again. Immediately my world was quieted down. There were no more noisy and distressing discussions on the virus, and gradually my mind gained peace, and I could even hear the pulse of time. Once again, my life was assuming a healthy rhythm, and I could spend my time in a more constructive way. So I decided to disconnect the internet most of the time and only use it when necessary. Consequently, I could concentrate more on my work and physical exercises, and every time when I accomplished the tasks, I could taste the sweetness of my productivity. Now I realize my internet addiction could be even more harmful than the coronavirus, and, ironically, it is the pandemic that has confronted me with this issue.

The fatigue from long-time online work also makes me embrace nature again. From April to August, I have watched different seasons passing by my window: the spring snow that gorgeously floated around, the first touch of green that sprouted out of bold tree branches, the pink May flowers that sent off a delicate fragrance in the wind, the full moon that was shining peacefully in the midnight sky, all making beautiful paintings and attracting me to go outside for a walk. Though my daily walking route remains quite the same, all the trees and buildings seem to be a view I never get tired of. My phone is stuffed with photos of different shades of green of trees and grasslands, under blue or grey sky, in sunny or rainy days. I have never missed a single chance to take these photos.

After a month of stay-at-home life, I decided to visit my school. As in my apartment, all the trees and flowers on campus looked so fresh and dear to me, and I simply had no chance to put my camera back in its case. I passed by the classroom where I taught for a half semester. The students' laughter still echoed in my ears. Now its door was attached with rules of entrance during the pandemic. There were few people around, and only some carefree squirrels happily jumped here and there. Like them, I began to enjoy a campus of my own in such beautiful weather. With no people around, I could jump in the air for an amazing selfie photo or stop my car on the deserted street to take more extraordinary pictures. My walking tour mingled

Emerson's peaceful communication with nature, the great escape from work fatigue, and greedy photo captures of each eye-catching view. The pandemic ushers me to the wonderful virtual world, but, in the meantime, attracts me to return to nature, once more. This seems to be a sustainable new life balance.

Of course, my life in the pandemic also involves endless search for facial-mask deals online and YouTube explorations for dozens of new ways of cooking potatoes. More imminent, the financial crisis and political conflicts between China (my home country) and the US has worried me so often and so much. Despite these worries, however, I try to see things positively, just the way I welcome the coming of a new virtual world. I believe many of its advantages are irreplaceable and could be further developed during the pandemic and preserved even after it. Like a successful businessman who grows richer and grudges every penny he spends even more, I now cherish each day of my healthy and beautiful life more than ever, trying to adapt to the new lifestyle and seize new opportunities. As I believe, there is always hope for a better life.

11

Some Lessons and Tales: Moving Classes Online in the Advent of a Crisis for Which No One Signed Up

Isaac Ewuoso

Thursday, March 12, 2020. Afternoon. Final week of class before spring break at Oakton Community College, Des Plaines, a suburb of Chicago, Illinois, where I teach composition classes as I do at Harper College in Palatine. At this time of day, it had been fairly typical to engage in conversations with peers in the faculty office. Many adjunct professors circulated COVID-19 tales about their other colleges' latest reactions to the pandemic and the possibility of college closures across Illinois. Some of the rumors were finally given real legs. At Oakton, the bold heading on the staff email sent by the college president read: "COVID-19 Preparedness and Prevention Update." The missive raised more questions than answers. This was the first email that marked the beginning of a series of others that would be sent later regarding CO-VID-19-related updates, revisions, announcements, and other clarifications. Classes are moving online. What that meant, specifically, the challenges, for students and faculty alike, was not all clear by the end of the day. Hindsight, as the adage goes, is 20/20, and this seemed to ring true in the spring semester of 2020, a COVID-19-plagued semester. My reflections and some of the conclusions that I can draw from this learning semester are recorded in this Documentarian tale.

THE GREAT CALL TO MOVE CLASSES ONLINE WAS TOO ABRUPT, AND STUDENTS RESPONDED WITH VARYING DEGREES OF PROTESTATIONS

First, it was the phone conversation I had with a student. It left me wondering about freedom of choice and learning, how some students might be perceiving the great commission to move classes and instructions online when cities across Illinois were beginning to implement their own lockdowns. My exchange with a student, whom I shall call Henry, was one I remembered vividly because he had made it palpable to me that he was not enthused about online classes, and his "I did not sign up for this" complaint stuck. It was just the first one of the several excuses I would later get from students like him who were lagging behind as they complained of the tidal waves of the pandemic hitting them on different dimensions.

The reality of the situation, brought about by a pandemic never before experienced by any educational institution, has caused me to reflect on the rejoinder "I did not sign up for this" to understand some of the reasons why some of my students struggled to stay motivated or stopped attending my class altogether as crisis began to take its toll on the country around mid-March. Henry is a very sharp student and a freshman who had recently changed majors. He made insightful comments during our face-to-face class meeting, a week just before the national lockdowns across colleges were taking effect. When our class moved online in the first and second week, he turned in discussion-board posts and essay assignments that were beyond exceptional. He did not seem to have any problems understanding assignment prompts or instructions. But after I had assigned a group assignment, reviewed it in one of our Zoom class meetings, posted the recorded session in the announcement section on Blackboard, and reached out via email to a couple of students who did not seem to be active in our online discussion forums, some students responded with reasons and some others did not, like Henry. In the course of the semester when I followed up with Henry, again, through a phone call for not turning in work or cooperating to work with his peers, it was because his internet service was becoming too slow, as it was being used by multiple people in his household who were working from home and schooling from home. Henry was one of those students who was silent and not proactive to inform me of their struggles. So, I decided to give those students a phone call. They recounted their individual difficulties in the pandemic age to me.

RESPONDING TO THE CALL TO MOVE CLASSES ONLINE IS STILL A LEARNING CURVE

As I reflect on my last week of teaching face to face before colleges nationwide went into lockdowns, many of my peers were as uncertain as the administrators attempting to provide staff and students guidance on what to expect regarding school closures. One college where I teach gave faculty four days to transition to online instruction. Another extended student spring break by one week to give faculty time to plan and prepare students for online classes. But whether it was a four-day or a two-week grace period to transition online, this was fraught with its own set of problems. It was more work. Not all my students responded gung-ho to the call to continue their composition class online. Many complained that they did not like virtual classes. Preparing students for an online class also means anticipating particular problems students might encounter and problematizing, to a sufficient degree, to mitigate virtual teaching problems. Susan Ko and Steve Rossen excellently observe in *Teaching Online: A Practical Guide* that learning online can be as exasperating for the student as for the instructor, particularly for those taking an online course for the first time. Suddenly thrust into a world in which independent or collaborative learning is heavily stressed, students accustomed to traditional classroom procedures—taking notes during a lecture, answering the occasional question, attending discussion sections—must make unexpected and often jolting adjustments to their study habits (293).

First-time students or freshmen will have their own learning curves to conquer in an online learning space. Whether it is their personal preference for collaborative or individual learning that is emphasized in the online class, students have to make changes to their studying patterns, ones that they are so used to implementing in their face-to-face classes. This means that students' learning preferences and learning styles can and will be impacted. Some students have particular strengths in a face-to-face, collaborative environment where they might easily get away without doing the assigned reading prior to coming to a class session and where live classroom discussions and instructor's response to questions and answers might help them make do with the high-stakes assignments. But those students who are inclined to work individually or have to complete assignments and activities in an online class as an individual, have more responsibilities to complete the assigned readings and activities, and demonstrate their own individual knowledge by completing high-stakes assignments.

Never had I seen as many students struggle in a class as in this plagued semester. Again, I cannot help but recall the words of the student who said, "I didn't sign up for this!" No student in my class signed up to take the class online but was given that option as the only practical choice because face-to-face classes were overruled by local and national lockdown edicts in the middle of March. Never mind the almost daily announcements and clarifications of these announcements on Blackboard or Desire2 Learn (D2L) that I gave. Never mind the repeated class emails and individual emails that I sent. Never mind the recorded Zoom or Google Meet meetings and live ones that occurred during the regular face-to-face class sessions. And never mind assignment instructions that made references to previous activities or suggested how students should begin the project that I created. Many students struggled in an online class that, rightly, they did not sufficiently plan for or sign up for voluntarily. As such, holding them accountable for that which they had no control over (they were either given a few days to two weeks to transition) did not seem fair. Just as it was involuntary for me to teach my composition classes online, the world was not given any advanced warning and involuntarily went into lockdowns to flatten the curve of the virus spread. In retrospect, I would have had more scaffolding activities to assignments that had been originally designed for a face-to-face classroom to be adapted online. If I saw COVID-19 gradually making its way to the United States as far back as January 2020, I would have signed up for my class to be delivered online and jettisoned my face-to-face lesson plans!

THE INTRICACIES OF THE CALL MADE SOME SYLLABUS POLICIES HARD TO SET IN STONE

To my students, I made it clear at the onset of my classes that I do not accept late work and that this policy is non-negotiable, with the exception that a student who has a reasonable excuse will have given me an advance notice that he/she cannot turn in the work by the due date. But the pandemic made me reconsider this rigid policy. After all, they have more readings and scaffolding activities to complete online. I hesitated to begin grading students' work quickly without getting a near unanimous assignment submission and would often push the deadline back in the hope that some of them would consider it a second chance and submit their work. But some did not. In consideration of the pandemic's impact on my students, I had no choice but to be flexible with expectations to the extent that I felt doing so was fair to others in the class as well.

SOME STUDENTS VIRTUALLY INCOMMUNICADO HAVE DIFFERING COMMUNICATION CHALLENGES

There were aspects of preparing students for online learning, made complicated by the lockdowns which prevented in-person classes and the doleful daily news of the pandemic, for which I could not prepare. Ko and Rossen correctly note that "students' problems fast become those of the instructor as well. Instead of teaching their course, posting information, and responding to legitimate queries on the discussion board, instructors often find themselves trying to troubleshoot technical queries for which they have minimal expertise" (293). Add to this, my repetition of instructions given for an assignment, clarification of directions to help students find class readings and materials, and mediation between individual students working on group projects and who have reached an impasse in communicating with their peers. But I was concerned about retaining my students and not losing anyone from my class. My first reaction was to send out a mass email to find out if students intended to continue the class online. I followed the recommendation given to faculty by the English department chair at Oakton College to drop some lessons and assignments, and as a consequence, lower the total grade points for my class to relieve students of some of the heavy workload they have, coupled with the anxieties that they now have due to the endless negative news of COVID-19. I could only assume that many of my students' attention had been diverted. How do I capture their attention? How can I reassure in the midst of a constant stream of news information predicting darker days ahead? These were some questions I thought about. It seemed that I was competing for their attention and reaction with my regular emails and announcement just as much the news of the day was.

I contemplated many decisions. I opened and read a beautiful email from the director of developmental composition at Oakton. He recommended that instructors "keep things as technologically parsimonious as possible" and "stick with 'familiar' media as much as possible" instead of "introducing the learning curve of fancier technology that's new" to the instructor and the students. I latched onto these words, devising a plan to make follow up calls to students whose online presence had plummeted. I discovered many reasons why some students had stayed incommunicado. While they did not feel comfortable speaking to me about their individual problems or difficulties in an email or during a question-and-answer session on Zoom, many would do so in a text message or in a phone call I made to them or that they made to me. I began calling and reaching out individually to as many students as possible the more I became familiar with their individual pandemic struggles affecting their class participation.

Most of the students I "lost" were the ones who stayed electronically incommunicado with me, and I did not have much success trying to reestablish communication with them via individual emails and phone calls. But I found some success in helping students who were struggling to complete assignments or to follow assignment instructions when I began texting and calling to speak personally with them. But with my classes, I had to send an announcement to my students, follow that up with a mass email, and at times a direct message. It was not uncommon to learn that some students had forgotten about the meeting, had not remembered the Zoom login information because they did not read their email, or some new issue or development had taken place at their homes or workplaces that had prevented them from joining. The more I used low-tech means to communicate with them, the more I found out about one or more problems they were having that they did not feel comfortable discussing in an email or Zoom. In fact, most would not say anything unless I asked them. Once I knew of some students' situations or difficulties, I would give them the benefit of the doubt that they may be struggling to keep up with my class due to their unique problems. Many of my teenage students were dealing with issues that typical working adults go through: break ups, moving, working long hours, child care, etc.

WORKING AS AN ADJUNCT FACULTY IS RISKY; IT HELPS ME UNDERSTAND THE CHALLENGES PART-TIME WORKING STUDENTS FACE

The precarity of working as an adjunct cannot be stressed enough in an unprecedented time such as this. As Meghan Zahneis points out in her piece for *The Chronicle of Higher Education*, "The COVID-19 Crisis is Widening the Gap Between Secure and Insecure Instructors," adjunct instructors have a lot to worry about: health insurance, fair compensation for course redevelopment online, student evaluations that will be used to determine their career future (never mind that many of them were given a short notice to move their classes online), decreased wages or job loss due to fallen student enrollment and the current economic tailspin. In one stunning revelation, Zahneis quotes a part-time faculty in her piece saying, "it was made explicit that part-time and non-tenure-track teaching will be the first to be cut in the fall semester if our enrollments decline." I pondered this implication, included the implication of not being around at the end of the academic year, of being put to the back burner as other faculty that are full time or have seniority are prioritized with class availability preference, of not being compensated sufficiently for the extra work of moving my classes online and using my own equipment for my work. But my reason for working as an adjunct is not because I have to, but because I want to. I love teaching. With the uptick in unemployment rates across the country, many of my students were affected. According to a *BBC Business* article "Coronavirus: Young People 'Most Likely to Lose Work' in Lockdown," more young people are likely to bear the brunt of job loss or to see their income drop due to the pandemic. This rang true in the spring semester as some of my students were furloughed or had their hours at work cut short. But even the ones lucky enough to retain their jobs because they worked for an "essential business" like Walgreens, Target, or Walmart, complained of the impacts from having to work longer hours. This category of students struggled to complete or turn in their assignments on time. Their virtual presence suffered as did their discussion board posts and responses.

PANDEMIC "REFLECTION ASSIGNMENTS" ARE WINDOWS INTO HOW SOME STUDENTS STAYED SANE

Documentation, in my view, does help with reflective practice, not just for students but for the instructor as well. Every semester, I have found it helpful to learn about students' perceptions of the class by having them complete a reflection essay as the last assignment in the class. It was my plan at the start of the semester when I had set in stone the self-reflective questions students in my composition classes that students were going to respond to. The advent of COVID-19 led me to reconsider my plans. I made them write about how the pandemic impacted them academically and discuss their strengths and weaknesses about writing. For my students, in many of the reflections they turned in, I got to read the various ways they were impacted and responded to the crisis. There was the student who said the pandemic meant he had to look after his daughters and participate in an online class as a virtual learner, something that he hates. But there was another student who said that the news coverage on the pandemic was a distraction to him from his studies. Nonetheless, he admitted that the readings that he had to complete and the discussion posts to which he had to respond, were a good distraction from the news coverage. There was a housewife, a first-year college student, who admitted to having a preference for a face-to-face class because she appreciates the physical college environment rather than an online class. The student admitted that, with the class moving online, she appreciated that it got her out of her comfort zone to work online on projects with different classmates.

Some students had contrasting perspectives. There was an interesting reflection essay I got from a student who said being in a face-to-face classroom keeps him even more accountable. The mere presence of other classmates sitting at close range and the presence of a professor in the classroom, keeps him more accountable than in an online environment. Working from home, the student revealed, was just too comfortable and often leads him to procrastinate more about completing an assignment—that he chooses to play video games when he needs to be studying. There was another student, a returning adult, who said that the last time he took a college class turning in handwritten papers was the norm. While he prefers face-to-face classes, he admits that he found working in an online class, especially with peers with whom he is able to form a good rapport, helpful. This is because he benefits from the work done with them on a collaborative project. But there was this one student who revealed that while he was unprepared for an online class and his family had to upgrade their internet due to it being used by many members of his household, which slowed it down, taking an online class was a good prep for what would have been, had the pandemic not struck, his first online class in the summer, a course he had planned to take. There was another student who revealed that the pandemic placed a huge strain on her personal, academic, and financial life. Though a freshman, the student confessed to being nervous, not being too tech savvy, and being surprised and impressed that she thrived in the class. There was a student who disclosed that while he was always a procrastinator and tended to work on his assignments very close to the due dates, the virtual class led him to make adjustments to his typical routines and to begin working early on assignments that he had to complete. Then there was another student who admitted to learning more about the importance of independent study as face-to-face instructions made him laidback.

Reflective assignments can be a two-way communication between students and instructors. But these reflection essays were also feedback for me on what students would like to see more in a composition class in the middle of a pandemic: more grammar exercises and challenging assignments that will enable them to expand their vocabulary. I have learned to be more creative with assignment designs and have even gained ideas from students who use available free tools and resources online to complete their assignments. In one class, I assigned a project that would have students working in groups to create an identity for their group's business proposal: one student used a free online logo designer that he had found online. I shared the link with the rest of the class. Some students established group texts as a simple means of staying in touch. Other students worked in Google docs and gave members of their group the shared access to edit and revise the work. The lessons and tales from this pandemic-driven semester are far from over; if anything, they provide us with mirrors that continue reflecting the light of our situation and that of our students.

WORKS CITED

"Coronavirus: Young People 'Most Likely to Lose Work' in Lockdown." *BBC News*, BBC, 19 May 2020, https://www.bbc.com/news/business-52717942.

Ko, Susan Schor, and Steve Rossen. *Teaching Online: A Practical Guide.* Routledge, 2017.

Zahneis, Megan. "COVID-19 Crisis Widens Divide Between Secure and Insecure Instructors." *The Chronicle of Higher Education*, The Chronicle of Higher Education, 18 Mar. 2020, https://www.chronicle.com/article/Covid-19-Crisis-Widens-Divide/248276?cid=wsinglestory_hp_1a.

12

Building Strength in an Uncommon Time

Catherine Lamas

In early March, I decided not to attend the 2020 CCCC Convention. It was not worth the risk to myself and my family to travel to Milwaukee. This decision was difficult because I was scheduled to present material at the CCCC Convention and the TYCA event. Instead, I moved on to a new chapter in my career that included remote teaching and the documentation of the experiences intended to keep education alive for many students. It is difficult to adequately summarize the psychological state I was in during this early period. My schools shut down one week before the convention was set to start, so the period of the Documentarian activity took place in the midst of what I call my "fog phase." Although I agreed to maintain my role as a Documentarian, I found it hard to concentrate on the daily tasks of recording my experiences. However, this activity did help to keep me focused at the onset of the COVID-19 pandemic, and I am thankful that I captured these thoughts.

I saw my Documentarian role as an essential part of the "commonplace" dialogue set to take place. My presentation for the CCCC covered the idea of creating a "safe place" in my classroom where students are free to discuss the fears and challenges of attending college. The 2020 CCCC Convention was an event where I could discuss commonality and inclusiveness not only for students but for all of us in higher education. Shifting to the online platform, forced us to create this "commonplace" in a virtual setting, and our feedback might serve to connect and influence other professionals in our discipline. Ironically, only a handful of participants accepted the challenge to document this unprecedented time in our history.

My position as an adjunct instructor does not always provide the opportunity for me to take part in a reflective discussion or share my perspectives with the department. I teach at four public colleges. I am a freeway flier, and although I do not have the coveted tenure, I still aim to "share the vision," make my "voice" known, and take part in the collegial behavior of the department. I attend conferences to network with my peers and learn from them, but we also need to have access to the entire collegial conversation. Nathan F. Alleman and Don Haviland characterize my actions by claiming that part-time faculty, "recognized and valued informal venues that validated their sense of professional voice and belonging overall as important to creating a collegial environment" (537). Contingent faculty desire collegiality, but we lack this membership and don't have the same level of interconnectedness within our respective departments. My teaching status is the premise for my engagement with the CCCC community because I have greater access to diverse thoughts and ideas than in my home organizations. My Documentarian activity provided an excellent avenue to share with others my pandemic ordeal during this time of uncertainty.

I woke each day in disbelief and functioned in a fog. As the COVID-19 situation unfurled, I could not grasp my inner feelings nor the magnitude of this sudden catastrophe. Everything seemed surreal, and there was nowhere to hide from this *Twilight Zone* episode. I knew this was coming—I had warned my face-to-face classes to prepare for virtual instruction. We tested the process to access Zoom sessions, I reminded them to check Canvas often, and I told them to stay focused. I reassured them that I cared about them and that they should contact me with any issues they encountered so that I could help them through the course. Like a mother preparing her children for school, I armed them with advice to navigate the coming waves and torrents of the "thing" that none of us had ever experienced. I wasn't scared, nor was I prepared for my rollercoaster of emotions that would unfold in the coming weeks, including the trauma about to creep into our lives.

Trauma is real, and we have all been traumatized by this pandemic—it was a lost job, it was a disabled student thrown into a course he never asked to be in, it was a family living in close quarters and enduring the volatile emotions that come from being "caged in." Yet within this madness, we were asked to teach and get our students to the finish line. Those of us experienced in teaching online courses were asked to help other faculty get up to speed in a matter of days. Ironically, many of us called to action were from the contingent staff, and we willingly obliged for multiple reasons. As Alleman and Haviland state, "lack of long-term job security and their desire to contribute to shared departmental goals often made

NTTF [Non-Tenure-Track Faculty] easy to exploit since they had dual incentives to capitulate to departmental asks and expectations" (540). Our desire to engage while protecting our positions drove us to action. The department was in triage mode with the urgent cries of "help me figure out ZOOM!" "How do I create online quizzes?" "How do I keep kids from cheating?"; and the list goes on.

Interestingly enough, in our panic, we did not see the world entirely through the eyes of our students. We tried to patch things together to get our work done and worried about our teaching needs over our student outcomes. It was not until I began the Documentarian role that I realized my teaching approaches needed some adjustment. This trauma put us in survival mode; it scarred us, but it also strengthened us.

DOCUMENTARIAN EXPERIENCE

I planned on an active schedule during the CCCC Annual Convention, and at a minimum would have taken part in the following manner:

- Wednesday morning would have been spent at the TYCA event, and I would have presented material on the topic of Student Retention.
- On Thursday, I would have gotten up early and walked to the venue for the General Opening Session of the convention, scanned the program for presentations that covered First-Year Writing topics, and taken part in some networking opportunities
- On Friday, I would have delivered my presentation on College Student Fear Factors, followed by visiting the poster session and taking part in some dialogue with the poster presenters. The next stop would have been to the publishers' exhibits to examine new offerings for the upcoming academic year. By the end of my day, I would have felt pleased that my presentation had taken place.
- Finally, on the last day of the convention, my time would have been spent attending one or two events, and then I would have headed to the airport to return to Los Angeles. On the plane trip, I probably would have reflected on the entire convention and the networking that took place. I enjoy networking with others, where I can learn from my colleagues and share my ideas. This knowledge assures me that we all have the same passions and interests, regardless of where we teach.

Instead, pandemic activity shaped my week in ways I had never imagined. The week brought challenges and successes in various ways.

- On Wednesday, I spent time redesigning four courses for online learning. As a "Freeway Flier," I work at multiple schools, and one school only allowed three days to convert our courses to an online format. To this day, I can only say that I worked in a numbed state of mind. These days reminded me of the days when my father died, because there was the same sense of sudden loss and trauma; life would never be the same. I knew I had to plow my way through personal and professional obstacles to lay the groundwork for the next ten weeks. There was "noise" everywhere because four colleges kept reminding me to take care of our student needs beyond academic work. But wait!

  ○ Who was taking care of us (teachers)?

  ○ Why was it up to me to make sure they (students) were taken care of?

  ○ Aren't they adults? Can't they take care of themselves?

  ○ I have needs too!

  "Stay at Home" orders came on this day. Now I was confined to my home with limited access to peers and academic dialogue. I pushed myself to concentrate and create content that would be accessible for students who were already "at-risk" in my courses. I had one course working through a five-week job-shadowing activity. Those students had to get to the finish line and successfully meet the course learning outcomes. In my Wednesday evening post, I wrote: "Honestly, I am exhausted from the amount of news and trying to make sure my content is going to really help my students."

- Thursday was not much different from Wednesday. I spent my day at the kitchen table, where I prepped courses and graded midterms. The daily news and email storms derailed me, so I limited my access to those outlets. I had joined a "pandemic teacher" group on social media, but that proved to do more harm than good, because it was a lot of "panic" chatter and whining about the situation. My schools were offering numerous webinars on remote teaching, but it was overwhelming to teach and attend "professional development" sessions. Managing the barrage of input becomes an everyday challenge to stay sane and not succumb to data overload. My day closed with the following thoughts: "I am feeling pretty good in terms of getting my classes in shape. I fell behind when trying to process world events, and now I feel relieved that I am nearly caught up."

- On Friday, I continued to work in a "vacuum" with little interaction with my colleagues. I saw a post on social media that discussed the challenges of not having an actual home office—I am one of those persons. It was hard to concentrate when televisions were blaring, and other family members were vying for workspace. Staying focused was not easy, and I looked for an accomplishment to celebrate every night to avoid getting caught up in a downward spiral. My day ended with this thought: "I feel quite accomplished and relieved that I made big gains in the prepping of my courses for the remainder of the year."

- Saturday brought the end to the Documentarian journaling activity. This day was a day of random action, because I needed a break from my usual structure. The weather was good so, I took a longer than usual walk to get fresh air while clearing my mind of the issues of the week. I completed a few school-related tasks. Not much to write about today—just a day to unwind and reflect. I noted in my Documentarian feedback that I had gotten tired of answering the same questions each day. I was tired of the monotony of the task given the limited opportunities we had in the "Stay at Home" mode. I did manage to end the day on a positive note with the following thought: "I feel pretty good about my day because I split my day pretty evenly between school and home activity."

Small accomplishments kept me moving:

- I spent the entire week making sure all my courses were fully prepared to "run" in the new model. During the week, I converted four courses from the face-to-face mode into online learning communities. I added some "extras" to these courses by curating some open sources that would help my students grasp concepts in a way other than reading texts and PowerPoint charts.

- The accomplishments for the week included Zoom sessions with my high-risk students and a feeling of some control. In each session, I made sure to provide a warm welcome to our new mode of learning, reassurance for those who felt uncomfortable in the new format, and I did my best to ask about their well-being before the start of our virtual instruction. I was conducting a balancing act between students who were comfortable in an online environment and students who were not prepared for this new environment. I spent a lot of energy coaxing the students to stay engaged, but I was competing with students who suddenly lost jobs, students who now worked overtime, students with children, and students who became ill with COVID-19. These problems became part of this learning situation.

POST REFLECTION

I chose to write from my usual workspace at home. Even with the "Stay at Home" measures, I maintained most of my usual routines to remain grounded. I usually teach about four classes in an online learning environment, so the cut-over to entirely online instruction was not too difficult. I have a schedule that helps me stay ahead of the demands of an online class. Since I am an introvert, a focused routine helps me "re-charge." This routine is essential to my thought process because it provides a sense of control. When I am "re-charged," I can focus on my tasks, including my writing and emotions.

Initially, I believed my emotions were pretty static during this journey, with only a few fluctuations. Now, I suspect I may have been hiding my inner feelings because too many people depended on me. So, while I felt my mindset was positive, I speculate that I was masking my emotions as a type of defense mechanism. In reality, my mind was all over the place. By the end of the week, I did find the Documentarian survey a little monotonous because my activity did not change. The "Stay at Home" orders contributed to a sense of isolation and did not allow for much deviation to report.

Working in isolation prompted me to take a closer look at my teaching goals. I have high expectations for myself and my students. I was a high performing student, and I believed all students had the same calling. But now that we were all on the same playing field of "the unknown," I began to rethink my priorities and expectations. I thought about the impact my course materials and assignments had on my students. Perhaps, I was unreasonable in some of my assumptions about student preparedness and inner drive. I recalled a comment made by a colleague who stated that all of our years of learning and teaching made us experts, but we can't expect our students to have that same expertise that took us years to build. I spent time reflecting on my philosophy and adjusted assignments to meet the educational need based on the student population and course outcomes. Since I expect my students to reflect on their work, so should I.

Along with assessing my expectations, I contemplated my pedagogy. I realized that my classroom "top-down" approach that hinges on lectures and "pushing" out information led in-class students to be overly dependent on me. I am successful with the online students when it comes to dialogue and collaboration, but not as successful with the in-class courses. Student engagement became a problem when I tried to switch in-class students to practices that were not familiar to them. I need to use activities in the classroom that I use with online students. I also recognized some of my online course material could be more thorough in detail for ease of completion. Typically, I use open-ended instruction and various collaboration assignments in both formats, but I realized I need to incorporate more meaningful inquiry and experiential learning activities in all my courses. I had grown complacent with my approach, and this needed to change. I have a lot of work ahead of me to revamp my courses for better retention and student success. This reflection has served as an "energizer" for me.

RETROSPECTIVE

We are still in an "Uncommon Time," but now that we have reached the end of the spring pandemic semester of learning, I can say that I have grown as a writer and a teacher. I was in the same survival mode as my students. The uncertainty had its traumatic effects on us, and not knowing the next steps in our day-to-day living was challenging for me. I could imagine my students sharing the same challenges, so I worked at creating assignments with meaningful rhetoric, and I worked to alter my way of communication. I carefully chose my words to form clear, student-teacher correspondence. I was deliberate in my dialogue, and I learned to listen to myself more closely as I directed my students through this learning experience.

Sharing my story may help others realize that during this time, we may have had similar emotions and experiences. This type of knowledge is vital for many of us—especially those of us who are contingent faculty and of various ethnic backgrounds. My "temporary" status puts me in a different category than those who have tenure. This faculty divide was evident in the demographics of this activity. As I reviewed the demographics, I was disappointed though not surprised by the contributors to this data collection. We need a well-rounded group of educators to keep this data from being biased, yet over 70% of the Documentarians were part-time educators. I wonder why we did not get a more significant contribution from the tenured faculty. There is an unspoken divide that I often witness between "full-time" professors and contingent faculty in my teaching institutions. In a study conducted in 2017, Cipriano and Buller support this observation by stating that "a third or more of the [study] respondents observed a decline in collegiality—sometimes moderate and sometimes severe—as faculty members moved from untenured to tenured positions or from teaching and research roles to administrative roles" (16). Can we assume this perception of tenured faculty to be accurate? Within the academy, we need to ensure there is a collaborative mindset among all levels of teaching status and demographics. I can attest to being shut out of a SIG meeting at the 2019 CCCC Convention because I was not a member of that community, and this was a disheartening incident.

I hope that the next generation of Documentarians will include tenured educators who are willing to take their time to share their experiences from their secured positions. Our profession will become more robust and more equitable when all parties come to the table to share knowledge, expertise, and creative dialogue.

CONCLUSION

CCCC 2020 is history, and education was turned on its head. Some of us fared better than others, and we have all come away with some battle wounds and lessons learned. I have learned that all my students need a better structure in the remote learning environment to succeed. I also learned that we could not "save" everyone, and it's okay to let some students go. Some of my "high-risk" students stopped participating, and this included a student living in a half-way house who showed great promise. I am spending the summer researching high-risk students in online learning communities to meet their needs in the upcoming school terms. The fall will provide another opportunity for me to get things right for our students.

Going forward, we need to reconcile the needs of contingent faculty to ensure there is no burnout. Attending to students' personal issues and academic demands was exhausting to accommodate. If I were a tenured teacher and only taught at one institution, this might have been manageable. But this is not the reality of the "Freeway Flier." I balanced eight courses during this crisis, and it took a significant toll on my well-being. We can't expect teachers to embrace all student issues, yet this was an ask by my administration. Too much bend and shift to accommodate student requests will break the teacher. Is it worth the effort to teach in these insane circumstances? Will contingent faculty be recognized for "plugging" the holes? Only time will tell, but despite the unknown, most of us will be back online because we care about education and student success.

Was I as positive as I earlier mentioned? Probably not. But it was a way for me to compartmentalize the many emotions I experienced during this time in our lives. Earlier, I said that this *Twilight Zone* episode reminded me of the death of my father. Shock, disbelief, sadness, survival—it was a packaged deal. Ultimately, we moved on to the "new normal," and I wistfully looked at "what was."

WORKS CITED

Alleman, Nathan, and Don Haviland. "'I Expect to Be Engaged as an Equal': Collegiality Expectations of Full-Time, Non-Tenure-Track Faculty Members." *Higher Education,* vol. 74, no. 3, Sept. 2017, pp. 527–42, https://doi.org/10.1007/s10734-016-0062-4.

Cipriano, Robert E, and Buller, Jeffrey L. "Does Tenure Affect Collegiality?" *The Department Chair,* vol. 28, no. 2, 2017, pp. 15–16.

13

Feminist Mishmash: COVID-19 CCCC

Heather McGovern

THE KNOT.
A few months out, as I reflect on my pandemic journaling for the CCCC Documentarian project, Spring 2020, and informed by academic research (*Science*) and journalistic reporting (*The Atlantic, Nature, Forbes, Slate, The New York Times*) about the effects of social distancing on women, and on mothers, in particular, both personally and professionally, I see what I wrote in March through that lens.

In fact, I realize that I blithely wrote this, "There really aren't any clear trends in what I say about my feelings. They jump around . . ." on April 2, as if in apology—because, well, women are taught to apologize, and it is a tough habit to break—and in apparent dismissal of my writing, even in repudiation of my emotions.

Rather than a dismissal, those words are, while not The Point, A Point. My Point.

The observations in my journals about what I planned, what I accomplished, and how I felt are a tangled hair knot: a scramble. They're likely not a mash up, because that would be more intentional; they are not a hodge-podge because the things in them matter: they are a mishmash.

They reveal the snarl of daily life for parents—but especially mothers—in the United States. The knot is exacerbated by the pandemic, but it exists, always.

There are other, more important stories to tell, and to which to listen—those of adjunct faculty, worried about losing their jobs. Those of people with disabilities, worried their very lives would be (again) deprioritized. Those of people of color, once again used by the rest of us—disproportionately affected by infections and deaths by COVID-19 and by the economic pain of the pandemic.

But they can tell their stories, and I will read, and listen, and learn. This is my story—although it is not mine alone, for I am sure many will find their own daily realities reflected in it.

JUMBLED

My journal responses are a jumble. They go back and forth between personal, family responsibilities, and professional responsibilities and accomplishments.

Here are a few examples:

Worked upstairs, walked with daughter, worked upstairs, took break went outside, to bedroom for sheets and laundry, to kitchen for dishes, worked upstairs, walked with husband, worked upstairs, walked with daughter, worked upstairs.

Or, in a much lengthier, more detailed passage:

I replied to late work from students. I succeeded in connecting with several students, and one preceptee, which was great. A student MIA since March 9 has replied to SOMEONE and we're trying to rope him back in. I recruited others to help gather data for the 5-year consultant. I did part of the Task Force work, which I think I can finish tomorrow. I walked with my husband to pay for and sign for our taxes. I walked with my 11-year-old, and have over 10,000 steps for the day—that and sunshine likely help my mood, too! I didn't have to help anyone with lunch today as we had leftovers again from last night. Both kids finished working on school work very early, so I had computer availability nearly all day. I made a Loom video to tell students about their homework and loaded it—three students have viewed it. I also set up a one hour drop-in-with-your-pet Zoom time during class time tomorrow. I talked to my peer mentor. Our provost sent out a message about class evals and tenure track faculty, and I asked my dean and union about adjunct faculty and teaching staff. Then, my dean and union officers talked with the provost and got her to agree that anyone can permanently delete this spring's evals if they like. That will help ease the concerns of so many of our adjunct faculty, who've been talking to me on Facebook and via email about how worried they are about not being hired again if their spring evals are bad. I also sent out an email about withdrawal as I've gotten lots of questions about it. I'm trying to walk a fine line, as program coordinator, to be present and connected, but also not annoy people or give them more work. I did make a Google Form to use potentially for withdrawals and sent it to a small group, haven't heard from them yet. I found online and ordered a beginning embroidery kit, and got a colleague who does speculative fiction to recommend a book (and she also recommended a camp) for my 13-year-old. I did two loads of laundry and ran and emptied the dishwasher twice, but now our sheets and dishes are clean. I also took the compost out, threw away the chair pads eaten by squirrels and put out others ones—not really the right size, but they'll let people sit outside on nicer days. Didn't call the parents, so need to do that still. Did review all of the personnel committee letters for new comments and revisions.

One day I observed,

Ended up basically jumping from one task to another, feeling as if I wasn't really following a plan. Then, observed I felt surprisingly exhausted by midafternoon—emotionally drained—and was having trouble wanting to respond and to respond positively.

I don't know why I found my emotional exhaustion surprising the day I wrote it. It certainly doesn't seem surprising today! Of course jumping around from one activity to another like that feels exhausting—because such rapid-shifts-in-tasking are exhausting.

My husband also works from home. He has for several years; he is just now more at home, not in the "morning office"—a coffee shop—or a shared work space in Philadelphia, frequented once a week. I think in March he helped the kids get lunch once. Never breakfast. Never dinner for the family. But he rarely helps with dinner, although he is a better cook than I am—and isn't up for breakfast. He issued one reminder to the girls to practice their band instruments, after I asked him to please do so, so I wouldn't sound like a nag. I did the grocery shopping, took a daughter to the dentist, did our CSA pick ups, gathered materials for and talked to our tax accountant, and canceled appointments. He took one daughter to two in-person, social distancing, off-ice practices, picked up ice cream for me for Mother's Day, curbside, and pizza—but those in May, not March. Not April. I checked the girls' online grades. He did not, safe in the knowledge that I was doing so. I ordered materials for Easter baskets, made 90% of phone calls to both of our sets of parents, ordered graduation presents, and mailed books and cards. But, then, I'd do most of this work without the pandemic—a difference is that in normal life, the girls get their own lunches, and we're not low on food requiring actual cooking rather than assembly.

He did other things—picked out a new lawn mower, and updated some financial records, for instance—redid a sound system, and more. But, as is typical in the division of men's labor and women's labor, most of his was one-time, while more of mine was recurring (dishwasher, cooking, laundry, daily check-ins about schoolwork). More of his was visible—a new lawn mower!—and more of mine was invisible (online delivery of a box of adhesive bandages).

I don't think my husband has been emotionally exhausted, except maybe two days—related to tough professional days, like having to let a colleague know he was being furloughed.

Even just making sure everyone had an electronic device to do work or school was exhausting—and my husband NEVER gave up, never even thought to give up, either his laptop or phone to anyone else:

> I did better at following my planned plan today than yesterday. That is probably because today isn't a teaching day. Also, both kids finished school work very quickly so I had more computer time.

Or

> I received texts or emails from nearly half the class, and my peer mentor struggled to answer questions in the Group Me. And I had a lag in response because my daughter was using my phone for her homework and didn't notice the texts coming in right away. It was frustrating.

I'm emotionally exhausted regularly, in large part because of kinship work—both in the family, and the professional equivalent—the mentoring, formal and informal, and checking in with colleagues, that falls more to women and people of color and other marginalized groups in the workplace as well as at home. See the list of work/family items in Table 13.1 for some parallels.

Table 13.1: Parallel activities in work/family duties

Work	Family
Student is worried about her mom, as the student feels she must keep working at Dairy Queen, but her mom just finished with chemo and so is high risk.	Didn't have to help anyone with lunch today as we had leftovers again from last night.

Work	Family
Spent nearly an hour in the morning talking to a mentee, worried about the switch, hoping for pass/fail grading, worried about her student evals, and just needing to talk to another adult human who isn't as stressed as her husband currently is.	. . . plus I did get the chicken baked (and potatoes—easy as they require little prep and both go in the oven). Also cooked frozen cranberries into sauce and helped daughter make pumpkin muffins for more breakfast and snacking variety.
Start a list of faculty who can take over other classes if or when some of our faculty become sick and can't continue to teach.	Ran out of leftovers for lunch, and no bread, so had to help husband find frozen burrito.
Also texted with colleague who had excellent personal news.	Happy that my 11-year-old had a video chat with a friend while they ate popcorn and watched a movie together, then made forts together, and that my 13-year-old had a video chat with two friends and so was more animated, happy, etc. Letting the latter stay up much later than normal right now to do this (got off phone at 10 when normally lights out is around 9).
Our provost sent out a message about class evals and tenure track faculty, and I asked my dean and union about adjunct faculty and teaching staff. Then, my dean and union officers talked with the provost and got her to agree that anyone can permanently delete this spring's evals if they like. That will help ease the concerns of so many of our adjunct faculty, who've been talking to me on Facebook and via email about how worried they are about not being hired again if their spring evals are bad.	On couch with 11-year-old daughter, who is panicking about nothing to eat in the house. She will make a quesadilla—by nothing to eat, no frozen waffles or pancakes—plan to bake bread (also out) and make pancakes to freeze this weekend. She and I each already ate apple cinnamon oatmeal, and I have coffee.
One student joined [Zoom office hours] just to say he hadn't done his work because he and his family had to stop by the CDC and then go see his grandmother, dying in her nursing home. I could hear his parents arguing in the background.	Need to call in-laws or parents and check on them, family friend in Seattle to check on him, elderly neighbor.

Work	Family
My peer mentor is living on campus still [I helped him through the process, or he would have been homeless, as he is emancipated] which he said is eerie. He's been going out for food although he has a meal plan and could eat on campus. I think he enjoyed talking to someone! [He stayed on Zoom for nearly half an hour after class just to chat.]	Lend phone to daughter for Zoom meeting with her skating coach and other skaters (audio on her phone doesn't work).
I should have finished this [the Documentarian evening survey] last night, but I was exhausted, had a student call even after 9 p.m. (he couldn't call earlier in the day because of his National Guard duties) and didn't think I could do the survey justice last night.	Also did two loads of laundry—washing towels more frequently with virus (and we all have allergies so fear we wouldn't recognize early symptoms) so more laundry.

UNRAVELED

Things were, and are, jumbled. But others unraveled. Professional opportunities disappeared—including the planned travel to and participation in CCCC, an inability to stay in attendance at a Zoom Teaching Circle Meeting because of two high-priority phone calls that interrupted it, and a planned in-person consultant visit for a five-year program review.

Some of these unravelings have led to more work—a stretched out, virtual consultant visit, still on-going, or advising that took place over a month instead of mostly in two days.

I can't get the conference—as a regular conference, with me away from work and home and focused on learning and listening and meeting people—back. There will be others, but never this one, in this way. It is a small loss—and worth the cost, to protect lives—but it is a real loss, perhaps more so because—in large part because of my parenting/family responsibilities—I don't attend CCCC annually, but instead more once every three years or so.

I also unraveled a bit with emotion—and that, too, often at least in part, gendered:

I spent an hour awake in the middle of the night ruminating about my children being orphans because we all get coronavirus and my husband and I die. . . . I had to make a mental list to update making sure people know who should be the girls' guardians if we die.

Or

My 11-year-old noted that we can barely see our state (NJ) under the red circles outwards from us on the maps.

My husband has reported no such sleep disruptions, nor has he been the primary person sharing the world of the pandemic with the kids.

TANGLED

My days are always a bit of a tangle, with work and family intertwined . . . work and work out before breakfast, go to work, leave earlier to run kids to activities, and work on my laptop while they're there.

Physical distancing during the pandemic simply exacerbated that. Now, there were no times physically at the university during which I could be just a professional. To help meet my students' changing needs, I even relaxed normal boundaries for the work day and week that I maintain.

And demands of the home changed—to include, at times, teacher (for my middle school children), and dramatically increased cooking/related cleaning responsibilities.

Although in the first week of physical distancing, it seemed like I'd have more free time, not commuting, that time quickly was gobbled up—and now physical distancing brings with it so many new tasks that it takes as much or more time as the original job. I had to create a new online withdrawal process, answer questions about it, and remind people about it. I had to support adjunct and full-time faculty in my program shift to online teaching, as Program Coordinator. Instead of just explaining the day's homework in class in two minutes, I had to create short videos for students, at their request, about the homework. I had to differently prepare classes, redoing some lesson plans I've reused for at least a year or two, and spend more time teaching as if with a dozen independent studies, instead of one group. And that work continues—meetings to shift orientation and registration online, supporting faculty in preparing to potentially teach online for fall term, contacting students to change their grades, as needed, to Pass or No Credit.

GRIEVING

One day I wrote, in my plans for the day,

> Hope to not be so emotionally exhausted, but maybe that is part of living through a pandemic, perhaps especially as a program coordinator—as a leader with others leaning on me, or looking to me for questions I can't answer.

The same could be said about parenting in the pandemic. Will you go back to school? I don't know. Probably not. Can you go to summer camp? I don't know. Probably not. Will we go on vacation? I don't know. Probably not. Can you get your hair cut?

The pandemic has been a series of processing my own mourning, usually on my own, but sometimes with my family, a friend, or a colleague, and then helping others process it. I cut back on my news exposure after the day I wrote this:

> The U.S went over 100,000 sick. AHHH!!!! And I read an article about the human toll in Italy that made me cry and cry, reading about families losing multiple members, Red Cross workers going to houses and removing sick people and disinfecting themselves before the next house, cremating bodies as coffins stack up.

I didn't write that my 11-year-old freaked out when she saw me crying over the article. I was the person deciding how much of the news to share with the girls.

My family has been lucky. My husband and I are both employed. Only one person in our immediate or extended family has, at this time, had COVID-19, although we've known many people with COVID by now. No one we know well has died, yet. There are smaller losses: my husband has taken a pay cut, a colleague and I made a pact to read only one the-death-of-higher-education article per day so as not to be paralyzed by fear about our careers, and friends and relatives have been furloughed or are unemployed.

Upon reflection, in April, I observed that I experienced five main stresses: 1) emotional responses to the growing number of sick and dead and stress of students and children and family members and colleagues, 2) stress caused by changed routines for everyone (students, children, me, husband), 3) stress caused by sharing electronic devices with kids (phone and laptop), 4) stress caused by additional/different work (more laundry/cleaning/different and more cooking, different prepping and interactions with students/colleagues), 5) stress caused by worrying about/helping kids and colleagues and students and husband and self and parents and inlaws and elderly neighbors and additional emotional labor with students, colleagues, family members, kids.

I wrote:

> Lots of stress, given the rapid change, and having to so often say "I don't know—nobody knows."

HOLDING ON

I think just accepting that we were—we still are—on a wild ride of change, and we can only just hold on—and we don't even know if making it eight seconds will be enough—is about what I can do right now.

WORKS CONSULTED

Agarwal, Pragya. "How Is the Pandemic Going to Affect Gender Equality." *Forbes*, 31 Mar. 2020, https://www.forbes.com/sites/pragyaagarwaleurope/2020/03/31/how-is-the-pandemic-going-to-affect-gender-equality/#79eaec25dfdd.

Donner, Francesca. "How Women Are Getting Squeezed by the Pandemic." *The New York Times*, 20 May 2020, https://www.nytimes.com/2020/05/20/us/women-economy-jobs-coronavirus-gender.html.

Gould, Emily. "The Trapped-at-Home-Mother." *Slate*, 14 Apr. 2020, https://www.slate.com/human-interest/2020/04/motherhood-quarantine-domestic-labor-balance.html.

Lewis, Helen. "The Coronavirus Is a Disaster for Feminism." *The Atlantic*, 19 Mar. 2020, https://www.theatlantic.com/international/archive/2020/03/feminism-womens-rights-coronavirus-covid19/608302/.

Minello, Allesandra. "The Pandemic and the Female Academic." *Nature*, 17 Apr. 2020, https://www.nature.com/articles/d41586-020-01135-9.

Staniscuaski, Fernanda et al. "Impact of COVID-19 on Academic Mothers." *Science*, 15 May 2020, vol. 368, no. 6492. https://doi.org/10.1126/science.abc2740.

14

Growing Up Again (and Again)

Shauna Chung

"Leave the door open for the unknown, the door into the dark," writes Rebecca Solnit in *A Field Guide to Getting Lost*. "That's where the most important things come from, where you yourself came from, and where you will go" (4). In early 2020, these words would've tasted sweet on my tongue and lit a fire in my belly. Eager to maintain momentum after passing my comprehensive exams and ready to pursue the research questions for my dissertation project, I would've taken Solnit's call as an ontological challenge: be open to the unknown and step bravely into the dark of your PhD journey.

And then COVID-19.

What began as rumors I and my first-year composition students thought were "just overreactions" quickly turned into a WHO-sanctioned pandemic. The rapid rate of infection in big Asian and European cities was difficult to imagine against the rural Southern backdrop of our day-to-day. Next thing we knew, our university president announced that the physical school campus would close after spring break and move to online learning until April 5. As words like "social distancing" and "flatten the curve" became part of the vernacular, that return date moved to "who knows?" Then came the theories bordering conspiracy: the National Guard is mobilizing, the entire nation is locking down, toilet paper gathering is essential. Erring on the side of caution, I found myself at the local grocery store, picking up frozen pizza, canned beans, and other inexpensive foods with generous expiration dates. I paused to snap photos of the barren shelves where toilet paper, paper towels, hand sanitizer, and disinfecting wipes once sat. Things were starting to sink in, albeit slowly.

With my pantry gradually resembling a doomsday prepper's and with only my own mouth to feed, I was ready to weather the storm of pandemic as I had all previous hurdles as a single, twentysomething graduate student: alone. Thoughts of self-isolation seemed daunting until I realized that this "new normal" hadn't dramatically changed my daily routine. I was already moving about my day alone; sequestering myself in an on-campus office to read, write, and grade alone; bringing work home to do alone. The threat of coronavirus, I thought, was just another PSI unit in the pressure cooker that is graduate school. As a serial, introverted "yes" person and with the job market looming in the periphery, I'd been so busy spreading myself thin that being lonely never crossed my mind. I was adulting, damnit.

This image of myself came crashing down when my father (a man who calls, maybe, twice a year to make sure that I'm still alive) summoned me home, a three-hour drive away. "Your mom and I just heard that states will go on lockdown soon, so you need to leave your place and come home immediately," he said matter-of-factly. This request posing as a command didn't register at first. "Home" was my apartment, my academics, my teaching. I hadn't called my parents' home "home" for well over seven years. I had a job that allowed me to pay rent and buy frozen pizza. I had a life wholly outside of the ecosystem I grew up in, which enabled me to try on versions of myself barred throughout childhood. I resisted the summons for a few days, registering it as an affront to my singleness and my ability to care for myself, until I learned that my brothers were also returning home. The youngest, a senior in college, got evicted from campus housing when his school moved completely online weeks before mine. He said premature goodbyes to his friends of four years, packed up his belongings, and moved in with my parents. His girlfriend, unable to return to her home state due to travel restrictions, moved in as well. My other brother, a fourth-year medical student, would also be en route as his clinical rotations and final classes had either been canceled or relegated to Zoom. The choice now was between canned beans and my complete family, the latter being an extremely rare occurrence. With academic conferences canceled and the rest of my semester transitioning online, I could make this move. COVID-19 kicked the door open and made "home" the unknown. I chose to go through the door from where I'd originally come.

Giving myself a two-week limit, I drove home and set up camp in my childhood room, immediately feeling like a kid in an adult's body. *You're just here to humor dad and convince him not to worry*, I thought. A younger me I barely recognized smiled through a picture frame someone had placed on a nightstand. Nostalgia tugged at the heartstrings, but my head quickly reminded me how different things were now—how much that little girl let go of in favor of becoming her own, thinking differently and for herself, pursuing a career in the humanities that her relatives didn't understand because it went off script. In an effort to preserve that distinction, I projected a rather self-inflated "I'm busy" ethos to my family. While I did have a terrifying to-do list, I was more desperate to keep pace with a self-imposed academic tempo than I was with acclimating to their dynamic. Plus, I didn't want to be a bother. Even though I'd been invited to the house, part of me felt like I was disrupting. I was an extra mouth to feed, an extra body leaving dead skin cells on the floor. Who would want to care for and accommodate that?

This question and my other personal hang-ups immediately took a back seat as the news cycle took center stage. I watched as Italy's pandemic-related death count reached an all-time high and Spain's began to rise exponentially. A few days after my arrival, I learned that CO-VID-19 cases were in my parents' county as well as in the one I'd left behind. With grandparents nearby and a father continuing to work in the medical field, the threat of infection was no longer something we saw on the news in a different country. It was at our doorstep, maybe even on our hands as we scrubbed soap for twenty seconds any time we touched something. Our relatives in South Korea, seeing case numbers in the US double and triple each day, offered to mail us hand sanitizer. I expressed mutual concern for their safety and health, but they told me *geogjeong-ma*, don't worry. Their country had somewhat contained the virus, had tested thousands of people, were actively contact-tracing infected individuals. Mine had just become number one in the world for most confirmed cases.

With each passing day, my academic life and wounded pride receded like a wave returning to the ocean, back to the overwhelming unknown that I thought I could skillfully sail. This new unknown was lethal, tearing through the globe with unprecedented speed, filling my belly not with fire but with knots. I worried for my nurse and doctor friends and family who were in need of proper personal protective equipment. I worried for my peers with family and bases overseas, their countries' borders disallowing reentrance. I worried for my colleagues with dissertation defenses coming up and threats of Zoom-bombing on their minds. I worried for my students who didn't have access to necessary technologies, whose parents were contracting the virus and/or losing their jobs, whose books and notes were captive in dorm rooms to which they couldn't return, whose mental health issues worsened by the day. I worried for family friends who'd recently closed their bistro and laid off several employees. I worried for the mail carriers, the retail workers, the furloughed, the immunocompromised, the elderly; the list continued. Fear nursed the worry and gave birth to paralysis. I tried to accomplish academic tasks—things that felt so important a week ago—but couldn't focus. My reading and writing seemed useless in light of the pandemic and what people around the world were going through.

"I'm sorry I'm so useless," I said to my mom as we washed dishes together one evening. She paused and put down a soapy dish.

"Why would you say that?" she asked.

"I feel like I'm not pulling my weight. I'm not paying you rent or buying groceries. I feel bad that you and Dad have to take care of me during this crazy time," I explained, picking up her dish and rinsing it.

A beat of silence.

"You are *ridiculous*," she replied, laughing and also looking a bit heartbroken. "This is not a place where you have to earn your place. We asked you to come here; we didn't want you to be alone in your apartment. I have zero expectation for you to 'pull your weight,' whatever that means. Nobody knows what's happening right now. We're all in survival mode. Just exist, ok? That's all you need to do right now."

She opened another door to the unknown. How do I "just exist"? If I'm not contributing something meaningful, responding to a call, or checking something off of my to-do list, what am I? What purpose do I have?

And then I heard myself, a quiet voice that prompted more questions. Did I actually believe that deliverables and productivity defined my worth? Were the "take a mental health day" and "be kind to yourself" emails I sent to my students just paying lip service? Was the stress of academic life, the incessant push to work, work, work, the motivator of my daily behaviors and action? To what end? At what cost?

The world was exploding and here I was having a full-blown existential crisis. And over someone expressing care—someone telling me that I wasn't a bother, that I didn't have to prove something or overthink to feel worthy and accepted, that I could just be as I was for a second instead of anxiously mapping out my next ten steps.

In this space of sounding out the unknown, I caught a first honest glimpse of myself. She was tired and burned out but still running on fumes. Since energy was in short supply, she was obsessed with efficiency, growing impatient with things like flowery adjectives and essays that didn't make "the point" immediately clear. She forgot that she enjoyed meandering narratives and getting lost in ideas. She forgot that her brothers were an absolute joy to be around. She forgot that productively engaging with her parents required time and energy, resources that she'd channeled exclusively to academic outlets. She realized that her identity and goals were still in flux, still uncertain. In some ways, she was still a child in an adult's body.

In light of these reflections, I took a day off for the first time in a while. A Saturday. A 24-hour timespan to listen to podcasts, walk outside, cook a meal with my siblings, and sleep without setting an alarm. Gradually, I began measuring out a few hours each day to actually connect with someone or something, not out of obligation or to check a box. I privileged a FaceTime call with a friend undergoing a fourteen-day quarantine over knocking out another reading. I left my room and started studying with my brothers who were also in the throes of academic work. I was able to help console my brother's girlfriend when she lost her job. I celebrated my birthday with friends over video chat on Facebook. I swept debris out of the driveway after tornadoes decimated areas just miles from our house. I helped care for an injured baby turtle that my brothers found in the rubble. We rescued and adopted out four puppies that someone abandoned in the woods near our house. My family learned how to play Exploding Kittens. I geared up with gloves and a disposable mask to go grocery shopping. I helped prepare dinner. I watered my mother's tomato plants. I folded my father's laundry. I called my grandparents.

Two weeks home turned into six. Now fluent in the rhythms of my family dynamic, I moved about my day with new, more balanced routines. I still worked to check things off of the to-do list and fulfill my professional commitments, but my evenings often ended in conversations with people rather than anxious nights alone. Perhaps this was life now, one where I opened myself up to other people and sought daily community more actively. Maybe a bit of togetherness, whether virtual or in person, is what we all needed to get through this horrific moment in time.

It wasn't until shelter-in-place orders started lifting that reality slapped me in the face. *No*, it said. *This isn't life now—this was a rare and fleeting moment to figure something out. The world continues to break. It's time to return and rebuild.* I knew the easing of restrictions wouldn't be a return to the way things used to be and would only be a first step in a much longer process that would require careful, deliberate steps forward. At the same time, it signaled that I could not stay as or where I was. Though I wouldn't be gallivanting in crowded public areas, I wouldn't be forced into isolation anymore. My dad wouldn't have an argument for me to remain home with everyone. With my FYC course wrapped up and my research study ready to go, there was nothing keeping me from going back. So, I set a departure date and began packing up my things.

Before leaving, I cleaned my room, making sure to leave as few dead skin cells behind as possible. As I vacuumed, scrubbed, and tidied up things, I felt the ghosts of my adolescent selves follow me. They held my adult hands as I remade my bed with washed sheets, winked at me through picture frames on my nightstand. During my first night home, I feared them—feared turning into them again. I'd worked so hard to forage my own way, to sluff off the identities prescribed throughout childhood and early adulthood, to prove that I was a grownup who could hold her own. I'd conflated return with reversion.

Reversion, however, occurred the first few weeks when I returned to my apartment. With a new frozen pizza stashed away and only myself to account for, I threw myself back into the old routine and the emerging concerns I witnessed through my computer screen. My parents' home and lessons of togetherness quickly became a memory that I found easy to forget as my isolated environment prompted me to work. Wrinkled sticky notes with to-do lists dotted my desk, replaced by fresh ones written in anxious scribbles. Days would pass before I'd see another face besides my own in the mirror or leave the apartment for fresh air and vitamin D. The time I'd previously allocated to personal conversations or walks around the neighborhood morphed into a few extra hours to be "productive." As I made progress on projects, formed a new dent in my carpet from standing at my desk all day, and credited this alleged productivity to the extra effort I was exerting, I began thinking, *Did I just waste six weeks at home?* Within days of my return, the pendulum had swung back to go, go, go.

And then I began writing this essay.

In late March and early April, the CCCC Documentarian Team administered five morning and evening surveys, each hitting my email inbox the same week I drove to my parents' house. What began as my obligation to a box I semi-arbitrarily checked to be a volunteer Documentarian at the Conference on College Composition and Communication soon turned into a lifeline as I wrestled with what it meant to be "home" during a pandemic. Revisiting my answers to the survey questions—e.g., what do you hope to accomplish today, what emotions are invoked by your reflections, describe the scene around you, etc.—I read another unrecognizable version of myself. Who was this person calling a "walk in the sunlight" an "accomplishment"? She expressed feelings of gratitude for the opportunity to "tune my ears more intentionally to those around me." She even described and reveled in the sound of people snoring in the next room, the familiar scent of floral shampoo, the buzz of a light as she sat at a desk in her childhood room to write about the mundane moments of her day.

Another door opened.

Shortly after re-reading my survey responses, my mother called out of the blue. We hadn't talked since I'd left. I answered, feigning happiness to mask feeling annoyed by this unanticipated cadence in my work rhythm. I had this essay to write and other deadlines to meet.

"What are you up to?" she asked.

"Oh, you know. Just the same routine. Busy, busy," I replied, hoping my repetition would signal something to her. "Is everything ok?"

"Mmhmm, everything's ok. I was just calling to call," she said.

"I see." The happiness façade and my patience were beginning to unravel. "Well, I'm glad everything is ok. Do you need anything?"

"Nope, I don't need anything. Are you eating ok? Have enough food?"

"Yeah, I'm fine."

"Well," she added after a brief lull, "you seem busy. I'll let you go. Just wanted to hear your voice."

"Ok, sounds good! Talk to you later, Mom!"

"Also—"

"Yes?"

". . . never mind."

"No no, say it."

"Just—don't forget to be human."

I hung up feeling slapped in the face again, unmoored by another profound one-liner from my mother. At first, the hackles went up. "Don't forget to be human"? Didn't I meet my "being human" quota after giving up so much time to be with family? Wasn't I the *most* human in the family since I was dedicating my professional life to the *human*ities? Doesn't my scholastic striving for attuned, empathetic, civic-minded rhetoric speak for itself?

No. No, no, no.

Why feed the academic machine human messages and not offer the same to my mother? Why do this "human work" for everyone else except for the ones who are the closest? Why talk the talk and obsess over research questions that seek empowerment, connection, and understanding when I cannot apply these concepts in a simple phone call or to myself?

The memory of my COVID-19 quarantine at home, an event that was never in the cards, screamed these questions into my ears and offered a new ontological challenge. The past, which I learned was a very dynamic present, called me not to revert but to re-version myself by stepping perpetually into the unknown of my humanity, a process that could not happen on an island unto myself. It forced the willingly unacknowledged parts of my daily habits into an uncomfortable consciousness. I came to realize that though self-sufficiency and hard work were key to surviving graduate school and an academic career, they weren't the measure of all things or sole characteristics that secured my worth and defined my interactions with others. I'd known this in theory all along; I'd heard it articulated by my professors, colleagues, and in books I read. Believing it, however, required re-versioning the child who would always be growing up again and again.

WORK CITED

Solnit, Rebecca. *A Field Guide to Getting Lost.* Penguin Books, 2005.

15

Documenting Our Solastalgia: A New Landscape

Maggie Christensen

As 4Cs week (March 25–28, 2020) progressed and so did news of the pandemic, I found myself working during our second week of "spring break," which was designed to give faculty time to prepare for the unprecedented move to remote learning. Situated in the middle of the country, we had the benefit of observing from a safe distance the effects of the virus in more densely populated areas. We were well-prepared and actively trying to "flatten the curve," we hoped. During this week, the gravity of the pandemic began to sink in with me as I began the journey from disbelief and shock, toward grief—and then fear. That week the US hit a major milestone: over 100,000 known COVID-19 cases, more than anywhere else in the world. We were all still getting used to isolation, listening to daily briefings from officials, and waiting for the next shoe to drop; we knew it was supposed to get worse before the situation could improve. Two months later, we would reach the grim mark of 100,000 deaths.

Obediently, I remained at home, at the same desk and chair, with the same students and faculty—but everything felt different. My graduate students, several of whom are themselves teachers, struggled to express their feelings as they experienced the by-now familiar symptoms: fatigue, lack of motivation, inability to focus. One local high-school teacher, weighed down by events, sent me this email, representative of so many others that week:

> I feel I need to tell you that I am struggling quite a lot mentally and emotionally with everything that is going on. I'm sure you feel that way, as well. I feel overwhelmed, buried, and like I have no routine or control over anything. I've tried to research, but my mind just gets filled with other distractions and thoughts. . . . I'm just trying to be transparent here. I want to do well, but I feel like I'm spinning out a bit and I feel overwhelmed. I'll do my best, but right now, [the project] most definitely won't be where

it should be. Sometimes I feel as if a weight has been placed on my chest. Is it just me? Others seem to be dealing with this just fine. . . . I suppose I wasn't built for coping with global pandemic.

I replied supportively, I hope. None of us is built for pandemic. A general malaise seemed to have settled over the whole city, expressed so effectively by my student. We are all #AloneTogether, which is not exactly what Sherry Turkle had in mind when she wrote a book with the same title. Sitting at home alone on the day I was supposed to be presenting at 4Cs, reading this student's earnest email, a wave of profound loss and sadness overcame me, a longing for life to return to the way it used to be. The landscape had indeed changed, perhaps irrevocably.

As I sought to comprehend the changing landscape of my teaching, working, and living, the term "solastalgia" seemed appropriate to try to name what I was experiencing. Generally used in reference to climate change, solastalgia is a neologism coined in 2003 by Glenn Albrecht, an environmental philosopher and retired professor of sustainability in Australia, to capture the feelings of loss and grief when one's home region is altered by climatic or environmental devastation. Albrecht defines solastalgia as "an emplaced or existential melancholia experienced with the negative transformation (desolation) of a loved home environment." Albrecht explains how he developed the term:

> Solastalgia has its origins in the concepts of "solace" and "desolation". Solace has meanings connected to the alleviation of distress or to the provision of comfort or consolation in the face of distressing events. Desolation has meanings connected to abandonment and loneliness. The suffix -algia has connotations of pain or suffering. Hence, solastalgia is a form of "homesickness" like that experienced with traditionally defined nostalgia, except that the victim has not left their home or home environment. Solastalgia, simply put, is "the homesickness you have when you are still at home." (para.8)

In my case, the "distressing events" caused by the pandemic, while not necessarily impacting the physical environment, nonetheless profoundly affected a different kind of landscape: my teaching, working, and living environment. Sheltering in place, I was "homesick," longing for my familiar worlds and routines which were replaced by a gnawing sense of uncertainty and fear. Like many of my colleagues and students, I was experiencing solastalgia.

Beyond the daily interactions on campus with students, faculty, and staff in classes, meetings, and ubiquitous hallway conversations, I also missed the important milestones, moments that enrich a semester, giving my job texture and purpose beyond the classroom. I felt nostalgic as the day for each event passed by, practically unnoticed: 4Cs, the incoming graduate teaching assistants gathering, the department honors ceremony, the defenses and capstone meetings. I acknowledged each of these familiar touchstones as they came, non-events now beyond our dramatically reduced world. The sense of solastalgia pervaded my days: I kept saying, "Normally, I would be doing such-and such," until these comparisons with "normal" have finally given way to a recognition that things will never be the same. And that realization hit me hard as I experienced frustration, loss, and grief.

Among communities that experience solastalgia, the dramatic change and prevalent uncertainty in a once predictable environment can be especially unsettling. On Friday afternoon of 4Cs week, I ventured out to campus to drop off some canned and dry goods for the food bank drive and also pick up some books and scan an article. Campus was eerily quiet, even for spring break, and it felt odd to be physically out of my house: everything was both familiar and unfamiliar. A sense of nostalgia swept over me as I surveyed the buildings (some old, some new) and considered my more than two decades here—all the people, all those memories. Then a vague fear crept in: what will the university be like after all this? What if we cannot or do not return? As I looked around the empty campus, this wave of solastalgia overcame me. The sun had returned, the air smelled like spring, but not a soul was to be seen. The landscape had changed, even though every building and tree appeared right where they always were. I know we are flattening the curve, doing what's necessary, but it feels disjointed—and jarring.

No one was in my building or the English Department to bring me back to "reality" in that moment, so I wrote to my students that evening, encouraging them to connect and check in, to write and seek hope.

One of my greatest joys as a teacher is listening to students process ideas for projects, often not yet fully baked, but full of promise and hope. That kind of uncertainty resembles a journey I take with students as they embark on a research project: they have a germ of an idea, but don't quite know where they will end up. Students often look to me for guidance, and in almost all cases I'm confident we can deliver them safely to their destination, generally having learned something through the experience. Another kind of uncertainty lurks, though, as we try to function and find a "new normal" in these unusual times: no one knows what will happen, and when they look to me for guidance, I do not have much to offer; I feel powerless. Many students and faculty are dealing with personal loss and incredibly difficult circumstances, as well. How do I balance these two very different kinds of uncertainty?

Much of the existential distress presented by COVID-19 left me feeling powerless and unproductive during 4Cs week. I was fascinated by my need (and my simultaneous awareness of that need) to attempt to grasp some sort of control when I was essentially powerless—most notably by cleaning up my desk and organizing my workspace. My thinking was that if I cleared the space, I would somehow clear my mind, but that action was futile. I found myself far more preoccupied with planning my next outing, and I sorely missed the days when going to the grocery store or campus wasn't such an event. On Friday of 4Cs week, I wrote, "The cautious venture out into the community feels very odd, scheduled, and intentional, compared to my 'regular' comings and goings, in which I often found myself popping in and out of stores or other businesses several times every day. Certainly, I am careful and deliberate in planning in ways that I never have before."

On Saturday I was supposed to moderate a panel at 4Cs, and my flight home would leave shortly after that. I remember being slightly worried about the quick turnaround time to catch the flight. I even checked the time from the hotel to the MKE airport to calculate the latest possible time I could leave the conference. How quaint all those plans seem now!

On Saturday evening during 4Cs week, in response to the question "What did you accomplish?" I wrote:

> For the fourth day in a row, this question nags at me—as if I must always be able to list my accomplishments, like a line on the CV. Earlier in the week I took great comfort in this question: it reminded me to take stock of all that I am doing amidst all the uncertainty and fretting. Today—perhaps because it's Saturday—the question feels more like a weight: what if my accomplishments today were not quantifiable? I curled my elderly

mother's hair for her and rubbed lotion on her dry feet; I gave my daughter some respite from her busy 3-year-old; I reassured a student that she would be okay in her comp class.

In my fatigue from Saturday evening's writing, I wondered if I was doing enough.

Solastalgia accounts for collective distress, but also—importantly—collective comfort, or solace, for the pain and uncertainty. Albrecht writes, "With a new . . . language to describe and 're-place' our emotions and feelings, powerful transformative forces are unleashed. Solastalgia is fixated on the melancholic, but it is also a foundation for action that will negate it" (para. 16). The pandemic has starkly reminded me that my job is less about grading and more about encouraging and comforting, both students AND faculty. In my role, I can be that transformative force.

How many emails have I answered from worried faculty who wonder what to do about the student who was doing fine in class until March and now they haven't heard from them? (Too many to count.) I try to answer each email patiently and with respect. I know my Dean of Students must cringe every time she gets a forwarded email from me: "Here are two more students we're concerned about. Please have your staff try to do a wellness check." We may not ever know what happened to them, even if the staff is able to connect with the student.

And being able to help students with their concerns is indeed a blessing. As always, I try to respond to emergent situations. I know in the coming weeks we will have plenty of students expressing concern about their work/school balance. And I will try to deal with each of these cases with sensitivity and support. In one situation from Saturday of 4Cs week, the student works in a grocery store and had been asked to increase her shifts to *60 hours per week* since she remains healthy. Not surprisingly, she feels overwhelmed and unable to keep up with her Comp II work. I connected with the student as well as her instructor, trying to provide options for completion of course and reassurance. I wonder, though, how many students never reach out and ask for help.

As we scramble to prepare for fall, the uncertainty mounts: how will our first-year graduate TAs learn to teach writing in this environment? I made the difficult decision to move them all to "remote learning" for fall. This option seems to me to offer the most flexibility, given the uncertainty. We have this summer to prepare these newest writing faculty for the road ahead, but this arrangement is certainly not what they signed up for.

I'm reminded how quickly life circumstances change—this time not just an individual circumstance, but on a widespread, community (and world-wide) basis. And how quickly we adapt to new norms, even as our memories or bodies resist. I'm reminded, too, about the power of spring, not just weather-wise (cold and stormy one day, sunny and warm the next), but also in its hope and promise of new life. In isolation, we desire to be part of something bigger, something more meaningful than ourselves. In this new normal, solastalgia encourages us to slow down and take stock, pay more attention to the simple everyday things we used to take for granted: going to the store, reaching out to a friend, playing a game. These prosaic activities turn out to engage the connections in life that matter. I believe that naming and defining our experiences with the pandemic will provide hope to find our way forward as we face even more challenging times.

On the Saturday of 4Cs week, my plan was a walk in the sunny morning. As we made our way to the (still open) park, my 3-year-old granddaughter—running with glee—tripped on the sidewalk and tumbled down, scraping her knees and elbow, and she cried inconsolably for her mommy. She couldn't be sidetracked back into the park scenario, so we turned around and hobbled home. In response to the child's insistence on seeing the doctor, my clever daughter wondered aloud if instead we should try to call the doctor. That day, she earned the Academy Award for "Best Performance in a Fake Telephone Call," in which she dialed the phone, waited on hold for the doctor, then told the doctor about her child's fall, asking for advice. After answering some additional clarifying questions from the "doctor," my daughter was relieved to report that her child did not, in fact, need to have a limb removed, nor did she even need to visit the doctor, but instead should apply the Elsa Band-aids and receive periodic snuggles. The child, satisfied, resumed her day, and all was well. For a moment, the pandemic cloud over all of us lifted, and sunshine poured in.

In that one 4Cs week, our weather moved from tentative spring back to winter, and finally landed on something quite close to summer—a typical lurching spring in Nebraska. Nature renews and transforms itself; ironically, the earth is healing right now because of the reduced emissions from human activity. My tulips have come and gone; they opened in glorious colors—yellow, orange, and red—and now are drying out. That week our magnolia tree did not bloom due to the timing of three days of hard frost; the buds were just coming out, and then all progress stopped. Some of the buds have fallen to the ground as hard brown clumps, but most cling to the tree which looks like a skeleton, and the green leaves are just starting to fill in the emptiness. Right now it is about 50–50, but I know eventually the leaves will win out, and next year the magnolia will bloom with exceptional brilliance. In a similar way, solastalgia's collective comfort will guide us from our currently unfamiliar and uncertain terrain into a new, transformed landscape. Hope returns through cycles, not necessarily through closure. And we have much more work to do.

Special thanks to Dr. Lisa Knopp, who introduced me to the term "solastalgia."

WORK CITED

Albrecht, Glenn. "The Age of Solastalgia." *The Conversation.* 7 August 2012, https://theconversation.com/the-age-of-solastalgia-8337.

16

Self-Reflexivity Is/As Resistance

Soha Youssef

My shoulders were tight from the heavy weight I had to carry at the young age of five. My little brain was constantly challenged every weekday from early morning until the school bell would announce a brief break before I had to revisit the books once again at home. My eyes were strained, gathering as much knowledge as they could until they were allowed to retire for the night. Soon, the sun rises, marking another day when I would do it all over again. And weekends only meant more time with books, reading, writing, and drilling.

Growing up, I was conditioned to be productive and to work hard. Arabic sayings such as "foul are the idle hands," and "those who work hard, succeed; those who sow the seeds, harvest" were often reiterated in my Egyptian household. Hard work became my dedication, my motivation, the source of my value, my self-worth. And nothing is meant to stand in the way of me being productive—not even family obligations. My parents, like most middle-class, college-educated Egyptians, saw a solid education as a panacea. One main asset of that solid education is gaining fluency in at least one additional language—particularly English, French, or German—on top of our native Arabic. To gain such fluency, I was sent to a Catholic, all-English school. By fourth grade, I added French as a third language, and in college, I studied German as a fourth language. Knowing so many languages did not make me any more special or prepared than my peers who share my social and economic statuses, and whose parents were first-generation college students. We, Egyptians, perceive language acquisition as a way out—out of a country that was colonized for too many years to retain an appreciation of its own Arabic, out of a limited and limiting income bracket that crushes one's potential, out to pursue the American dream. That fascination with languages is, indeed, one of the consequences of colonization. Taken to an extreme, our fascination turns into a misconception that speaking in tongues is evidence of modernity. But that pursuit of modernity mandates hard work. So, for me, work always came first.

That drive, I presume, is probably what gravitated me toward academia in the first place. Realizing now how intellectually demanding, emotionally daunting, and psychologically draining academia can be, I understand why I chose it as a career. Scholarship, teaching, and service: they are my source of bliss, my calling, as well as the root of my anxiety attacks—all at the same time and not necessarily in this order. That anxiety, though, is what I have always perceived as a healthy exercise. It is the anxiety that fuels and sustains my productivity. A sustained productivity keeps me normal, keeps me sane. And any disruption to that normalcy throws off my rhythm and breaks me down, all while inciting my self-guilt. That typical looming manuscript submission deadline, that infamous growing pile of student papers, that additional committee to serve on—all spike my heart rate and anxiety level—the healthy anxiety. It is only when something interferes with my productivity that I experience the other kind of anxiety—the destructive kind. Then, I catch myself gasping for air.

Though that breathing difficulty is not associated with COVID-19 on a medical level, the pandemic has definitely accentuated my anxiety and panic attacks, particularly during the first few weeks of the lockdown. To my surprise, as time went by, anxiety was replaced with clarity—clarity to perceive the problematics of not only the academy, but also of my own labor practices.

My first reaction to institutional orders to self-quarantine was a sense of denial—not of the fact that the world is facing a global crisis, but of the fact that I have lost grip. I was in denial of the fact that post-COVID-19 times brought about a new understanding of normalcy and what that notion entails. Like most academics who work against the tenure clock, I saw a once-in-a-lifetime opportunity in the lockdown. I left campus on March 13 not only with hopes to maintain my pre-COVID-19 productivity levels, but with aspirations to exceed such expectations. That is how delusional I was. Those aspirations were induced and further complicated by institutional and academic expectations of productivity. The promise of time abundance during the quarantine solidified my then-delusional state of mind only to realize my inability to accomplish even the pre-COVID-19 baseline productivity levels. And then self-guilt set in. Since I was slow to realize that the meaning of normalcy is shifting, I experienced a creeping sense of guilt that I was not making use of all the time that the lockdown afforded me. What complicated that sense of guilt was observations of fellow academics who were maintaining a daily writing regimen—exactly like they did pre-COVID-19. In honesty, their chameleon powers still mesmerize me. And those unhealthy comparisons between my dismal adaptation to post-COVID-19 new normal and the adaptation of others were not only maddening, but also counterproductive. I spent more time drawing comparisons than being productive. That abundance of time—though it did not allow me to be over productive—definitely afforded me self-reflexivity. Though I discovered I was continually incapable of achieving daily tasks, let alone being over productive, I began to realize the bliss of slowing down.

Being forced to actually sit down, take a deep breath, and watch my own life—for the first time—I got to experience my own life as a viewer, instead of an active agent; as an acted upon, instead of an actor. That sense of helplessness imposed by the virus turned out to be an eye-opener, providing me a clearer vision of my labor practices that were informed by my Egyptian upbringing, with its emphasis on perpetual productivity, and later reinforced by the American academy. It was like a curtain had been lifted to afford me clarity of vision. I found myself questioning academia's precipitancy—that tendency to place quantity before quality, to value the act of being productive over pondering, reflecting on, dwelling upon, and carefully examining (whether that is data or pedagogy or committee decisions). I found myself constantly working against the tenure timeclock rather than spending time with my research or pedagogy. And the quarantine afforded me the privileges of slowing down, of reflecting on my academic work habits, without worrying about my financial situation or employment stability. Unlike over forty million who have been impacted by the crisis, I am infinitely grateful that my academic status afforded me such privilege. The deeper I reflected on my work habits, the more I came to discover about myself as an academic as well as about academia and the profession. Soon, I realized that what I have always perceived as healthy anxiety is not healthy after all. I realized that it is perfectly fine to pause, to take a break, to slow down. I started to question academia's rush for productivity: we valorize it, and prioritize it over even our mental health. The reactions to the lockdown were a collective denial that that hierarchy cannot hold during a state of national emergency—denial that the right questions we should have been asking one another should not be about the progression of our writing and research agendas, but about our state of mind.

And I would not have discovered the bliss of reflecting during these difficult times had it not been for the prompted reflections that Cs' Documentarian role took the shape of following the conference's cancellation due to the pandemic. It was through those reflections that I was able to peek through a window to a sense of acceptance that slowly replaced denial, anxiety, and guilt that rippled as a consequence of the lockdown. Not only that, but the sense of solidarity experienced through those reflections was an additional privilege at a time when the majority of the nation experienced a lack thereof. The call for Documentarians to reflect on that particular moment in history created a sense of belonging and solidarity: knowing that all Documentarians are going through the same reflective exercises made me realize how tight the community is, which is a privilege that not all professions offer. And that sense of community and belonging, I have to admit, was much needed in that particular moment when loneliness and fear were the predominant emotions. That sense of normalcy, though fleeting, helped me during the journey toward acceptance—as I compose this reflection, about three months into the lockdown, it is finally sinking in that normalcy as we used to know and experience it is something from the past. It will be eventually replaced with a new normal that we may imagine now but will not fully comprehend until social isolation is lifted and we get to actually occupy other spaces than our homes. Though that sense of normalcy was fleeting, the reflective exercises that that moment created raised my consciousness about the true power of reflection as an act of resilience. While uncertainty can be maddening for most, engaging in reflective writing, I discovered, offers some clarity to the self and of the self, a way of making sense, of understanding the un-understandable.

In one of the reflective entries, I articulated the benefits of self-reflective writing, stating "daily reflections are helping me regain control over my own life, especially since I am aware that I have no control over the chaos outside my own house or beyond the self." Now, that sense of control presented itself in a heightened metacognitive awareness of my mental health as well as of the physical movements and practices that promote a healthy mindset. For instance, in the first reflection I expressed hopes to "forgive myself when I do not achieve as much as I am used to during regular work days. . . . [admitting that] It is a learning curve." In the evening of this same day, nonetheless, I fluctuated to despair and guilt when I expressed my failure to meet the personal expectation "to compose more than three paragraphs" on that day. My metacognitive awareness of my mental health also shows when I realize that "I am constantly having to remind myself that it is okay to listen to my anxiety and practice selfcare, [admitting] that it is easier said than done." Reflecting on my time management strategies in the second reflection, I noted that "my perception of the rigidity of [my hour-by-hour] plans has become more lenient and forgiving," identifying such self-forgiveness as selfcare. That evening, I admitted, "Even though the writing is happening slower than it does in normal working days, it is still happening—those little accomplishments I am learning to celebrate." As much as I started celebrating small writing progress, I celebrated my ability to take breaks from work and actually learn to spend "quality time with my spouse and Teebah, our dog," such as making a special dinner and baking bread with my spouse, watching a movie, or "bak[ing] a cherry pie for some indulgence [that] weekend." Another prominent pattern I noticed in all nine reflections pertains to my physical movement. In my post-reflection entry, I realized a particular pattern in my previous reflections:

> I found myself consistently mentioning Teebah, our dog, and how the notion of taking her for walks—an act that used to be a chore—is now "an out" from the quarantine. Since going on walks is one of the few outdoor activities still permitted, I found myself perceiving Teebah as the actor and myself as the acted upon. I used structures such as "taking walks with Teebah" rather than "walking the dog/Teebah." The walks became something I look forward to. They are reminiscent of normalcy.

But the yearning for normalcy as we once knew it does not dissipate, I now realize. Yearning for normalcy becomes particularly evident when I engage in mundane activities. Grocery shopping became an activity to equally dread and look forward to. Taking the risk of bringing home an infection, along with the groceries, is the one predominant thought I have every time I don my mask and gloves, and reach out for our reusable grocery bags. It might sound overly dramatic to admit that those motions, which are now part of the ritual, often bear a close resemblance to patriotism—only the country here is my own home, and the sustenance and safety of its residents is my duty. But that sense of patriotism is never pure and hardly altruistic. It is usually tainted with a selfish drive that is borderline celebratory.

Home—a privilege morphed into a prison. And leaving its confinement, though precarious, feels liberating, with a promise of temporary normalcy as we once knew it.

The pandemic particularly raised my awareness of my privileges as a tenure-track academic who does not have to worry about the next paycheck. My institution has not resorted to furloughs or layoffs—yet. There is always a yet. There is always uncertainty. But, right now, I am grateful for not being contingent, and that gratitude is a constant reminder about the status of my contingent peers who might be struggling to pay rent or make ends meet. My privilege is in a sense a reminder about the status of the academy—an academy that is embedded in capitalism, pretending that, despite the pandemic, it is business as usual, that our classes should seamlessly move online, and that our writing productivity is expected to hold—regardless of our privilege or lack thereof.

The very act of composing this reflection is an epitome of that urge for productivity—that urge that I was conditioned to for as long as I could recall. Productivity is my normalcy. In fact, it is because of such conditioning to be productive that it became my normalcy. My Egyptian upbringing equipped me with a thick skin for hard work and productivity in adverse conditions. I was taught from a young age that doing the minimum is not an option if I am to fully utilize my potential, attain upward mobility, or chase the American dream. That perseverance might have conditioned me to survive and thrive for nine consecutive years as a graduate student in America, earning two master's degrees and a doctorate, and then conjure the resilience (or gullibility) to make a conscious decision to seek a tenure-track position. Though that sense of perseverance that my parents instilled in me from a young age did condition me for hard work, it also desensitized me to the adverse psychological and mental consequences of that constant drive for productivity. That drive, since it is usually accompanied by a state of euphoria or intoxication, has blinded me to simple evident facts: I am almost always exhausted, I do not get enough deep sleep, I do not practice selfcare as deliberately or as often as I should, I am alienated from healthy socializations, and I do not spend much quality time with my spouse or with our puppy. Many might perceive my work habits as evidence of workaholism. And it took a global pandemic to sober me up. With the sudden change of space and pace, the lockdown forced me into a state of paralysis as I lost all control over my labor practices. What made it even more difficult to be productive is the daily habits that I self-created: religiously listening to NPR and watching the PBS news hour every morning, then sinking into sadness and despondence for the rest of the day. It took me a few weeks before I decided that remaining informed cannot come at the hefty price of my mental health. Reaching such understanding, I maintained my distance from the news. In hindsight, immersing myself in pandemic-related news placed me in a vicious cycle of anxiety and lack of productivity. And it was not until I started to put my reflections in writing that I realized that a pandemic was the worst time to chase my own normal, pre-pandemic rates of productivity. It was also the moment that I realized the therapeutic element of reflective writing.

Not only that, but I realize now more than ever that being conditioned to be productive is a privilege. It was privilege that conditioned me to be over productive as a middle-class Egyptian child, and it is privilege that now allows me to expect, and actually enjoy, a more moderate rate of productivity at a time when it is difficult for most to find the energy to do so. Not only do I find reflective writing, and the act of writing for that matter, to be enjoyable, but I also find it comforting. Reflective writing, particularly the reflections required in light of the newly-envisioned Cs Documentarian role, offered me a space to clearly track my movement as well as tune in to my physical comfort and ways it informs my productivity as I changed my work space during the lockdown. My new practices do not happen organically (yet) and have to be consciously self-driven: I am now more deliberate about taking walks with Teebah, since I am now more aware of the ways those movements help maintain my sanity and, consequently, my productivity. Through those reflections, I am now more cognizant that I am one of those to whom selfcare does not come naturally; it has to be intentional and calculated. At the risk of sounding frivolous, I now schedule baths in addition to the merely functional daily showers; I regularly do home facials; I have learned to enjoy my morning coffee in the outdoor morning breeze instead of rushing to my computer first thing in the morning and going through cycles of repetitively microwaving my coffee till it eventually becomes undrinkable. Reflective writing provided me a window to understand not only myself and my labor practices as a scholar-instructor and an academic, but also the academy and what it values.

If I am to name one lesson I have learned from this global crisis, it would be the bliss of self-reflexivity: of slowing down to question our individual labor practices, and of raising our awareness of our privileges (or lack thereof) as academics. Those privileges are meant to be shared with those who were particularly impacted by the pandemic and whose livelihood is threatened by its consequences. Though my experience is not generalizable, I doubt anyone could argue against the benefits of reflective writing and the value of constantly examining our own positionalities in any given situation. But if not all of us, academics, are privileged enough to be afforded the time and energy to reflect on the ways our productivity might have been impacted by the pandemic, then it is the responsibility of the privileged of us to ensure that our campuses have the resources to support the mental health of faculty members, particularly contingent faculty. Mental health awareness, support, and resources are even more vital now than ever. And perhaps it is time for all of us to slow down and exercise self care and mindfulness. If this is not the right time, I am not sure when.

17

"Tending to My Life": On Resilience and Academic Work

Charlotte Asmuth

Like many of my Documentarian colleagues, I use the term *work* often in my survey responses. Indeed, I mention work seventy-three times, nearly twice as often as the second most frequently used word. I attempt, at various times, to "sit down to work," "get back to work," "continue to work," complete "student assessment work," and so on. I refer to "my work" several times and my relationship to it. I mention "my actual work" once, ostensibly referring to academic work and not the work exerted during daily acts of self-care. In comparison, I mention writing (I should be working on a particular kind of writing, dissertation-related) only eleven times. I experience continuous anxiety about not doing the "right" kind of work: my dissertation work. At one point, I write, "I feel like my work is always shrouded in anxiety."

In spring 2020, as the World Health Organization declares a global pandemic due to the rapid spread of COVID-19, I am supposed to be starting my dissertation. Instead, I spend the final six weeks of the semester shifting my course online, reading everything I can about online instruction, joining Facebook groups with grim names like "Pandemic Pedagogy," commenting frequently on my students' writing, drafting emails, and offering reassurance, support, and extended deadlines to students—in addition to planning trips to different grocery stores that might not be crowded, worrying about at-risk family members and my students, becoming increasingly disturbed by the racist discourse some public officials take up when discussing COVID-19, and trying to engage in acts of self-care.

In spring 2020, I'm managing to teach and support my students. But my normal "sit down and work" method for academic writing is not working anymore.

RESILIENCE AND ACADEMIC WORK

The image below (Figure 17.1) captures my workspace on March 28, 2020, at 10:18 AM. I call the couch in this picture my "gray work couch" and it acts as my desk for now. Piles of papers, note pads, pens, my attendance book, and course materials for the class I teach reside on one side of the couch. The laundry, the cats, or I occupy the other side. Books propped open like tents are on the floor in front of the couch. I have to dodge them on the way to the kitchen. When I need to meet virtually with a student, I take a small, empty cardboard box into the living room and prop my laptop on this box so my screen appears at eye level. While I normally dress "professionally" for class (collared shirt, ironed and tucked in, dress shoes), I have given that up for quarantine.

Figure 17.1. The author's "gray work couch" on March 28, 2020. A small pile of laundry and two throw pillows take up the right side of the couch. A laptop, binder, planner, textbook, legal pad, papers, and two other throw pillows occupy the left side of the couch.

Shortly after taking the photograph, I gather the small pile of laundry on the couch and dump it on the bed so that I have room to sit on the couch. At night, I carry this pile from the bed back to the couch, not folding these clothes until a few days later. The pile is on the smaller side in the photo because, each day, my partner and I grab the clothes we need from the pile before transferring it from the couch to the bed. Each time I interact with the laundry pile, I think of the psychology professor in Paul Prior and Jody Shipka's "Chronotopic Lamination." When she writes at home, this professor "sets the buzzer on the dryer so that approximately every forty-five minutes to an hour she is pulled away from the text to tend the laundry downstairs" (180). As she deals with the laundry, she thinks about the text she is working on. This routine, a way of managing her attention, is an example of what Prior and Shipka call "environment-selecting and -structuring practices" (ESSPs), which they define as "the intentional deployment of external aids and actors to shape, stabilize, and direct consciousness in service of the task at hand" (219). Seemingly mundane practices like those of the psychology professor are ways in which agents can exert control over—or reshape-for-now—the material environments in which they compose. What Prior and Shipka's participants reveal is that academic work routines are influenced by dispersed practices, life histories, emotions, etc., some of which appear to have little to do with the kind of academic writing I am experiencing so much anxiety about.

Here, for example, is how one of Prior and Shipka's other participants, Melissa Orlie (a well-published academic), responds when Shipka asks about "intrusions" to her work routine:

> I don't see the tending to my life as an interruption [to my work]. Um, from the time, I remember it from being reading Marx as an undergraduate that I had this whole sense of, you need a really broad definition of work. And that the, *the conditions of work, you know, having good food, having the garden watered—all those things are about creating a sense of well-being for me so that I can work, and I don't consider them things not, you know, not to do, um, they're actually part of the process and I have to create time for them.* (222-23; original emphasis)

Orlie's philosophy of work is clearly influenced by her awareness that academic work is not only intellectual work—that caring for her body sustains her academic work, too. What stands out to me when I re-read this passage is how her description of her working life is so unlike most of the descriptions that are available in our field. Orlie's practice of "tending to [her] life" is part of her work. Graduate students are, too often, not beneficiaries of this kind of advice about work habits from faculty mentors.

There is some evidence that conversations about work habits happen between faculty advisors and graduate students (e.g., Tulley). But graduate students are rarely privy to richly detailed accounts of what day-to-day academic work looks and feels like. I don't point this out to blame my lack of scholarly productivity during the pandemic on the absence of these accounts, for I know that I am not alone in feeling "unproductive" during this time. I also believe that "being productive" in the recognized sense need not be our priority right now (as Aisha Ahmad argues in a well-circulated *Chronicle of Higher Education* article). Rather, I point this out because the pandemic has left me struggling to establish some semblance of a work routine without having had a particularly structured one in place before.

While many scholars in our field specialize in capturing, in granular detail, the working/writing scenes of everyday people, we have yet to consistently turn a critical eye to our own sites of work/writing and our own working/writing practices. Indeed, academic work routines are still very much occluded in our field and academia in general, emerging only occasionally and only for those who are listening and watching closely. Over the last few years, I've caught glimpses of colleagues' private work routines. A professor makes a passing comment in a graduate seminar about the role that procrastination plays in her writing process: "When I have article revisions to work on, cleaning the fridge becomes suddenly important." I see this same professor walk laps around the building during breaks in class. One professor's office door always appears locked as he prefers to work from home. In a writing group, another professor shares a draft of a conference talk that is in outline form and confesses that she's not quite sure what her takeaways are yet. An advisor tells me he removed his Wi-Fi card from his laptop during the hours he worked on his dissertation.

But none of these fragmentary observations are particularly helpful to me right now. I don't know how that procrasti-cleaning professor structures her work days, responds to reviewer feedback on her writing, or even how she manages a cluttered email inbox. And right now,

I'm hesitant to ask any potentially overburdened faculty mentors for their advice. Instead, to help manage my anxiety, I reflect on previous situations in which I have been resilient.

The first time I taught the 300-level course I'm teaching in spring 2020, I was mourning the end of a five-year relationship and applying to doctoral programs. Two weeks of class sessions were canceled due to snow days, so I was already trying to make adjustments to the course schedule on the fly. And then the pipes in the house I rented burst while I was out of town (attending 4C17, incidentally), flooding the downstairs. When I returned, the house was uninhabitable. I spent the next six weeks in temporary housing near campus while the house was being repaired. At the same time, I navigated the process of deciding which school to attend for my PhD, mentored new graduate teaching assistants, and tried to finish teaching two classes, one of which I had never taught before and wasn't entirely sure I was ready to teach in the first place. My primary source of comfort, my dog, was not allowed in my temporary housing, so I arranged for my ex to care for him. Occasionally, I snuck him into my room for an afternoon. Sometimes, I brought him to my classes and the Writing Center, where he quickly became the "Writing Center mascot" and a source of joy for students who took photos with him. The day before I left for 4C19, during the semester when I was finishing my doctoral coursework, my dog died.

These experiences remind me that I have worked during challenging times before and that I have gotten through these difficult times. I need this reminder right now, when my anxiety about completing my dissertation and entering a potentially bleak job market persists. Right now, like Melissa Orlie, I am "tending to my life" (Prior and Shipka 222), even if some parts of that life have been put on hold. And yet, I can't help but wonder how different my current work habits might be if faculty mentors had openly discussed their own work habits with me.

WAYS FORWARD: "INTRUSIVE MENTORING"

About six years ago, my MA advisor offered to talk about managing multiple academic projects at the same time. We were sitting in his office and I was running through a few ideas I had for a potential research project for my MA thesis. I said, "I have a few things I want to work on, but don't really know how to juggle them." He replied with something like, "That's something we can talk about. I'd be happy to talk about that sometime." I nodded as his offer hung in the air. I was perhaps too unsure of how to initiate such a meeting (and unsure of what to expect he would say, which is precisely why I *should* have taken him up on this offer) and neither of us brought it up again. Not taking him up on his offer remains a big regret.

In the conclusion of *How Writing Faculty Write*, Christine Tulley writes, "Beyond seminar papers and writing for publication/digital publication courses in some doctoral programs, any additional graduate writing instruction within rhetoric and composition as a field has largely been the result of a one-to-one modeling" (150). She thus argues, "We need to go beyond just modeling how we write for our graduate students and actually teach them how we know how to do it" (150). By extension, I argue, faculty mentors ought to go beyond simply modeling their work habits (e.g., writing in the office, as many faculty do) to having frank discussions with graduate students about their work habits and how they developed these habits. It is especially important to have these conversations now because (1) they can foster resilience in graduate students and (2) given the uncertainty surrounding COVID-19, academics may be working from home for an extended period of time again. Thus, graduate students will be unable to witness faculty mentors who normally work in the office exhibiting productive work habits. Below, I provide a few suggestions for both faculty and graduate students about how to initiate these conversations.

Graduate students who wish to initiate these discussions with faculty mentors might find Tulley's interview questions, provided in her book's appendix, a useful place to start. In addition, graduate students might approach their advisors with questions such as the following: How do you structure your work time? How do you balance pressure to publish with your other responsibilities? How do you respond to reviewer feedback? Do your writing habits vary depending on whether you're writing for administration, teaching, or publication purposes? What does blending self-care and academic work look like for you? Can you tell me about a time in your work life in which you felt resilient? What did that look like for you?

To that end, faculty mentors should volunteer responses to the above questions before they even have to be asked. Additionally, faculty can introduce mentees to the concept of "environment-selecting and -structuring practices" and illustrate this concept with examples from their own working lives. (I have done this in undergraduate courses

I teach and students find the idea that writing environments affect composing practices fascinating.) Faculty can also share and discuss draft versions of journal articles with the accompanying cover letter, reviewers' comments, and their responses to their comments. I realize that doing so requires a certain amount of vulnerability, emotional labor, and time, but this practice aligns with recent calls in our field for faculty to "[m]ake academic practice and conventions accessible" (Mckoy et al. para 3) and to have more open conversations about their relationship to work as well as their experiences with failure (Driscoll et al.; LaFrance and Corbett). To be clear, I believe that had I received a form of the proactive "intrusive mentoring" I'm advocating for here, I might already have a structured work routine in place or a flexible set of strategies on which to draw to structure my work.[1] While this routine would likely need to be adjusted during the pandemic, it would give me a place to start and I might not feel so adrift.

While I have provided suggestions for graduate students about how to initiate conversations about work habits, the burden of this labor should largely fall on faculty, especially because marginalized graduate students already take on an enormous amount of emotional and material labor, compounded by their economic and institutional precarity (see Colón; González; Kumari; Madden et al.; Mckoy et al.; Tang and Andriamanalina). For example, Lida Colón describes the extra work Black graduate students often take on, tapping into networks like Digital Black Lit and Composition (DBLAC) to find support for their research interests and "their entire selves outside of the academic space," because their graduate courses do not center Black scholarship and their institutions are predominately white.

---

1   In the 1980s, academic counselor Walter Earl coined the term "intrusive advising" to describe "deliberate structured student intervention at the first indication of academic difficulty in order to motivate a student to seek help" (28). Earl's model involves inviting probationary students to reflect on "factors that most contributed to the[ir] probationary status" and to work with their advisors to develop a plan of action for increased academic success (see pages 31-32). Earl seems to be motivated by deficit assumptions about students, however: his theory of "intrusive advising" operates from the premise that students' "[d]eficiencies" in orienting to university life are "treatable" if students can be taught certain skills (30). By contrast, I use "intrusive mentoring" (a term others have used before) to refer to a proactive form of support for graduate students that both makes academic practices explicit and aims to change the institutional structures in which graduate students work.

The conversations I allude to above are not easy and will look different depending on the mentor and mentee. Furthermore, these conversations require an enormous amount of trust between mentors and mentees, which is not necessarily easy to establish. As a non-binary, queer, white graduate student, for example, it is hard enough for me to establish trusting relationships with mentors when I am repeatedly misgendered by them. It can be even more challenging for BIPOC graduate students to establish trusting relationships with mentors in predominantly white institutional spaces.

Thus, I argue, graduate faculty need to view supporting graduate students' work habits as an equity issue in our field. While the conversations I describe above are a good start for making work practices visible and more accessible to graduate students (and, if desired, subject to revision by graduate students), they are still not enough. "Ethical mentorship" should be formally institutionalized and not limited to one-on-one mentoring sessions (Mckoy et al.; see also Tulley 150). Mentoring graduate work habits must be built sustainably into graduate programs and graduate writing courses, even when those courses are not "Writing for Publication" courses. At my institution, no writing group was formally established within my program until a visiting scholar took on the labor of doing so. It remains to be seen whether this writing group will continue without the presence of this visiting scholar.

The global pandemic has disrupted all of our working lives in some way. Some graduate students (and faculty) will again be forced to work from home when they are unaccustomed to doing so, have increased child care responsibilities, or do not have access to a quiet space to work. How can faculty teach graduate students to take up useful work habits and care for themselves during times of collective crisis? How can faculty support graduate students' work practices when both their own and graduate students' working conditions are increasingly precarious and inconsistent? Now, more than ever, it may be especially difficult for some of us (not to mention our undergraduate students) to restructure our working environments. But it is crucial for faculty to support graduate students as they try to do so, for the futures of junior scholars, and by extension our field, depend on it.

WORKS CITED

Ahmad, Aisha S. "Why You Should Ignore All That Coronavirus-Inspired Productivity Pressure." *The Chronicle of Higher Education*, 27 March

2020, https://www.chronicle.com/article/Why-You-Should-Ignore-All-That/248366.

Colón, Lida. "Don't Talk About It, Be About It: A Model of Material Support for Black Graduate Students." *XChanges: An Interdisciplinary Journal of Technical Communication, Rhetoric, and Writing Across the Curriculum*, vol. 15, no. 1, 2020, https://xchanges.org/dont-talk-about-it-15-1.

Driscoll, Dana Lynn, S. Rebecca Leigh, and Nadia Francine Zamin. "Self-Care as Professionalization: A Case for Ethical Doctoral Education in Composition Studies." *College Composition and Communication*, vol. 71, no. 3, 2020, pp. 453–80.

Earl, Walter R. "Intrusive Advising of Freshmen in Academic Difficulty." *NACADA Journal*, vol. 8, no. 2, 1988, pp. 27–33.

González, Caleb Lee. "Emerging through Critical Race Theory Counter-storytelling in a Rhetoric and Composition Graduate Studies Context." *XChanges: An Interdisciplinary Journal of Technical Communication, Rhetoric, and Writing Across the Curriculum*, vol. 15, no. 1, 2020, https://xchanges.org/emerging-through-crt-counter-storytelling-15-1.

Kumari, Ashanka. *Remaking Identities, Reworking Graduate Study: Stories from First-Generation-to-College Rhetoric and Composition Ph.D. Students on Navigating the Doctorate*. 2019. University of Louisville, Ph.D. dissertation. ThinkIR, https://ir.library.louisville.edu/etd/3206.

LaFrance, Michelle, and Steven J. Corbett. "Discourse Community Fail! Negotiating Choices in Success/Failure and Graduate-Level Writing Development." *Graduate Writing Across the Disciplines: Identifying, Teaching, and Supporting*, edited by Marilee Brooks-Gillies, Elena G. Garcia, Soo Hyon Kim, Katie Manthey, and Trixie G. Smith, WAC Clearinghouse, 2020, pp. 295–314, https://doi.org/10.37514/ATD-B.2020.0407.2.12.

Madden, Shannon, Michele Eodice, Kirsten T. Edwards, and Alexandria Lockett, editors. *Learning from the Lived Experiences of Graduate Student Writers*. Utah State UP, 2020.

Mckoy, Temptaous, Hannah Rule, Dawn Opel, Karrieann Soto Vega, and Ashanka Kumari. "CCCC Statement of Professional Guidance for Mentoring Graduate Students." Conference on College Composition and Communication, November 2019, https://cccc.ncte.org/cccc/resources/positions/professional-guidance-for-mentoring-graduate-students/.

Prior, Paul, and Jody Shipka. "Chronotopic Lamination: Tracing the Contours of Literate Activity." *Writing Selves/Writing Societies: Research from Activity Perspectives*, edited by Charles Bazerman and David R. Russell, WAC Clearinghouse, 2003, pp. 180–238, https://doi.org/10.37514/PER-B.2003.2317.2.06.

Tang, Jasmine Kar, and Noro Andriamanalina. "'Rhonda Left Early to Go to Black Lives Matter': Programmatic Support for Graduate Writers of Color." *WPA: Writing Program Administration*, vol. 39, no. 2, 2016, pp. 10-16.

Tulley, Christine E. *How Writing Faculty Write: Strategies for Process, Product, and Productivity.* Utah State UP, 2018.

18

A Controlled Freak-Out: Mentoring, Writing, and Parenting during COVID-19

Katrina M. Powell

A CCCCS THAT MIGHT HAVE BEEN

I signed on to be a CCCCs Documentarian with enthusiasm. I was excited to document my CCCCs experience this year as I anticipated it would be similar to others. My first CCCCs conference was in 1998, and I've attended or presented at most of them since then. I wanted to write about how I read through the program with delight as I choose sessions to attend, meet with friends and colleagues both at sessions and at art museums, and, as my role has changed over the years, attend a social for graduate students and alumni from Virginia Tech.

If I had traveled to Milwaukee, I was scheduled to facilitate a workshop for ATTW on Tuesday afternoon about building alternative archives. All the workshop facilitators were scheduled to have dinner with Cheryl Geisler on Tuesday evening—I'm very disappointed about not doing the workshop and not attending that dinner. The participants scheduled for my workshop are working on amazing projects and I was so excited to meet them and learn about their work. I also would have attended the Consortium of Doctoral Programs in Rhetoric and Composition and met with Steve Parks before the Documentarians reception event. Steve and I are working on a collaborative project together and we were going to strategize our work for the coming months. We're used to working over email and the phone, but it would have been great to meet in person. I also would have attended the *CCC* editorial board meeting, attended a variety of presentations on research methods and displacement, and attended presentations of graduate students and alumni from our program.

One of my most favorite things about going to CCCCs is spending time with my best friend from graduate school. She lives in Milwaukee, and teaches in the UW system, so I may have gone to her house, caught up with her kids and spouse, and discussed the higher education situation in Wisconsin. I have so much respect for anyone teaching in Wisconsin these last years. From my friend I've learned about the grassroots efforts that she and her colleagues have engaged in for years to bring equitable labor conditions to all faculty. Now that the pandemic has threatened the financial stability of many colleges and universities, many are turning to their experience managing dire situations. She's an excellent faculty member and I'm inspired by her determination and grit during what has been an impossible situation. She's also really fun, funny, and caring and it's a joy to be near her. I was deeply saddened not to see her at CCCCs this year.

Another thing I usually do at the conference is look around in lobbies and hallways for particular people to say "Hi" to. These are people who I don't know well enough to share lunch or even have a long conversation, but with whom I'm acquainted and like to check in. One of these people is Shirley Logan. She's retired now so I'm not sure if she would have been there, but I love seeing her at CCCCs. She was the first person to hire me to teach technical writing and encourage me to pursue an academic career. Over the years when I've seen her at CCCCs, she remembers me and she asks how I am and about Virginia Tech. I'm always impressed that she remembers me. She was one of my first mentors in the field, encouraging me to apply to PhD programs, valuing my experience as a technical writer and introducing me to other graduate students. With the increased political activism in the last few weeks, I have thought much about Shirley, her mentorship, and her leadership in our field.

WORKING FROM HOME

With the cancelation of the conference and the move to online instruction and working from home, I was glad that the editors decided to continue the Documentarian project. I teach autobiography and write about archiving and research methods, so I lean toward valuing this kind of archival role. A question that I thought about throughout this time was whether the role of Documentarian and the time to write/reflect in this way has something to do with privilege. I wondered if most of my fellow Documentarians were graduate students and junior colleagues, and, if so, what does it mean that the role falls to them? I wondered if it mirrors administrative, committee, and mentoring work in our field that is often taken up by junior colleagues and underrepresented groups. And as the writing prompts asked us to consider where and when and under what conditions we were writing, I was acutely aware of my own relative privilege, both as a senior faculty member and as a person in my community with the means, ability, and kind of job to work from home.

Figure 18.1. Black cat sitting by a laptop and computer monitor on a desk by a window with a blooming redbud tree in the distance.

During the lockdown, I wrote every day in the same space (Figure 18.1). Though I had just moved when the pandemic was gaining full steam, I think this would have been true anyway—I tend to write in the same spaces. However, I normally write in my campus office as well, since I'm in the office often for administrative duties. The routine of having the same space at home really helped provide me focus and comfort. And the heightened awareness, both because of the pandemic and because of the prompts from the Documentarian editors, brought into sharp relief its necessity and also the privilege I have as a writer and academic to have such a space with equipment, a comfortable chair, high-speed internet, my books. So many do not have one or any of those things. Many of our students who are asked to complete courses online this semester do not have adequate internet access, and I was reminded of the work of Cindy Selfe and Gail Hawisher from long ago, which asked us to consider equity in technology and online instruction. Many of our faculty were prepared to teach online, but many were not and have faced high levels of stress in addition to the stress of the pandemic itself. There will be lasting repercussions of this moment as we continue our work toward equity in educational and technological access and as we face the coming fall semester with hybrid or complete online instruction for the foreseeable future.

Not long after the conference was canceled and our classes shifted online, my son's school closed as well. In those early days, I tried to keep up a routine to help my son break up the day. His life has been the most changed within our family—no school, no face-to-face interaction with friends, no baseball practice—just him and his parents. So, by intentionally scheduling my day in relation to his day, I hoped it would help his days go by faster. As a family, we had conversations about our situation relative to other families and tried to recognize how we could be in a position to help others. I thought a lot in those early days about how I hoped to get some work done, and I wanted to be a source of strength for my family. When we look back on all this, I wanted my son to remember some fun things like board games and family movie nights, but also, I wanted him to be aware of the ways his experience of the pandemic could be different from some kids in the community.

While my son didn't need help with homework, he did need help managing his grief and loss of not going to school every day and interacting with his friends. But we didn't know he was grieving until much later. He seemed fine at first, as we strictly adhered to physical distancing and staying at home. I will spend much more time over the coming years wondering if we did the right things for him. We know our home space was safe and spacious and equipped for access, but we worried and continue to worry about the impacts of the stress and uncertainty for him and his friends.

In those early days of working from home, the days ran together. We started to not know if it was a Tuesday or a Friday. I wrote one day in my reflection, "There's a random roll of gorilla tape on my desk—not sure how it got there." Another day I wrote, "I think I must be in acceptance mode. The last two days I've been grumpy, but today I was more myself because I've settled into the reality that this will go on for months, and I may as well get used to it." There were early days when I thought it would end and we could go back to working and schooling, but as time went on it was clear things would never be the same. Now that the fall looks different, we'll all likely be home again, and we're making plans to do things differently as a family.

I can tell I was very enthusiastic in the first few reflections and then I became tired or emotionally drained. The announcement of a state-wide shutdown was pending, my teenager was realizing the finality of the decisions to close his school. It was hard to write reflections during this time but I'm so glad that I did. I asked my graduate students to do some similar exercises in their researcher's journals as they faced re-imagining their projects now that their human subjects research had been paused. I asked them to give themselves time to mourn the loss of the project they'd imagined, but to also reimage the project so that they could progress. I also encouraged them that productivity expectations might need to be revised. This has been a delicate balance for myself as a writer and as a mentor to undergraduates, graduate students, and junior colleagues. I feel like the timing of being asked to do these reflections couldn't have come at a better time, as they were helpful to me to center myself so that I could be available to students as they navigated similar feelings and issues during this time. It's really incredible that this Documentarian role was established THIS year. The timing was uncanny, actually, and it reinforced what I've tried to teach and write about reflexive practice as a teacher, writer, and researcher.

MENTORING

While I attempted to build a routine both for the home and for my own writing, every day there are a number of emerging issues to address. The most pressing issue was helping graduate students as they transitioned to taking and teaching their classes online. I was not doing the difficult technical support work, but as director of the graduate program, I fielded many emails and calls as graduate students navigated being both an instructor and a student. There were many emotional phone calls as graduate students worried for their health and the health of their families, and whether they would be able to finish their course work while figuring out online instruction. They are all devoted teachers themselves and wanted so desperately to be good teachers to their own students. As the tension really built during March, I wrote this response as one of my reflections for the Documentarian writing prompts:

> I've been in a sort of ordered chaos freak-out sprinkled with the calm that I know graduate students need to see from me. So, I give them lots of advice about how it's going to be ok, how they *will* progress in their degree, how we will get them to graduation, how their committees will be flexible, and that their projects will still be viable and interesting even though their human subject work has been paused by IRB. I try to be calm for them, a strategist for them, and at the same time I feel their same stress and worry. I'm really glad I took a meditation class this fall.

Figure 18.2. Picture of blooming lavender irises next to a garden wall and big rock.

Being available to advise graduate students is really important to me; however, it's really difficult work. Before the pandemic, I sought out a variety of self-care strategies (Figure 18.2) so that, in turn, I could be available to students and junior colleagues as they pursue their programs of study, write their dissertations, and navigate the tenure track. The pandemic made this work all the more critical, and I thought often about the timing of having some skills in meditation to help myself be present and aware.

While writing the Documentarian responses, our state had not yet issued a state-wide lockdown, but it was imminent and felt ominous. Our administration was telling us to be prepared for it. In March I wrote, "I don't really know what 'prepared' means in this situation. I have experienced backcountry camping, not a pandemic. I have experience in overcoming trauma, but not the sustained trauma of a pandemic. I've been thinking a lot about the survival training course I took at a military academy. I've also been thinking about which bags/backpacks to use if we have to leave." Now that I'm writing this essay a few months later, I can see that I wasn't overreacting in March. On top of that, the killing of unarmed Black people, not a new phenomenon, continues. It's so bad that we're risking our lives to protest—both because of the police in riot gear and because of the potential spread of the virus. While I had been more hopeful about things in May, I've fallen back into despair that's very difficult to climb out of. So, self-care and resetting are skills I have to return to again and again. I joined GirlTrek.org's 21 Days in History walking meditation. GirlTrek founders Vanessa Harrison and Morgan Dixon, now with more than 600,000 followers, started a walking meditation for twenty-one days in June. Each day, Vanessa and Morgan walk while discussing an important African American woman in history and how their work has impacted them as women and as activists. I've joined them as a form of self-care and also as a way to listen and learn for additional ways to participate as an ally.

One of the issues I've worked on for years is reliable summer funding for our graduate students. Our graduate students are on a nine-month contract. Most seek summer jobs away from the university, but international students are limited in what kind of employment they can do based on their visa restrictions. This long-standing financial concern became even more pressing with the impacts of COVID-19. I'm happy that we were able to secure funding for all the students this summer. It took a pandemic for this change to be made, and I don't know whether it will be sustained.

WRITING: AS A PRACTICE AND AS A FIELD

Writing during this time has been critical to help me settle my mind. That the questions from the Documentarian editors asked us to think emotionally about how we're handling the day brought to the forefront the impact of the emotional drain that the pandemic has on all of us, even if to varying degrees. The reflections helped me realize something very important. Before the pandemic and the lock-down, I had grown increasingly weary of all the committee meetings that are often not productive. Then I had my first Zoom meeting after a couple of weeks of not seeing anyone, and I was never so excited to see my colleagues. After not meeting with them for several weeks, the meeting was energetic, friendly, compassionate, productive, and efficient. So those two things combined—the heightened awareness from reflection prompts about missing people, together with a new lens through which we're now having Zoom/pandemic meetings, has really been something to think about as we move forward. This relates to another discovery. I'm left with a desire to slow down. I love my work, I love our field, and I love the people I get to work with, not only on my campus, but across the country. Because the pace in my department has been so hectic in the last few years, I had forgotten how much I feel that way about the work. This moment of isolation and the opportunity to reflect as a Documentarian during this moment has reconnected me to these feelings, and I am profoundly grateful.

Since March, many of the issues I faced in those early days are the same now, except classes have ended and some of the stress has ended. However, that stress has been replaced or amplified by increased police brutality against Black people. Many of us are protesting, and I wonder if we're in the streets because we can't gather in our homes in the same way we might have. We've come to a breaking point, and our weariness and sadness over the pandemic means we have no more tolerance for what's been going on for generations. I don't really know. But attending a variety of activities and seeing all the statements of support coming from departments, colleges, and universities and other organizations, makes me even more grateful for the training I've had in the field of rhetoric and composition. We're not a perfect discipline, but at the heart of my pedagogical training, both in graduate school and from colleagues with whom I work, is a commitment to inclusive pedagogical practices. Initiatives like DBLAC and NextGen are all signs that our field is and has been on the pulse of culture, history, and equity and the ways that writing, composing, and research have a role to play in these issues, even if, as a field, we have much to do ourselves to improve our discipline. Having served as director and committee member on many dissertations, having chaired a search committee last fall, and having served as mentor to graduate students and colleagues both formally and informally, I have hope for our field as our colleagues insist on our action and will be capable and responsible leaders and scholars. I knew this before March, but with the opportunity to write about it, I have a renewed commitment to our field and our colleagues.

19

Harnessing the Magical Properties of Collaboration for Transforming the Neoliberal University

Shelagh Patterson

Shelagh Patterson

FROM DOCUMENTARIAN POST REFLECTION, APRIL 6

I am sitting in my kitchen as dusk deepens the blue of sky. Between the still bare branches of the trees, a white moon, almost full, slowly rises. It was on Friday, March 27, that I realized the collaborative possibilities for positive social transformation to which being a Documentarian suddenly created access. *At first I was just following the instructions and answering the questions. I felt hesitant about writing anonymously as a Black scholar in a survey created by and primarily for white scholars, but then the survey became a structure and a community in my life at a moment in time when I had lost so much of my structure and community due to the switch to online teaching. The voice in the survey became my friend.* Joyce Elbrecht and Lydia Fakundiny explain how collaboration creates additional consciousness in their wonderful essay "Scenes from a Collaboration." The essay is written in the voice of Jael B. Juba, the fictional author of their collaboratively written novels, as she reflects on her own existence. The jail be the juba. *The jail is the process of collaboration to which Elbrecht and Fakundiny chose to submit and through the shared commitment something additional and fictional, but not less true or real, comes into existence.* For the Documentarians, the jail was the surveys, twice a day (and now also this reflective survey, soft lavender background), and the jail, the survey, is the juba, the magic—what Chela Sandoval would call the within, yet beyond. *Sandoval extends Louis Althusser's theories to argue that "the citizen-subject can learn to identify, develop, and control the means of ideology, that is, marshal the knowledge necessary to 'break with ideology' while at the same time also speaking in, and from within, ideology." Sandoval then positions US third world feminists, including Gloria Anzaldúa, Audre Lorde, Paula Gunn Allen, and Nellie Wong, as concrete examples of a consciousness that "permits functioning within, yet beyond, the demands of dominant ideology"* (44): the immense energy required to break with ideology from within the swiftness of our hegemonic neoliberalism; the beautiful collaborative energy generated by Julie, Bump, and Bree that they open to a larger collective. Their juba becomes ours.

Writing as a Documentarian participated in the work of processing my situation/events over the week of writing in empowering me to the location of my resistance within the university where I am currently employed. I feel filled with joy, magic, hope, clarity of purpose, and strength. I welcome the gift of structure, the bold imposition in our daily lives at home rather than at a conference—but this as a choice we could make—unlike our jobs which was not a choice. I feel grateful to be part of a makeshift community with our attention turned to this moment. I feel grateful for the scholarly expertise to be present and articulate about the power of our collective and with a praxis to tap into and amplify and be amplified. When I realized that the survey was getting in the way of my work routine, I changed the terms of engagement, but there was nothing stopping me from doing so. I see that as a turning point in the journey, which enabled me to harness our Documentarian juba for sobriety and quitting smoking, *a baseline for radical action as the only Black full-time instructor in the first-year writing program in a public university in northern New Jersey; I have been worried about the toll on my health of resisting white supremacy in the university.*

Last week was a little rough spirit-wise, but not too bad. I was missing smoking and became mildly irritable. But I have good discipline and can break the addiction in a week without too much misery. Ten years ago, I took a photograph of the glass door of the Thomas Merton Center on Penn Avenue in Pittsburgh. It had a palm card taped to it with the words "Radical Sobriety." *I had never heard the phrase before, and while the date for the event had passed, the palm card sparked a meditation.* Then when I moved to Newark, sobriety was a valued practice in our activist communities. I was sober for two and a half years so that I could adjunct, develop a scholarly praxis for social justice, and finish the dissertation. There is a story of the night and day of the decision which includes moonshine at Skippers, one of Amiri Baraka's spots, and a Fanon conference at Columbia in the morning. Anyways, I need to move back into that level of productivity. I've been lost in grief for almost two years, but this *"pandemic is a portal"* (Roy). I am committed to build within, yet beyond the new directions higher ed is using this pandemic to push through. I know sobriety is a skill I use to enjoy working hard. I know I have been relying on nicotine as a toxic surrogate for joy. I was able to use my expertise in writing collaboration to identify the likes of Jael B. Juba whom I courted to discipline my health and self-care as a baseline for building resistance, which is what I learned to do from US third world feminism and from new countrypeople-warriors who extend our praxis. My writing as a Documentarian exponentially increased the quality of my health and wellbeing which grounds me for resisting and reshaping the neoliberal waves gathering in our universities.

~~~

"I myself, a creature of these wilds, experience a degree of dementia much of the time and have come to welcome the old and familiar, its temporary duration exposed like an outdated, weathered signpost twisted by the season and pointing earthward—old and familiar, and a reminder to stay on the lookout for the likes of me, hardly distinguishable in the vastness of these fictional wilds except to the scouting eye of the venturesome reader."
–Jael B. Juba

FROM THE MORNING AND EVENING SURVEYS, MARCH 25 - MARCH 29

It's Wednesday so I start teaching at 10 a.m. and then teach again at 11:30 a.m. I feel far from the question because already this Wednesday was different from a regular Wednesday because I was going to be at Cs and had created online classes for my students. But, a new layer of difference has been revealed, and so which regular, because our regular was before the now-regular of social distancing, so in that regular I am at the conference, but there was a regular for this week before this new sense of regular. On a regular workday, I grade some papers; I teach two classes; two days a week I have office hours; I eat at least two meals a day; I probably will binge watch in the evening before going to sleep. I brush my teeth, maybe floss, send work emails (not in that order perhaps), "Yet to cite the everyday that holds up civilization is immediately to become aware of how it is tangled in, woven from, constituted along with the rhythmic recall of the epic" (Delany 255).

I was looking forward to today. Last year was my first Cs, and I became a member of the Black Caucus. This year I am one of the facilitators of the workshop "Real Talk: Using Personal Narratives and

Embodied Experience to Reimagine African American/Black Rhetorical Studies." I was excited because my family celebrates difference and wanted to share our strategies for communicating and building love across our differences, particularly as it relates to continental, color, gender, and sexuality differences.

When I have a backlog of essays to comment on, like I do today, I just plow through them one by one, and take breaks as needed. I have to remember to intentionally schedule by the hour for my office hours at 10 a.m., which also reminded me that I also have to remember 8 a.m. (which I missed by thirteen minutes) to listen to *Democracy Now!*

The general weariness of too many papers to comment on.

The regular worry that my stamina is not up to the task.

My city is in lockdown. Our mayor used the crime-mapping technology to map COVID-19 hotspots. My neighborhood has additional restrictions. We are not allowed walks except for emergency or essential shopping. All of the city has a curfew from 8 p.m.–5 a.m. We have already been feeling the forces of gentrification. Which businesses that have closed will not reopen and what will be in their place? I worry about people suddenly unemployed and how many have jobs or statuses that might prevent them from receiving government assistance. I worry about the rise of domestic abuse.

~~~

In the kitchen still, I smell the smoke from the grill and hear Melissa Ethridge's live concert. My green glass Pellegrino bottle sits on the table beside me. The action is typing. The action is breathing. In the lot on the other side of my backyard is a grey garbage can with a plastic bag caught and fluttering in the wind like some sort of animal.

"Andrew Cuomo is no hero. He spent years slashing hospital capacity."

My day looked like I had planned although I never did leave the kitchen as my workstation. I did do my daily trip to the cherry blossoms. I didn't grade as many papers as I wanted.

Sit. Move. Sit. Move.

While sitting my fingers move as I type.

My eyes move as I read what I type.

My chest moves as I breath.

Sometimes I quietly speak the words.

I had a sobering realization. As a full-time contingent instructor of first-year writing, life hasn't changed much. If anything, not having to go to campus and teach classes makes life easier. The classroom is my joy, but it also takes a lot of energy and coupled with the work of reading and commenting on essays, I am often exhausted by evening. Without spending energy in the classroom, I feel rested, but my time hasn't changed. I just have more of it: to spend reading, commenting on, and grading student essays. It's not comforting to realize that the demands on full-time contingent faculty require us to live lives of social isolation.

~~~

I'm still finishing up grading those thirty essays. I also have to take my trip to the cherry blossoms for my project and post yesterday's. I am a day behind now for two days in a row. If I do not go running today, I have to go running tomorrow.

"Thirteen Deaths in a Day: An 'Apocalyptic' Coronavirus Surge at an N.Y.C. Hospital"

These surveys are a stability for me right now. Something to look forward to. I also find them challenging because I haven't read the Q&A doc. It scares me that my thoughts through this form may become aggregated data that I have no control over: a difference between creative writing and comp-rhet narrative. I have decided we are allies, but we don't know each other well yet. I wish I didn't have so much to grade so that I could organize my days in ways that would allow me to perform more for this survey—the way I would've been able to do in Milwaukee. I am also thinking about a friend's post about how we should be organizing and not grading as much. I also feel this survey is a structure for me, the way my classes serve as a structure for my students. Because of this survey, I decided to floss this morning so I could report that I had flossed rather than carrying the need to floss with me all day and then never getting to it.

Do you have any questions for us? Anything we can help with at this moment?

Nothing this morning.

~~~

Friday!

I did things a little differently today. I got through a bunch of essays before filling out this survey. The energy and concentration these surveys invite had been leaving me with less for commenting on essays. I plan to go for a run, do my cherry blossom project, which I didn't take footage for yesterday, and grade more essays. I also hope to join a family Netflix watch party of *Self Made*. I wasn't originally going to do that, but I realized that it connects to the work I was planning to do in the Wednesday workshop and becomes a way to connect with family and continue the intellectual work of Cs.

I am feeling good. It is always helpful when a concrete task is already behind me, and it's still morning.

The kitchen, the kitchen, the kitchen. WFUV on the radio. Sun in the window. Glass water bottle by my side. Sparkles whisper as I unscrew the top and tingle as I take a swig.

~ ~ ~

A Black history calendar from 2008 hangs on the slim strip of wall between the window and the door to the backyard, open to the frontispiece. Above the caption, "The Chicago Defender" in large cursive font, is a decorative gilded purple frame. Within the frame is a black and white picture of a young Black boy carrying a large bag that looks like a basketball, in the background a brick building and a tall copper lamp post. The boy holds a large newspaper in front of the bag. I stand up to read the title of the headline: I can't quite make it out. WFUV on the radio. Glass water bottle empty beside me so I better go get that. Sparkle. Don't get me going on the state of my water (forgive the pun).

"Total System Failure: Congress Pushes $2 Trillion Pandemic Bill. Will Dems Allow 'Corporate Coup'?"

Today was magical. I finished grading a class in the morning and then emailed a class an extension in the evening after making good headway. A student texted me for feedback this evening because she works on the weekends. I wanted to ask her where she was working because so many are not right now; the ones who are, are labeled essential. What is essential? And who decides? But I simply texted her that I'd read it right away and then it was truly fantastic, so I was texting her how much I loved her first paragraph, etc., while also writing feedback on Canvas. At the same time, I was trying to get onto the cousins' Netflix party chat for *Self Made*. I took a run. First got cherry blossoms footage. During my run I bump into a bestie and her dog just finishing their run. And she was able to hook me up. Friday at the conference, maybe I'd be with friends having a drink. This would be the fun survey. Three days in and late at night.

It's so complex right now. There are a lot of things happening and my role is education which is deemed essential in its ability and inability to move online. I have concerns about how my domestic space has been turned into my workspace. I have concerns how easy the shift.

I received an email from HR that said they paid me extra for March 20. I could either have the overpayment taken out from the next paycheck or the next two. The mistake was made because all tenure track faculty receive backpay from our new contracts, but the full-time contingent do not. For a moment, HR must've thought we had better contracts than we do.

~~~

This was Saturday!

I was planning to go to a morning panel and then take the bus to Kenosha to visit my sister, niece, and nephew before flying home.

I did it differently again today. I accomplished everything I needed to accomplish before doing the survey. My hopes and achievements are one and the same: farmer's market, finally finish that grading, morning survey. I guess then it is the morning, if I am filling out the morning survey. What do I hope to accomplish today? I hope to spend time reading the email about the survey and the types of questions we are encouraged to ask ourselves as we respond to the surveys. I hope to do a performance for the evening survey.

Time was suspended as I finished my backlog of essays. Now, time is expansive as the day unfolds again in morning to evening, the time between surveys. How long will that be? This is exciting new territory that happens in the moment of collaboration when a collective is formed through temporal commitments: the act of collaboration creates another temporal dimension besides the standardized one. So here I am at the end of my day, and it's morning. To quote the art collaboration that created their own calendar: "What happens when you make time expand? Or lead it to take the shape of your dreams?" (Lara).

Awe, humility, joy

The scene around me is light blue with a grey border at the top and a colorful border patterning different shapes all the same size at the bottom. I type into a white text box above a blue line. The font is sans serif normal black. The laptop is on my lap, and my cat is on my calves. I am on the day bed in the office/television room with magenta walls, the womb room, in the center of the house on the second floor. There is a lamp on the bedside table with an arts and crafts stained glass pattern. There are two empty highball glasses manufactured to look like crystal and two empty mugs. Short ones. One from my Gran's house in Scotland, a pattern of brown oblongs and loops.

In the day that has passed I had contact with some students over email. I went to the market. Chatted with the farmers some of whom have become dear friends. Last week was stressful. Those of us who knew each other kept social distance while the crowds had trouble. Today everyone was more relaxed, so it was easier to stand and chat, which I did. I also bought some donuts and brought them by my colleague's house. This wouldn't have been planned if I was writing this in the morning. This other day that's about to unfold, I don't know if I'll have contact with anyone.

I plan to find out if I've been doing this assignment wrong! I'm nervous for the final survey performance, but in a good way.

~~~

I am in the living room. The curtains are drawn. A sliver of grey sky sneaks in in a slit. I am on my couch, a love seat. My journal is beside me, open and abandoned from last night's project never begun. My feet are on the brass and glass coffee table. "Elsie's Plate" is on the table beside me brought out specifically for tonight's performance. I kept its glass space helmet on so I could smell the moss and cedar as I write this evening about the day.

Today did not go as planned. I did read the Documentarian materials. The email on March 18, 2020, "New Opportunity for CCCC 2020 Documentarians," is a beautiful invitation to community in a worrying moment in time and set the tone for how I approached these surveys. Then I drank too much gin, woke up late. Because I used the temporal commitments of our collective survey to expand time, in one dimension it is 11:10 a.m. on a Sunday morning. In the dimension of our survey, it is still Saturday evening, thus the day is what unfolded between the morning survey and the evening survey. I listened to the vinyl soundtrack of the *Night of the Living Dead* performed by Morricone Youth. There was a moment of hope on side A that went well with a passage from the email, but I didn't have the wherewithal, and still do not, to properly document the connection.

How did you use your time today?

Drunkenly.

Excited to decide that alcohol is not going to be a part of my self-isolation in these times of social distancing. The curfew makes it easy. All I have to do is get to 8 p.m., then the state does the work of self-discipline for me #silverlining #pandemicfascism.

This was totally the best. If you are the survey as well as the creators of the survey, in your open collaboration the juba formed is the form. Have you read Elbrecht and Fakundiny? 'Til we meet again and in what form.

FROM DOCUMENTARIAN POST REFLECTION, APRIL 6

Wednesday through Friday, my mornings and evenings were in the kitchen, where I am right now. The pattern was consistent—I would wake up, I would work at the kitchen table on my laptop, and then in the middle of the day, I would go for a drive to the cherry blossoms and maybe for a run in the park or a quick shopping. Saturday was different. I wrote in different spaces: in the morning which was actually the evening as the temporal possibilities of collaboration created an alternate dimension, I was upstairs in the office/den which I call the womb room. In the evening, which was actually on Sunday morning, racing the noon deadline, I was in my living room. The alternate temporal dimension started coming in to play on Friday morning when I did my grading first and then filled out the survey. This suggests that, when I am getting through a backlog of essays, I like to just wake up and plow through them until I run out of steam. The consistency of location suggests I like consistency. I like windows, and my workspace is pretty seamlessly integrated into my domestic space, a horror through which I'm not quite sure what to do with the ease of living. When I realized that the survey was getting in the way of work—the survey also being work but a kind for which I don't normally create space during the semester—I needed an alternate temporal dimension. As I built the alternate dimension, geography also became dynamic. I seem to have different needs for different types of work. It seems I need an alternate temporal dimension and different geographies to balance scholarly creative work with teaching commitments. It also suggests my desire for collaboration as I used the occasion of collaboration to expand time as my research has taught me to do.

CODA, JUNE 8, 2020

I am sitting in my dining room that I recently turned into an office/classroom. I pushed the table right up against the wall and brought an old window, wood frame and all, down and propped it on the table against the wall. I can use it as a white board, but right now, I have printouts of the reflection survey taped to it—so I can see the whole in a single frame. I have a white peony with the most intoxicating scent in a glass bottle next to a newspaper sculpture of a rose a former student gave me as part of her end of semester reflection a few years ago. I am listening to "Shambhala Moon" on repeat, a favorite from twenty years ago when I hung with the Nudgie Music crew in the village bought this morning from an online marketplace. The contradictions of our lives are many. I have been sober for months, minus a few days here and there. I wasn't able to quit cigarettes during the semester, but I'm doing pretty good since the semester ended.

This afternoon I took a break from writing and drove downtown to the Justice for George Floyd protest. For weeks now across the country and world people have been taking to the streets in protest to the brutal killing of George Floyd by Minneapolis police officer Derek Chauvin who pinned Floyd to the ground with a knee to Floyd's neck. A young sister caught the attack on a video that went viral and ignited the outrage brewing over the months of quarantine as the details of Ahmaud Arbery's lynching became more clear and the outrage of the senseless killing of Breonna Taylor, an EMT worker, by Louisville police as she was sleeping in her bed, and the outrage of the particular vulnerability of our Black communities dying from COVID-19 due to the continued effects of racism that is the foundation of our country's wealth.

People who know me will be surprised to hear today was the first of the protests I attended, and I left before we became a spontaneous critical mass and took over the streets in a march past City Hall on the way to Military Park. I'm normally out on the streets and sometimes even an organizer. But, I haven't been feeling well, and I am trying to honor lessons from my experience at Cs this year where I connected to the juba of the collaboration amongst Julie Lindquist, Bump Halbritter, Bree Straayer, and the rest of us Documentarians and named my site of resistance and activism the university. A week ago we were hit hard—the first-year writing program where I teach. We have a core group of instructional specialists, many of whom have worked here for over a decade, some even longer, who were integral in building the program, which was awarded a CCCC Writing Program Certificate of Excellence, and has been integral in founding our recently formed Department of Writing Studies. We had been told that all of our specialists up for contract renewal would be renewed. At the eleventh hour, a new decision was made, and five of us were informed in an emailed letter that they did not have their contracts renewed. The email was accompanied with neither regret, nor gratitude, nor acknowledgement of years of service. We are supposed to be the frontline of welcoming our students to the university. I do not even know if upper administration considers this an attack, and that an attack on one of us, is an attack on all, and an attack on the work we do, which is the work we do to lay foundations for student success. The waves of neoliberalism are sweeping through with a force.

We will resist. We will advocate for the reinstatement of our colleagues. We will advocate for teaching tenure lines for all FYW faculty. We will win.

WORKS CITED

Delany, Samuel R. "Epic." *Encyclopedia* Vol. 1, A-E, edited by Tisa Bryant, Miranda Mellis, and Kate Schatz, Enclomedia, 2006, pp. 254–62.

Elbrecht, Joyce, and Lydia Fakundiny. "Scenes from a Collaboration: Or Becoming Jael B. Juba." *Tulsa Studies in Women's Literature*, vol. 13, no. 2, 1994, pp. 241–57. JSTOR, https://www.jstor.org/stable/464108.

Lara, Ana-Maurine. "The Pënz Calendar." Pënz: (It's Pronounced Pants), 29 Dec. 2007, http://www.penzitspronouncedpants.blogspot. com/2007/12/penz-calendar.html.

Roy, Arundhati. "Arundhati Roy: 'The Pandemic Is a Portal'." *Financial Times*, 3 Apr. 2020, https://ww.ft.com/content/10d8f5e8-74eb-11ea-95fe-fcd274e920ca.

Sandoval, Chela. *The Methodology of the Oppressed*. U of Minnesota P, 2000.

20

Hitting Pause on Productivity: Finding Mindful Labor in Quarantine

Gabrielle Isabel Kelenyi

On March 11, 2020, the University of Wisconsin-Madison suspended in-person classes beginning March 23 through April 10 in light of the COVID-19 pandemic. I was in my Economies of Literacy class when the email popped up on my screen. As the discussion wrapped up and the news spread throughout the class, we ended with uncertain plans for the future: we'll figure out what our class looks like in the coming weeks; for now, enjoy your spring break.

Enjoy your spring break. I can do that. My partner and I were headed to visit my dad in Chicago for a few days and take engagement pictures. It would be nice to spend time in my childhood home, check in on my dad, get some work done on my midterms, and take some sappy pictures with skyscraper backdrops. It would be nice to step just slightly away for just a brief moment from the many roles I play as an aspiring academic and primarily enjoy being a daughter, a friend, a partner (with just a little bit of student, as always). A few days into break, though, the university extended the suspension of in-person classes through the end of the semester, and instructors across campus were thrust into bringing their courses online. My spring break was no longer a break as I processed information from my professors as a student, my supervisors as a grad student employee, my undergraduate students as their instructor, and the university at large. I did my best to stay on track with my original plans for break and accommodate the changing demands of my position as a graduate instructor, a TA at the Writing Center, a student in my courses, a novice researcher, and a colleague in my program.

This was what everyone was doing, though. And somehow I felt strangely confident in my ability to weather this unprecedented storm. I wasn't pleased about any of the new demands on my time, but I calmly put my head down and continued working despite my original plan to enjoy my spring break by taking a break. Plans change. And, in my focus on communicating changes in my course calendar to my students, implementing changes to my strategy for my midterms, and integrating lifestyle changes to my daily routine, I missed the fact that most of those changes were not self-determined.

And then I began reading for next week's classes. For the Economies of Literacy course, excerpts from researcher Melissa Gregg's monographs *Work's Intimacy* and *Counterproductive: Time Management in the Knowledge Economy* were on the syllabus for the coming week. And reading these excerpts from Gregg while working from home during and coming off a spring break that wasn't a break made these texts even more intensely relatable and appropriate than I think they would've been otherwise. I couldn't help but recognize how my "efficiency training" immediately kicked in when faced with unprecedented change. Unexpectedly, after reading these excerpts, I was worried and agitated by my instinct to press on unaffectedly, to remain productive and not question the blurring lines between work and home. I just . . . kept working. Why wasn't I feeling anything other than the impetus to continue working?

When things began to shut down, like many, I looked at it as an opportunity. Quarantine meant more efficiency, right? Finally, I will have more time to do this and do that, to catch up and get ahead. But I soon realized that time isn't extended in quarantine—I don't get more of it. Despite not having to travel to and from appointments and responsibilities, I didn't find more time to accomplish all of the things on my to-do list. That didn't stop me from adding more items to that list, though.

And then, all of a sudden, about two weeks later, I seemingly couldn't just keep going. This is odd for me. All of my intersecting identities—student, educator, writer, woman, person of color—are persistent. I do not stop; I persist. But instead of confident, I suddenly felt hopeless . . . I stared listlessly at my computer screen and then at my to-do list and back again at my computer, unsure of how or where to begin. I closed my laptop and opened a book. I read the words, but I didn't understand them. I tried changing positions: a new seat at the dining-room-table-turned-communal-workspace, a respite on the couch, the uncomfortable desk chair in the other room. I returned to my place at the dining room table and opened my laptop once again. I stared at my inbox. What now? Would I be stuck here forever?

~ ~ ~

I imagine similar questions have crossed other people's minds during quarantine: What now? In fact, in an overwhelming fit of despair, I asked it out loud to my partner: Will it be like this forever? It doesn't hit everyone at the same time, and it might not have hit you, dear reader, yet, but quarantine can bring up some pretty existential questions. Answers in quarantine can be pretty illuminating.

Before the pandemic, I treated every day as a challenge. How much could I possibly squeeze in? How many things could I schedule between 9 a.m. and 6 p.m.? Down to the minute, I would jam task after task into my daily planner. I would power walk through the hallways of the English Department, up and down the streets of campus. I would arrive at meetings, classes, appointments out of breath but ready to work. And then I would happily cross each item off my list, feeling more motivated to forge ahead as each item was checked off, strategizing and prioritizing my way to accomplishing everything on it. There was no greater sense of accomplishment than coming home at the end of the day with everything complete. There was also no greater sense of anxiety than coming home with more things to do and obsessively strategizing to find a way to do them and still be present at home. In my efforts to fit everything into a typical workday, I chased after the "work/life balance ruse" that Melissa Gregg elucidates in *Work's Intimacy*; however, instead of achieving true balance, I was swept up in "work's enticing and seductive dimensions" (5-6). As a result, I unknowingly yet acutely struggled with what she terms "presence bleed," or the "consciousness of the always-present potential for engaging with work [that] is a new form of affective labor that must be constantly regulated" (3). Except, I didn't know how to regulate it. I still battle against a constant consciousness that I could be accomplishing more and against the instinct to strategize how to work more. I feel an almost insatiable need to produce in order to feel whole, in order to avoid feeling anxious.

I deeply identify with the senses of pleasure and accomplishment that professional work produces in today's era as aided by rapid and extensive technological advances that Melissa Gregg writes about in *Work's Intimacy*. The "psychological appeal" of work for me was exacerbated by the turn to technological platforms in response to workplace and state-wide shutdowns in the face of the COVID-19 pandemic. That is, as a high school composition teacher and now as a graduate student, I've been trained in the "disciplinary techniques" of "self-monitoring and individual goal-setting," but the autonomy of such positions "come at a price: to constantly prove responsibility" (13). So when quarantine began, I was still out of breath. I wasn't power walking through hallways or up and down the streets of campus anymore. Instead, I was zooming through meetings, weaving in assignments, and sending out emails. My planner was filled to the brim, and I continued to find ways to fit as much as I could into my day. No pandemic would stop me; in fact, I would transcend it. Quarantine wouldn't change anything but where I'm working. I would continue being the concurrent student, educator, colleague, writer, partner I had always been—reliable, impressive, efficient, persistent, and breathless.

As a result of the rapid shift to online instruction and learning, I acutely felt the "presence bleed" (*Counterproductive* 12) that has resulted from the technologically-aided turn from an information economy to an attention economy. As neoliberal ideologies influence education at every level, promoting individual responsibility, market-based competition, and quantifiable success, teachers and students—of which I am both—find themselves in incredibly precarious positions, especially in the face of COVID-19. In order to keep my job, I must respond well to the pandemic-amplified "productivity imperative" or suffer the "cumulative effect of cost-cutting measures that urge employees to 'do more with less' and 'work smarter, not harder'" (3). As such, I must quickly develop new effective habits and lean on technology to continue producing—to continue teaching, writing, discussing, participating, replying, attending, etc. My fight-or-flight response to the heightened precarity instigated by higher education's reactions to the COVID-19 pandemic was to fall back on what Gregg calls my "efficiency training," which "encourages workers to see themselves as capable of separating from the pack and with the right motivation, destined for a prosperous future, even in times of economic distress" (75). And as Gregg illuminates, the potential issues posed by separating from the pack—and predominantly exercising our capacities for intimacy/connection "in the pursuit of competitive professional profit," as a result—may eventually lead to being "unable to appreciate the benefits of intimacy for unprofitable purposes" (*Work's Intimacy* 6). I can attest that it has proven extremely difficult to achieve work/life balance in the face of the imperative to be available for faculty and students, to make it work beyond "normal" business hours (what are those nowadays, anyways?), to unquestioningly make sacrifices in order not to move up, but simply maintain my status, because 1) there are no longer clear boundaries between work and life, and 2) I believed my efficiency training would continue to serve me well, despite the unprecedented circumstances. Without clear boundaries, professional productivity has come to mean progress and living my personal life has come to mean a pause in that productivity. As a result, productivity for professional progress has begun to take precedence over what seems like pausing for personal connection. I was indeed becoming "unable to appreciate the benefits of intimacy for unprofitable purposes" (6).

Gregg writes that "presence bleed captures both the changing behavioral dimensions and professional expectations in communication and information-heavy jobs" (*Work's Intimacy* 2). As a millennial in 2020, as a woman of color, and as a scholar-educator, I'm not sure I've known any other behavioral dimensions or professional expectations. I've come up in an age of precarity that makes it possible to take advantage of worker-citizen-consumer-learners like me. And so, originally as a high school teacher and now as a graduate student, I have consistently found myself wondering why that is, torn between two cultural economic voices:

- the quiet, calm voice that advocates for being understanding, for being a team player that does her part, and
- the outraged voice that says I shouldn't have to take on this much and tolerate the invasion of work into so much of my life.

I've realized the first voice as efficiency trained (*Counterproductive* 75); it responds to the productivity imperative (3) and performs executive athleticism (54). That is, this first voice "accepts personal responsibility for productivity" (73). This is how middle-class neoliberalism raised me, shapes me: it's up to me to do my part in order to keep being productive and therefore keep progressing; teamwork and productivity are how I make myself marketable.

The second voice, on the other hand, is trying to practice mindful labor (*Work's Intimacy* 16) by recognizing the hegemonic status of time management on my professional and personal life (*Counterproductive* 55). The second voice is working against the influences of an "age of maximum flexibility" and against giving in to the "feelings of instability, threat, and fear" that advances in technology have played on over the last few decades (18). It seeks to honor the power of collectivity in establishing career competence, in being good worker-citizen-consumer-learners. As time wears on, both before but especially during quarantine, I am becoming more aware of the "immaterial" (or invisible) labor (*Work's Intimacy* 13) involved in the responsibilities that come along with the coexisting positions I hold as a graduate student, an educator, a researcher, a partner, a woman, a colleague, a writer, a daughter, a sister, a friend.

Despite recognizing being torn between these two voices, the first one consistently won out. I didn't realize it until now, but I had formed an unhealthy obsession with accomplishment. I struggled to stop accomplishing—I mean, who wants to stop accomplishing things? I liked being breathless because it meant I was getting things done. However, I believe this second voice represents "an emerging practice of mindful labor [that] can introduce ethics to the pursuit of productivity" (*Counterproductive* 16) that is beginning to take hold in me, especially as a result of the sweeping lifestyle changes COVID-19 has introduced. With more and more time in quarantine, I'm coming to realize the truth in Gregg's assertion that "time management is inwardly focused; its project is personal enhancement rather than care for others" (75). I don't want this to be my sole focus anymore; instead, I want to practice radical care for myself and for others by practicing mindful labor—labor that honors the idea that "solidarity and power are formed through the collective imposition of work limits" (*Work's Intimacy* 4).

Thus, a few weeks in, I realized that quarantine was not the opportunity I thought it was. As the number of cases and deaths grew and the stay-at-home orders increased and the social distancing measures strengthened, I tried to simply press on with my daily routine like the good efficiency-trained scholar-educator I had always been. As I was bombarded with news of the United States' fumbling efforts to flatten the curve, desperate attempts to protect the economy, and disparities in protection and care exacerbating long-held inequities in our country, I tried to focus on what was in my locus of control—my to-do list. And that's when quarantine meant overworking myself, meant beating myself up for even thinking about taking a break, meant overscheduling and overextending myself more than ever before. I disregarded the idea that perhaps I needed to grieve the destruction the pandemic was wreaking on the world and the loss of self-determination quarantine imposed on my daily routine. I disregarded the idea that my body and my mind needed time to adjust to quarantine. I just needed to keep working and focus on the tasks in front of me. However, participating in the eight daily reflection prompts as a CCCC Documentarian highlighted for me how little I was moving throughout the day. The reflections highlighted how long I stayed in the same place, accomplishing all the things but seemingly getting nowhere, making no progress. It's a puzzling catch-22: powering through a to-do list without moving; staying in place while trying to push forward. Mentally, it's exhausting. And emotionally, it's confusing: why wasn't I feeling the same senses of pleasure and accomplishment for the work I was completing? Instead, I would come to the end-of-day reflections and feel defeated, exhausted, and disappointed for not having reached all of my (impossible) goals. I felt as if I wasn't using my time wisely, as if, all of a sudden, I couldn't be efficient.

Quarantine was a different opportunity entirely because, normally, opportunities are something I try to make the most of, even when they're unexpected. But what I'm learning from quarantine is how not to make the most of something, how not to make it work for me, how to stop strategizing, how to sit with un-accomplishment. I am learning how to question productivity as progress and prioritize reflection as pause. I'm learning how to be more aware of immaterial/invisible labor and practice more mindful labor that encompasses an ethics of (self-) care. To do this, I am trying to channel my motivation to be productive toward "unprofitable" ends, like setting up family video calls and reaching out to friends just to catch up. As the popular rhetoric goes, quarantine and social distancing isn't for me but for others. If I don't come out of quarantine having accomplished all of my professional goals, that's okay because quarantine isn't for more work or for profiting off of seemingly "more" time (what a joke!). Quarantine is for preserving life. It's to hopefully return to life as we once knew it or an even better one in which we prioritize and cherish connections for personal (rather than solely professional) purposes. I hope to come away from this with less of an inward focus on my own improvement and achievement and more of an outward focus on practicing radical care through building and maintaining positive relationships with myself and others.

Now, it's hard not to reframe these "lessons" as a new way of taking advantage, of making quarantine work for me. However, instead of accomplishing a new way to live my life that doesn't revolve around accomplishing or failing, I'm coming to terms with it instead. And I don't think coming to terms is the same as making the most of a situation. It's accepting it. It's turning away from a sole focus on progress and finding comfort in pausing, both by myself and with others. I may be catching my breath, but not necessarily by choice, and I'm reminded of all the people who can't catch their breath right now, who couldn't. Practicing mindful labor is one way to begin fighting for those most affected by COVID-19 because it undermines the neoliberal project of individual responsibility, competition, and measurable success. Instead, mindful labor can help us collectively come to understand and elevate the meaning and purpose (instead of just the profits) behind the work we do as well as the work we don't.

~~~

We won't be stuck here forever. But if we're fortunate enough to take a moment (or even to be forced to take a moment) to breathe, we should, because there are so many others who cannot. Pressing on unemotionally is dangerous and risky. Efficiency training and executive athleticism are only good up until a point; mindful labor, on the other hand, can clarify a sustainable path forward.

And through such a practice, I hope to know how to stop along the way, how to be more accommodating of detours, instead of finding myself hopeless and unable to move forward. If I take anything from quarantine, I hope it is to respond to events of the world with grace and compassion for myself and for others; I hope I learn how to be intentional about catching my breath and to be grateful for the chance to do so.

As a student, an educator, a writer, and especially as a woman of color, it's hard for me to sit with un-accomplishment, to be unproductive, because of a fear of letting my communities down. When you're tired, it's much easier to keep pushing forward when it's for people and causes you care about. And therefore, it sometimes feels all up to me to continue forging a path with and for others like me. If I don't do it, who will? I'm learning that it's those same communities who help me get unstuck and regain my confidence. When I unexpectedly rolled to a stop, it was other students, educators, writers, and women (of color) who told me it would be okay, who encouraged me to catch my breath, who reminded me that there's no such thing as oppression and inequity that can be overcome with just hard work, who showed me that it's not all up to me. Only in solidarity can we resist the influences of precarity, especially during this time.

WORKS CITED

Gregg, Melissa. *Counterproductive: Time Management in the Knowledge Economy*. Duke UP, 2018

Gregg, Melissa. *Work's Intimacy*. Polity, 2011

21

"You Good, Fam'?": Mindful Journaling and Africana Digital Dialogic Compassionate Rhetorical Response Pedagogy during a Pandemic

Rachel Panton

> I think our notions of what counts as radical have changed over time. Self-care and healing and attention to the body and the spiritual dimension—all of this is now a part of radical social justice struggles.
>
> –Angela Davis

Despite my disappointment of being unable to fulfill my original duties as a Documentarian for the Conference on College Composition and Communication Convention in 2020, my new role, as a result of the worldwide pandemic, had far more reaching consequences for my students and for me. When I first learned of the new responsibilities as Documentarian of 4Cs, one that required participants to journal about our daily experiences during quarantine when we would have otherwise been attending the conference, I was eager to participate. I maintain a business documenting stories of Black women's wellness and teach courses on meditative and mindful journaling in the community, so, needless to say, I am well versed in the mental, physical, spiritual, and communal benefits of reflective writing. Likewise, the framework of Africana womanism, which is rooted in holistic nurturing, has shaped my research and my pedagogical practice as a professor of writing in College Composition for over twenty years.

This new role, as a Documentarian of uncommon times, however, compelled me to slow down and deepen my writing and pedagogical praxis. Reflective and mindful journaling in a moment of actualized trauma, heightened my personal self-care practice, as well as my Africana womanist pedagogical outlook on care in the classroom, allowing me to be more present to my students' wellbeing and prioritizing the process of their writing over the growth and goals of their writing.

During a period of crisis, this new role, and the circumstances surrounding it, elevated my consciousness on student needs and my attention to their cognitive processes. It also grounded me in unexpected ways and allowed me to be a keener observer. These observations rooted me in the work of sacred writing and allowed me to engage in digital dialogic compassionate writing responses, both in my rhetorical responses to student writing and in personal written correspondence with them. Daily journaling of the chaos that was taking place in my own home, in my community, in the US, and in the world at the precise moment it was happening helped redirect my attention from grading and correcting to connecting and checking in, as I began personal digital dialogs with my students. In this way, I not only documented what was happening with me and my family during the initial quarantine, but also what was happening with my students and their families, and it altered my approach to teaching composition throughout the course of the semester.

The prompts that were given to us were similar to those in mindful and meditative journaling, which asks its practitioners to ground ourselves in the present before the act of writing begins. Similar to yoga, when participants are asked to feel their feet "grounding" to the mat or feel their sit-bones connecting with the earth, grounding requires that the practitioner becomes aware of the present moment, without judgment, so that in turn they remain flexible and fluid (Wenger). The 4Cs daily morning survey prompts asked questions like: "Describe the scene around you. Where are you in it? What do you see, hear, and smell?" These were questions of mindfulness, calling me to ground myself where I was and observe without judgment. Scott R. Bishop and his team of researchers on Mindfulness Based Stress Reduction (MBSR) maintained that mindfulness initiates a change in perspective when we are attentive to our inner experiences so that, "in a state of mindfulness, thoughts and feelings are observed as events in the mind, without over-identifying with them, and without reacting to them in an automatic, habitual pattern of reactivity" (Bishop et al. 232). Mindfulness allows space, then, for connective contemplation and breaking habitual, rote responses in exchange for a new outlook or fresh perspective.

Comparably, Mezirow's Theory of Transformative Learning teaches us that deep critical self-reflection, which transcends content knowledge achievement, raises our consciousness and aids in meaning making and effecting change, often in the spirit of social justice. Transformation, he explains, begins when one experiences a "disorienting dilemma" that sparks a pivot in thinking and an embrace of a possible self, one that requires a shedding or letting go of existing perspectives (22). In order to expand, however, old frameworks and habits of the mind must be replaced with new possibilities that rest in the hopefulness of change (hooks).

In response to the daily 4Cs survey, in the mornings I could be found sitting still, alone, coffee in hand, in the lush garden of a family matriarch in Miami. I would go there to do my morning rituals and prayers to my ancestors before the tsunami of anxiety and chaos came barreling toward me once my family awakened. There, I would pour libations, sing to my ancestors, conjure their energy, and ask of them, "What is mine to do?" as I recalled a litany of traumas they had overcome starting with the Middle Passage. Like Alice Walker, I felt myself longing for comfort, nurturing, and modeling in my [mother in-law's] garden. I was looking to the past to make sense out of my current circumstances and to create something new. It was in the garden where I grounded myself and tended to my own self-care before I was bombarded with non-stop media updates from elders in my family and WhatsApp notifications from worried friends, "Girl, did you see there were six confirmed cases at Nova? It's all over the news!" It's where I could catch my breath before I had to take on the role of provider, mother, counselor, second-grade teacher, professor, faculty advisor, etc. In the stillness of dawn, I listened intently to the chorus of morning songbirds and hooting owls. I witnessed the mango trees bearing unripened fruit.

These observations were reminders that I was part of a larger ecosystem, that I was connected to something much greater than myself, and that the earth was still and bountiful. The birds were carrying on with their daily lives, aloof to the president's latest briefing or predictions by "America's doctor." They weren't keeping track of death tolls and rising positive tests. They were simply in a state of being and for a few brief moments I was there with them. As a practitioner and priestess of an African Diasporic Religion (ADR), connecting with nature is an essential component of my spiritual practice and in "owning that space [there comes an] understanding that we have this intricate relationship with the divine, [and a partnership] with our brilliant selves . . ."(Harris 252). In these moments, I also envisioned my students and what they might be waking up to, what thoughts and scenes they might encounter, and I took a moment to silently acknowledge their circumstances. Although I wanted to be as productive as possible each day, my thoughts kept coming back to my students and their wellbeing.

Miller and Nozawa suggested that Loving Kindness Meditation is "ultimately, a meditation on how we are connected to people, animals, life, and all creation" (51). They raised the possibility that certain forms of meditation may serve to create or enhance direct pathways to love, care and concern between teachers and their students. Such a possibility could potentially shift away from a "stress-reduction" model of trying to control stressful emotions and toward exploring how teachers broaden their sense of interconnectedness with students and teaching environments.

Historically, for many Black women teachers, mobilizing this kind of care has become an act of preservation for "selves, communities, and social worlds" (Hobart and Kneese 2). This kind of radical care was not new to me, as I had long identified as an Africana womanist for many years throughout my career, but never had the feeling of care and the need to act/feel so visceral. In her article, "A Womanist Experience of Caring: Understanding the Pedagogy of Exemplary Black Women Teachers," Beauboeuf-Lafontant maintains that womanist caring is exemplified in the traditional role of the Africana teacher. She also outlines three characteristics of the pedagogy, including embracing the maternal, political clarity, and ethic of risk. Through an amalgamation of these three characteristics, Black women historically view "caring and mothering in [a] larger socio-historical [realm] . . .[and] in sharing knowledge we can also share power" (Beauboeuf-Lafontant 283). Likewise, journaling after pouring libations and paying homage to my ancestors helped me to make meaning out of the urge to connect with my students who were at the moment, all "at-risk."

My background in Africana womanism, coupled with journaling and self-reflection in the space of my spiritual practice, informed my teaching during the crisis in ways that sought to shelter my students by providing structure in the midst of adversity and preventing as much social and institutional failure as I could. In doing so, I resisted the entrapment of a mainstream, patriarchal, and disconnected notion of teaching and production—like the popular meme on the productivity of Isaac Newton and his development of calculus during the plague, which circulated social media during the onset of the pandemic and instead sought connectedness through digital dialogue with my students. Journaling, then, provided a sacred space, where I was able to remain attached: to my body, to the community, to the collective as opposed to fragmented, detached, and disconnected.

My concern was for the whole student not just for their academic wellbeing. I needed to convey to them in that moment, "I am not going to give up on you, I am not going to let you give up on yourself" (Dweck 203). Traditionally, caring in the Black family has been connected to what is happening in society by acknowledging struggles and sharing knowledge that gives the youth agency to resist oppression (Beauboeuf-Lafontant). In word and deed Black teachers express love for students by acknowledging the injustice that is happening around them while simultaneously manifesting the divinity within ourselves and honoring that same divinity in our students; acknowledging their strengths, their gifts, their talents, issues that are important to them. It seeks intimacy with and not aloofness to students, even though success is not guaranteed. Nevertheless, this kind of familial intimacy with students seeks to empower them, especially in times of struggle.

By the onset of the pandemic, nearly all of my students were feeling disenfranchised, uncertain, and traumatized. Overnight and without warning, their in-person classes ended abruptly and they were given three days to leave campus; to leave their independence, to leave their friends, to leave their dorm, to leave their student organizations, to leave their teammates, to leave their coaches, or to leave their host country. Those who returned home were now sharing spaces with their parents and siblings around the clock. They were sharing computers. Some became essential workers, taking on forty- to fifty-hour shifts in supermarkets to help out around the house. I had seventy-five eighteen-year-olds who were counting on me to not let them down and now I was challenged with maintaining connection and engagement virtually during a global pandemic. No problem.

Early on, it became apparent that some of my brightest students were struggling in this new online environment, as none of them had signed up for a distance learning experience. Likewise, my role as a writing instructor was intensifying literally overnight and I needed to make sure that any changes mid-semester were done in a student-centered manner with humanization and connection at the core. I had long adopted hooks's notion of engaged pedagogy and teaching to transgress by being authentic, present in the body, and encouraging students to move about the classroom creatively as well, but engaging students was proving to be challenging given our new circumstances. Everything went to a traditional online setting to immediately accommodate students who were now suddenly in different time zones or even countries. This meant that the social community we had spent ten weeks building was completely dismantled. As educators, we know that the social dimension of using our senses in a classroom and in our bodies are different once we shift to online learning. In face-to-face learning, both student and teacher are aware of audible and visual clues by each other. Online, students need to know that they are dealing with a human on the other end of cyberspace and this happens most often through digital dialog. For example, if students do not contribute to the discussion board, we have very little way of knowing if they have attended class or not and neither do the students.

I could sense students retreating behind the black boxes of our Zoom virtual classrooms, as most of them turned their cameras off. We began meeting live via Zoom a few days a week and I was offering office hours via that same platform, but most students had grown silent and stopped engaging. That's when I turned to email. I decided that first week that I would send virtual professor-pal messages to all seventy-five students. I personalized my notes and let my students know that I was thinking about them and their families. I wondered how they were doing—if they were well, mentally and physically, and if all of their needs were met. I didn't leave that up to administrators. I asked questions like, "How are you? How's your team doing? Are you able to work out? Can you get fresh air? Is the weather suitable?"

Being present meant more than checking to make sure they were discussing today's topic on the discussion board, it meant being fully present to their socio-historical experience, embodying the spirit of Africana womanism in a moment of crisis. As an "othermother" (hooks), I needed to know that my children were okay. I could not just act as if what was happening was normal and then say, "Okay kids, let's turn to page 35 of our textbooks and start chapter 2." None of us will ever be the same after this experience and I had to acknowledge where we were in the process. My "checking in" email was my proverbial, "You good, fam?" question acknowledging a familial bond, but not necessarily by blood, and one that asks, "how are you feeling in your soul?"

To my surprise, every one of my students wrote back to me and most commented on how much they appreciated the personal communication:

Student: I am doing as well as I could possibly be doing considering the circumstances. As a procrastinator at heart, online school would never be my first choice but I'm making do. I appreciate you reaching out!

I hope all is well with you. I know that I have been driving my parents crazy in our circumstantial house arrest, so I'm sending you all the vibes of patience and strength in this time when you have to focus on work as well as a child.

Thank you so much for reaching out! The effort you're making to make this "new normal" as smooth as possible is not lost on me.

Student: Hi Dr. Panton, hope all is well. At the moment, we're just working on articles for the orientation issue, nothing too fun :). I work at Publix too, and have been working 40-45 hour weeks with everything going on . . . *I appreciate you reaching out, not a lot of teachers have done that so it means a lot.* Stay safe and hopefully see you when we get back or next semester!

Student: Good Evening! . . .This transition is very tough, but I know that everyone is struggling. I'm hoping we get to come back to Nova one last time. Thank you so much for reaching out, it truly means a lot. I hope you are safe as well, and not too stressed with these course changes.

Student: Hello Professor Panton, I am doing well. Still trying to get everything together, unfortunately I have been a little behind. My job selected a few employees to continue to work throughout this pandemic, so I have been working nonstop. My family is doing well and are trying to take precautions. Thank you so much for checking up, I appreciate it. You are the only professor I have that has expressed concern.

My students' heartfelt responses informed my pedagogical practices moving forward. Collins explains that, "for Black women new knowledge claims are rarely worked out in isolation from other individuals and are usually developed through dialogues with other members of a community" (212). By reaching out to my students, my community, to inquire about their wholeness, I not only gained insight on their wellbeing, but also on their need for more compassion.

Despite my esoteric aspirations, however, I needed to grade. Journaling about it and receiving feedback from my students, however, helped me to move forward in a way that felt comfortable for me and fair for my students. I decided that I would take a compassionate approach to grading as well as in my rhetorical responses to their work. I could not be in my garden grounding myself through meditation and journaling and not pass on to my students the same comfort and nurturing I was seeking. Typically, I mark their papers on every page, highlight structural or grammatical patterns of error and attach a rubric that I fill in, commenting on critical thinking, content, organization, and language. All of a sudden, the usual feedback seemed like too much to dispense and too much for them to receive. I needed to grade but I focused on three holistic areas: The most effective area, the least effective area, and a suggestion in the form of a question. This approach made students aware of what was working, what needed improvement, and questions to consider for revision. I also began with encouragement:

> You're doing such a great job of staying focused through all of this, Javier! The most effective part of this report is your methods section, as well as your observation data in the results section.
>
> The least effective areas are the connections between international students and team camaraderie. Is there any secondary literature that could better connect the two ideas? Would it be better to discuss just camaraderie among team members?
>
> You got this. Fins up!

By not focusing on checking all of the boxes in my rubric, my hope was that this approach would lessen the overwhelm students were feeling and would engage them more in the process of their writing.

The goal of compassionate dialogic writing response pedagogy, as I understand it, is to help students feel less estranged from writing and to provide kind and helpful feedback. It also serves to allow the students to have voices and choices in their writing, instead of feeling silenced, judged and directed to write what the teacher wants. Compassionate Writing Response (CWR), then, aims to align itself with best practices of commentary in that comments are "Turn[ed into] conversation . . . do not take control of student's text . . . gives priority to global concerns . . . limits the scope of comments . . . gears comments to the individual student . . . and makes frequent use of praise." It also seeks to "establish relationships based on honesty and empathy that will eventually fulfill everyone's needs" (Macklin 5). In this way, CWR seeks to ask how we as teachers can help students learn instead of assuming that we already know. In our most recent moments of crisis, I had to admit to myself that I did not know what would be most helpful in the learning process of my students and I had to be willing to engage in dialogue with them to find out.

The Documentarian role of 4Cs 2020 facilitated critical self-reflection and meaningful connections with my students and my praxis. Documenting the onset of the pandemic through mindful journaling fostered stillness and grounding, in the midst of complete chaos, that tested my role as an Africana womanist practitioner and compelled me to consider the mental, physical, and spiritual wellbeing of my students more than ever at a crucial moment. It also allowed for sacred space to explore and elevate my existing spiritual and teaching practices to include a digital dialogic pedagogy that is congruent with the core ideals of connection and empowerment in Black women's liberatory pedagogies.

After the semester ended, I continued my journaling practice as it regarded my teaching and spent the entire summer creating an entirely new syllabus based on our current socio-historical circumstances and one that focuses on the processes of student writing rather than the production of student writing. This new course and syllabus on the rhetoric of health and wellness allows students the space to participate in low stakes mindful journaling and also facilitates documentation of the pandemic and the rhetoric of it as it is unfolding. My hope is to provide a nurturing environment where my students feel empowered through writing assignments and discourse that allow for mindfulness, compassion, and empathy in a world that desperately needs it right now.

WORKS CITED

Beauboeuf-Lafontant, Tamara. "A Womanist Experience of Caring: Understanding the Pedagogy of Exemplary Black Women Teachers." *The Womanist Reader,* edited by Layli Philips. Routledge, 2006, pp. 280–95.

Bishop, Scott R., et al. "Mindfulness: A Proposed Operational Definition: Science and Practice." *Clinical Psychology*, vol. 11, no. 3, 2004, pp. 230–41. *ProQuest,* https://doi.org/10.1093/clipsy.bph077.

Collins, Patricia Hill. *Black Feminist Thought: Knowledge, Consciousness, and the Politics of Empowerment*, 2ⁿᵈ ed. Routledge, 2000.

Dweck, Carol S. *Mindset: The New Psychology of Success.* United States, Random House Publishing Group, 2006.

Harris, Lakeesha J. "Healing Through (re)Membering and (re)Claiming Ancestral Knowledge about Black Witch Magic." *Black Women's Liberatory Pedagogies: Resistance, Transformation, and Healing Within and Beyond the Academy*, edited by Olivia N. Perlow, Durene I. Wheeler, Sharon L. Bethea, and BarBara M. Scott, 2018, pp. 245–63.

Hobart, Hi'ilei Julia Kawehipuaakahaopulani and Tamara Kneese "Radical Care: Survival Strategies for Uncertain Times." *Social Text*, 1 March 2020; vol. 38, no. 142, pp. 1–16. https://doi.org/10.1215/01642472-7971067.

hooks, b. *Teaching to Transgress: Education as the Practice of Freedom*. Routledge, 1994.

Macklin, Tialitha. "Compassionate Writing Response: Using Dialogic Feedback to Encourage Student Voice in the First-Year Composition Classroom." *Journal of Response to Writing*, vol. 2, no. 2, 2016, pp. 88–105

Mezirow, J., & Associates. *Learning as Transformation: Critical Perspectives on a Theory in Progress.* Jossey-Bass, 2000.

Miller, John P., and Aya Nozawa. "Meditating Teachers: a Qualitative Study" *Journal of In-Service Education*, vol. 28, no. 1, 2002, pp. 179–92, https://www.tandfonline.com/doi/abs/10.1080/13674580200200177.

van Gelder, Sarah. "The Radical Work of Healing: Fania and Angela Davis on a New Kind of Civil Rights Activism." *Yes!*, 18 Feb. 2016, https://www.yesmagazine.org/issues/life-after-oil/the-radical-work-of-healing-fania-and-angela-davis-on-a-new-kind-of-civil-rights-activism-20160218.

Walker, Alice. *In Search of Our Mothers' Gardens*. Harcourt Brace Jovanovich, 1983.

Wenger, Christy. *Yoga Minds, Writing Bodies: Contemplative Writing Pedagogy*. Parlor Press, 2015, dhttps://doi.org/10.37514/per-b.2015.0636

Afterword

"People Always Clap for the Wrong Things," Or, Labor, Time, and Writing Have Always Been a Feminist Issue

Holly Hassel

Recollections from an Uncommon Time: 4C20 Documentarian Tales is both history and present, both a snapshot of the field in a moment of crisis, and the start of a larger experiment.[1] As the contributors of this volume illustrate richly, individual experiences of the pandemic—even within the relatively privileged class of academic workers—varied greatly, and the stories that are told in this collection illustrate both the mundane and traumatic experiences of colleagues who participated. I read these pieces alongside each other and feel their

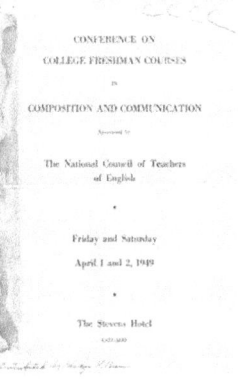

grief, anxiety, self-flagellation, and anger. I also read renewed commitments to work, to self-care, to family, and to gratitude.

What else stands out to me as the program chair of CCCC 2021—in which Julie Lindquist and I collaborated to continue the Documentarian feature—is how the intersections of labor, time, and writing have always been a feminist issue. The 2020 COVID-19 global pandemic revealed, more than other events in recent history, how the inequitable resource of time, and how the inequitably distributed value attached to labor, is raced, classed, abled, and gendered. Broadly, the *New York Times* reported as early as April 2020 that "One in three jobs held by women has been designated as essential, according to a

---

1   The line "People always clap for the wrong things" is from *The Catcher in the Rye* and was the title of my MA thesis, an application of existentialist philosophy to the novel. As I started to sketch out this essay, somehow I seemed to be drawn back to it as I read and reread the Documentarian tales, and as the process of conference planning unfolded, folded, and refolded again.

New York Times analysis of census data crossed with the federal government's essential worker guidelines. Nonwhite women are more likely to be doing essential jobs than anyone else" (Robertson and Gebeloff). I do not think that the academy is exempt from this inequity.

I think about the question asked in the introduction to this collection: "What *is* a conference experience?" (10). And I also ask, "what *is* a conference?" and I also ask "What and who is a conference for?" These questions undergird the experiences of academics and of writing teachers (specifically) and are essential to take up. The radical reimagining of our daily lives and how we do our jobs called for by the CO-VID-19 pandemic has given us the opportunity to think about and rethink about the answers to these questions.

Though Documentarians were not exclusively in non-presenter roles (many concurrently were)—Documentarians have a role on the program regardless of whether they have a presenter role-—it invites me to ask questions about how the Documentarian role is a feminist act, because it forces us to confront labor and time. Who, in a conference program and space, gets to write? Who gets to speak? Who talks and who is listened to? Who, with time and space in their academic employment, gets to spend time writing their own thoughts, making their own arguments, participating in a scholarly conversation, and who spends their time most days responding to the writing of others and meeting the needs of first-year students and their writing or supporting graduate teaching assistants, contingent faculty, and teachers of all employment statuses to do their work. Such tasks were enormously intensified in the pandemic, as Heather McGovern documents in Chapter 13, and as Miriam Moore's student's material reality illustrates in Chapter 8, responding to Moore's call to "spend some time thinking about the assigned reading and what it means for the way they viewed the world." "When? I mean . . . when? I have three kids and a husband and a job. I've love to sit and think about all this—but I have a life," said the exasperated student. Reflection and self-care are luxuries for the teachers and students whose time is not exclusively taken up by reading, writing, and reflection. I think about Seth Kahn's July 2020 *College English* article, in which he writes: "As long as faculty continue to proclaim to decision-makers that some kinds of teaching are less valuable than others, or than research, we can't be surprised when those decision-makers decide to mistreat faculty who teach—especially those who teach primarily lower-division general education courses" (592).

Likewise, if a conference is just about sharing research, then the vast majority of those who work *in the field of composition and rhetoric* (whose primary responsibility is teaching and supporting others' writing, of supporting the literacy development of new college students, of maintaining the curricular foundation of most English departments and independent writing programs that underwrite and subsidizes majors and graduate degrees)—do not get to be part of what conferences do. If we attached the same value to conferencing as we do to the field writ large, if conferencing is showing up and sharing your writing, your arguments, your research (which, in the system of rewards that values lines on CVs, impact factor, and prestige, can be one of the primary motivators for conference participation) then we are excluding most people in the field from the professional benefits of the annual convening of this organization.

The November 2019 position statement, "CCCC Statement of Professional Guidance for Mentoring Graduate Students," makes similar calls: "make academic practice and conventions accessible," and "validate and help students prepare for diverse careers," admonishing that

> . . . mentors should not invoke or imply damaging and unrealistic myths about what success on the (academic) job market must look like (e.g., that only R1 academic positions are desirable, that a national academic job search is the only way to secure satisfactory employment). Instead, faculty should work with graduate students to imagine myriad post degree options and follow students' leads on working to meet their goals.

The CCCC as an organization and in its publication continues to "call for" these ideological and attitude shifts—and yet its practices continue unchanged.

I think about Holly Larsen's award-winning article, "Epistemic Authority in Two-Year Colleges" published in *Teaching English in the Two-Year College* in 2019, where she continues the scholarly conversation initiated by two-year college teacher-scholars like Mark Reynolds, Howard Tinberg, Jeff Andelora, and others. Larson asks

> why aren't two-year English faculty writing and publishing to move the theoretical gaze onto our institutions, our students, our challenges? Should the burden be upon the shoulders of community college professors to discipline our teaching experiences into

theory if we are to become equal knowledge makers and contribute to the discipline of composition studies? (118-19)

If two-year college teachers are representative of the "teaching-intensive" faculty members, as I would argue they are, I think there is a clear line between the marginalization of lore, of practice, of teaching as ultimately a different kind of intellectual activity from research and theory, one that alienates those who write for publication and professional peers and those who read the writing of others, whether students or scholars.

I think about the TYCA Workload Working Papers and report, which, as TYCA Working Paper #5: Two-Year College English Faculty Professional Development Workload (2020) reports,

> Likewise, the workloads faculty shouldered—teaching loads, the particular labor demands of teaching composition, and service obligations—often left little time or energy for professional development, especially when faculty were expected to pursue it on their own time (and sometimes on their own dime)" (8).

Every time I see colleagues or strangers documenting their writing progress on social media ("wrote this many words today!" "Sitting down to write now!"), I think about what a luxury that is for most instructors of writing in the modern academic economy.

I'm writing right now, today, in a late-stage pandemic, because my husband took my two kids—both in virtual school—out of state for nine days, even though I currently work in a position that is structured with equal parts teaching and research. Writing this afterword has been on my to-do list for eight months. For most faculty in teaching-intensive positions whether they are contingent or tenure-track, it is normal not to think about one's *own* writing—but we think about the writing of others all the time, and they are also academics.

The Documentarian role means that *participating* is also *listening*. It is *paying attention* as much as expecting others to listen to you. It's absolutely unsurprising when I look at the demographics that Lindquist, Straayer, and Halbritter account for in the Introduction to this collection, whether gender, race, or employment status. It suggests something about who is expected to listen, and who expects that their voice will be centered by others. Serving as a Documentarian is a structured opportunity to observe and reflect, and to have that observation and reflection-informed text be valued (at least in this moment and in this collection) as a form of knowledge. As Xiao Tan writes in Chapter 3:

> I had never felt that what I do was lifesaving or game-changing. Not being able to see the immediate impact made me question how useful and worthy my work really is. But the Documentarian project gave me a new perspective of looking at my role in the world. As I may continue to feel vulnerable as a foreigner and racial minority, I can now scoop up the courage to think about what makes me scared in the first place, apart from the disease itself. I am also in a better position to voice my concerns and complaints and to expect that, together, we could right the wrongs.

What my hope is for the Documentarian role in 2020, 2021, and hopefully beyond, is that we create a space not for just those who participate in a certain way, centered and spotlighted. In the Documentarian role, we create a new opportunity for whose experiences can become centered in an online and print publication with NCTE's SWR series, but it could also signal that this is a new and valuable way of "participating in the conversation." That paying attention to what's going on, and then describing that phenomenon, is both a useful labor for Documentarians, but also a valuable activity in and of itself for knowledge production—what do we know about what we do?

In this way, the Documentarian Tales are also a fantastically useful data source for CCCC leaders to know more about what the convention offers its participants. Maybe it's doing exactly what it should, *but maybe it is not*. In the last year of collaborative conference planning 2020 program chair Julie Lindquist, she and I have had to think about how to do this important part of the organization's exclusively virtually, including the planning for a conference with an uncertain 2021 future, one that has to account for a year that just disappeared from the history of the CCCC convention, held annually since 1949. Initially, the Documentarian role launched for the 2020 conference followed the conference's call to "Consider our Commonplaces"—as a term, "commonplace" hasn't always been legible to general readers, and for me, I think about it as "something we take for granted"—some core elements of our practice that we just don't even question. What I loved from first reading about Julie's vision for the role was that it did exactly that—a commonplace about conferences is that they are a) in a place, b) where people go, c) to share their work.

And yet, all of these have been turned upside down, in ways that I think are needed. For example, going "to a place" has *always* been highly inaccessible for many CCCC members/academic workers: graduate students, contingent faculty, and independent scholars who have minimal or no academic funding; academics from under-resourced institutions like two-year colleges and some HBCUs and tribal colleges; disabled colleagues with needs that make travel uncomfortable, exhausting, or nearly impossible; parents of children at nearly any age whose care must be considered; caregivers of any other loved one who simply cannot be abandoned for four days to the care of others.

The Documentarian work of 2021 will, I hope, help us do even more to learn more about not just what *was* and wasn't in 2020, but about what a virtual convening will mean, do, and offer to attendees. Most of us expect that, somehow, we might return to "normal" and not the "new normal"—but what might we learn from the ways educators participate in Virtual 2021? Sessions are shorter, presentations tighter: recorded sessions means that the conference can be viewed, revisited and reabsorbed, and that attendees can (for once) go to multiple sessions in the same session block—even if it's not synchronously. What will this mean for a kind of *durability* of the conference, so different from the co-located conference model in which you're either able to be THERE doing THAT or not. As Shelagh Patterson writes:

> As a full-time contingent instructor of first-year writing, life hasn't changed much. If anything, not having to go to campus and teach classes makes life easier. The classroom is my joy, but it also takes a lot of energy and coupled with the work of reading and commenting on essays, I am often exhausted by evening. Without spending energy in the classroom, I feel rested, but my time hasn't changed. I just have more of it: to spend reading, commenting on, and grading student essays. It's not comforting to realize that the demands on full-time contingent faculty require us to live lives of social isolation. (ch. 19)

What would it mean to make space for—virtual or otherwise—the work of instructors whose primary activity is talking with, writing with, and reading work by the first-year student writers whose labor props up the entire field of writing and rhetoric. I'm interested in using and building change on the insights gained from the 2021 Documentarians whose insights have already made the material realities of writing teachers visible through their reflective tales.

And my hope, moving into the role of chair of CCCC, the organization, in the coming year, is that these Documentarian Tales (2020 and 2021) can become an additional kind of resource, a data source collected to tell us something about what IS at the conference—in the past, most ephemeral moments of professional activity have not had the same durability, except to the extent that new collegiate relationships formed were continued, or conference feedback turned into publication. What will this mean for how we make and use the knowledge shared at the conference? What will it mean that the accounts themselves become published knowledge? Maybe it will make room for a different kind of work activity, as Hanson notes: "[w]ork couldn't heal my pain, but reflection and changing my perspective could" (ch. 6). Nobody wants to change work into self-care, but maybe more of work—more kinds of writing—could be nourishing, valuable, reflective, and descriptive. Or as Cheryl Price-McKell asks in Chapter 9, "Can we draw insight, empathy, and knowledge from recognizing and inviting nonacademic identities into our work without apology or rationale?" Or as Rachel Panton writes, in Chapter 21:

> During a period of crisis, this new role, and the circumstances surrounding it, elevated my consciousness on student needs and my attention to their cognitive processes. It also grounded me in unexpected ways and allowed me to be a keener observer. These observations rooted me in the work of sacred writing and allowed me to engage in digital dialogic compassionate writing responses, both in my rhetorical responses to student writing and in personal written correspondence with them.

In other words, maybe the practice of listening to ourselves and to others—instead of talking at them—will cultivate attention to what we all know are a set of messed up values about labor—the activities we reward, the institutional values that are granted merit, status and resources; and what we are encouraged to spend our time on in order to be perceived as "part of" CCCC (it ain't teaching and service).

My hope is that—even as Virtual CCCC 2021 will be "less than" for those who are attached to the traditions of going to a place at a specific time—there will be something of a liberating function—that being at a place some time and then returning to review what you couldn't see in the moment will help us learn something about how to meet the professional needs of a broader group of literacy professionals in the field. The 2021 Documentarian Tales will be one part of helping us move forward as an organization toward a sustainable future.

WORKS CITED

Andelora, Jeff. "The Teacher/Scholar: Reconstructing Our Professional Identity in Two-Year Colleges." *Teaching English in the Two-Year College*, vol. 32, no. 3, Mar. 2005, pp. 307–22.

Conference on College Composition and Communication. "CCCC Statement of Professional Guidance for Mentoring Graduate Students." November 2019. https://cccc.ncte.org/cccc/resources/positions/professional-guidance-for-mentoring-graduate-students/.

---. "Program: First Conference." https://www.archives.library.illinois.edu/ncte/about/april.php.

Kahn, Seth. "We Value Teaching Too Much to Keep Devaluing It." *College English*, vol. 82, no. 6, July 2020, pp. 592–611.

Larsen, Holly. "Epistemic Authority in Composition Studies: Tenuous Relationship between Two-Year English Faculty and Knowledge Production." *Teaching English in the Two-Year College*, vol. 46, no. 2, Dec. 2018, pp. 109–36.

Robertson, Campbell, and Robert Gebeloff. "How Millions of Women Became the Most Essential Workers in America." *New York Times*. 18 April 2020. https://www.nytimes.com/2020/04/18/us/coronavirus-women-essential-workers.html.

Sullivan, Patrick M., and Christie Toth, eds. *Teaching Composition at the Two-Year College: Background Readings*. Bedford/St. Martin's, 2017

Suh, Emily, Lizbett Tinoco, and Christie Toth. "TYCA Working Paper #5: Two-Year College English Faculty Professional Development Workload." TYCA. https://ncte.org/wp-content/uploads/2020/11/TYCA_Working_Paper_5.pdf. November 2020.

Tinberg, Howard. "Community College Teachers as Border Crossers." *Teaching Composition at the Two-Year College: Background Readings*, edited by Patrick Sullivan and Christine Toth, Bedford/St. Martin's, 2017, pp. 334–41.

Afterword

Moments and Reflections from WPA Scholars on Race

Staci M. Perryman-Clark and Collin Lamont Craig

Recollections from an Uncommon Time: 4C20 Documentarian Tales is a window into a historical moment of human precarity, unforeseeable disruptions to everyday life, and concentrated efforts to make sense of how the realities of a pandemic disrupt our concepts of time, work, and community. As readers of this collection, we learned how colleagues managed the vicissitudes of the pandemic, wrestled with existential dread, and modified their everyday movements while feeling interrupted. We learned how they assessed and mitigated risks, said goodbye to students, left their offices with no clear date to return, scrambled to make plans for self care, and rethought what was essential to their identities and practices as teachers. We found their recollections echoing our own experiences as we ourselves came to terms with the pandemic as teachers and academics.

The CCCC Convention has been a common place for us as long-time collaborators, Black teacher-scholars committed to doing race work, and as narrators who have situated our stories within the broader context of scholarship on critical race studies and writing program administration. The conference as both a moment and a practice of professional development is part of that broader context. In fact, while writing this afterword, we also realized that our individual and shared conference experiences could be characterized as autoethnographic investigations of how race matters experientially, ideologically and theoretically in our field. In our first collaboration, "Troubling the Boundaries: (De)Constructing WPA Identities at the Intersections of Race and Gender," we too explored the questions that similarly serve as the impetus for this collection, but through a racial lens. Our questions read something like this: What is a conference to a Black scholar in the field? How do I respond to racist antagonism to Black scholarship at a conference? Why is a predominately white conference viable for me to attend as a Black scholar doing race work? When we documented our own conference accounts, we shared revealing stories about racial and gender microaggressions we experienced as graduate students while training to do WPA work. We wrote about how this work resonated as an embodied experience and shared it with colleagues at a CCCC's affiliated conference. Our storytelling was our space for sense making. It was our method for seeking answers to these questions as we would come to understand conferences as a rhetorical production of our discipline, as well as performative sites where we learned how to perform disciplinary identities. Sharing these stories was not void of risk. At the time of publication, neither of us were tenured and we were very early in our careers.

When the time came to contribute to *WPA: Writing Program Administration's* special symposium on whiteness and race studies, we courageously took on another opportunity to share new revelations about racial microaggressions after moving into tenure track positions ("Boundaries Revisited"). But given the limited amount of space of the symposium, we knew we needed to tackle racial issues in relation to WPA with a larger book project. Hence, *Black Perspectives in Writing Program Administration: From the Margins to the Center* was born.

In our first chapter, we reflected on the larger sociopolitical space in which we were "documenting" and situating our work. Like several contributors to *Recollections from an Uncommon Time: 4C20 Documentarian Tales*, we reflected on the very space and moments of composing our first chapter. At the time, we noted "the news of Castile's killing appeared in the media at the very moment when we were drafting this book chapter! Given these current events, there couldn't be a more kairotic moment to consider how they inform the rhetorical situation of Blackness in twenty-first century higher education" (2). Similarly, several contributors to *Recollections* reflect on the mass murderings of Black citizens and the political unrest surrounding the COVID-19 pandemic. As we said in our symposium contribution to whiteness studies, "the more things change, they still the same" ("Boundaries Revisited").

But things aren't the same. Perhaps things will never be the same. While themes identified in *Recollections* like aspirations, access, home, family, labor, and community identity certainly existed when reflecting on academic work pre-COVID-19 pandemic, and while these themes are often documented through stories, and in particular, "stor[ies] of diversity" (Introduction), it is critical that our field not only considers these stories as they document particular moments in time, as often grounded in broader sociopolitical contexts, but also, and more importantly, as a field, we must begin using our expertise in the method of "documentation," so that the stories we reveal and document, become some of the best models for higher education to adopt as it reaches disciplines and fields much broader than and different from our own. If there was ever a field to become the leading voice of what documentation should look like, it's definitely our own.

While every contribution to this collection reveals many common themes about academic life and work/life balances, for us, *Recollections* identified a few additional themes for how we as a field move forward with our disciplinary and scholarly lives in higher education post-COVID-19. For us, we need to reexamine themes of globalism and transnationalism, particularly in the ways in which they affect members of our scholarly and professional communities. If CCCC is indeed the largest organization dedicated to the teaching of postsecondary writing in the world, we can no longer treat globalization as an afterthought, not only during a pandemic, but also post-pandemic.

The documented accounts of student life in *Recollections* also call for us as a field to interrogate how we center student grit as a prime social and psychological variable to investigate when making sense of how students sustain their academic interests and successfully achieve their academic goals. Grit is a fairly new concept of study by education theorists that has been used to identify one of the many predictors that impact student learning and academic achievement. Within the context of writing studies, investigating grit translates into how we come to understand ways students maintain the rights to their own language in the face of white language supremacist pedagogies. It translates into how student writers maintain and affirm their preexisting and multiply literate identities while being asked to adopt the language of the university. It is reflected in how they persist in completing complex writing projects while physically removed from vital learning communities, holed up in their bedrooms, sheltering in place and waiting for a signal to return to their normal lives. And let's be real, grit is often used as a variable to measure the academic success of students from low income and underrepresented minority groups (Duckworth 2016, Kundu 2020). Instead of naming and focusing on the specific identity groups that we seek to address, "grit" becomes a coded term that scapegoats inequity and replaces its focus with merit and hardwork.

Recollections reflects the lived experiences of students finding ways to maintain focus, manage major adjustments to their learning environments, and persisting through a pandemic. These are students who navigate splotchy internet connections while distance learning from home, some are essential workers at their local grocery stores who courageously maintain their jobs, others are using technologically savvy ways to stay connected to their support systems. And what of their writing lives? They reorient themselves to new and foreign writing situations. They form group chats and study groups on Whatsapp and text peers in their writing courses to finalize plans for peer reviewing writing drafts. They write pandemic narratives that connect in-school literacies with their out-of-school literacies.

In our own pandemic experiences as teachers and administrators, students sought us out for help with a range of challenges unrelated to our class curriculum: from history projects students were completing in other classes when they failed to chase down the elusive professor for guidance; or for career advice when their overworked academic advisor seemingly resigned to leave their student advisees to fend for themselves. These students leveraged their grit when their institutions failed them. But what we see in these *Recollections* is a counter narrative of necessary adjustments and revised pedagogies in a critical moment of crisis: culturally and contextually relevant teaching approaches, writing teachers building spaces for classroom dialog for students to decompress and speak about nonacademic topics, offered information about COVID-19 related campus resources, personal phone calls to disappearing students from a concerned professor—all empathetic and humanizing teaching practices. And choosing empathy and humanity was just that: a choice. For some, it challenged us to make hard choices about how we teach writing in our courses, how we show up for our students, how we empathize with their lived experiences, and if we could choose their humanity over our rigid, inflexible teaching philosophies. Perhaps the rhetoric of the pandemic created a mirror by which we were asked to drastically look at ourselves as writing teachers, and to search and find humanity in our own teaching practices—to quickly come to terms with the reality that a humanizing pedagogical practice could be a matter of life and death for our students. What we experience in *Recollections* is a repertoire of situated literacy practices for this historical moment: locating and reading information for financial aid relief, using the right search terms while browsing the internet to find food pantries, following instructions for accessing Zoom rooms, learning how to craft the right email to non-responsive teachers, learning the measures for social distancing and how to properly wear a mask, or where to locate Wi-Fi hotspots in the city if you didn't have reliable internet at home.

More critically, what the pandemic taught us if you failed at learning these literacies while Black, Brown, or Native is that the inevitabilities of death and dying are higher. When reading across these documented recollections, we realized the necessary work of protecting student grit. We realized that writing teachers can and must build learning environments that foster students' collective agency. And this means creating a range of contingency strategies for classroom engagement, learning new technologies, performing innovative, and flexible pedagogies that are sensitive, affirming and inviting to students' lived experiences. It means expanding literacies that reach beyond the boundaries of writing assignments and classroom practices and leans into the contours and conditions of students' everyday lives. It means leveraging our institutional networks and community resources as gatekeepers, mentors, "othermothers" (Panton, Chapter 21) and department chairs in order to build learning environments that bridge out-of-school and in-school literacies.

Recollections reminds us that creating and expanding opportunities that contribute to academic success is a viable approach for cultivating the agency that students would need to adapt to the rhetorical situation of the pandemic. So this is our point: perhaps we might use these "recollections" as rubrics for theorizing how we can protect student grit. Perhaps we should more actively interrogate ways that we ask students to exploit their grit when they face structural, institutional, or existential challenges. How might we shift the gaze away from student grit and shift our focus towards cultivating and fortifying the structural elements that foster students' collective agency? We must materialize equitable, social justice oriented supportive systems within our writing classroom, departments, and discipline that allow our students to achieve the collective agency to claim their rights to their own language, to center and leverage their non-normative literacies in the writing classroom, and to affirm their stories and counter stories as viable sites of knowledge making and theory building.

Another theme this collection takes up is the concept of professional and faculty development, a topic that is also near and dear to our hearts as WPA scholars and faculty developers. This collection reveals that it's time that we start equipping our discipline and institutions with sufficient professional development, not only as it pertains to teaching, learning, and writing pedagogy. We also need to develop stronger faculty development programs that help us navigate healthy professional lives, working conditions, and working relationships. As scholars trained in humanist fields, we need to affirm scholarship to provide us with opportunities to remain fully human: to celebrate victories however large or small, and to confront challenges, failures and grief without guilt. Many of the stories in this collection afford us with such an opportunity: It is a gift we need to receive and keep.

Recollections from an Uncommon Time: 4C20 Documentarian Tales calls for us to revisit our teaching philosophies, to identify the gaps, and ask new pedagogical questions. It asks for us to interrogate how and where we have been limited in our imaginations in how we build and sustain writing communities and write in community. Perhaps this is a moment where we reimagine the viability of our pedagogies, our writing departments, our conferences, our office hours, our race and equity task forces, our academic journals, our theories, and our field missions to "cultivate interdependence and collective responsibility, interrelationality, resistance, antiracism, care, mutuality, and healing," especially for the sake of our students (Albracht ch. 7)—especially in a historical moment when our democratic processes, voting rights, and race-based curriculums are under siege by conservative political projects. Rachel Panton's meditations on an Africana womanist pedagogical outlook on care in the classroom calls for us to center engaged pedagogy as a viable approach for ways of seeing our students, "what they might be waking up to, what thoughts and scenes they might encounter" (ch. 21) and how we might acknowledge their pandemic related circumstances as intricately connected to their well-being, not just as individual humans enduring an unprecedented challenge, but as fully embodied learners.

Finally, this collection provides us with the opportunity to identify professional development opportunities for leadership development. As WPAs and academic leaders, we need to identify and apply organizational strategies that confront crisis management, decision making, and risk management. This collection offers one of the firmest reminders that how we handle crises and decisions can have life and death consequences. Our field needs to look carefully at public-facing documents to ensure that we live up to the values by which we purport to live. We need to think more critically about how we communicate and document decisions beyond the typical institutional lip service and damage control rhetorical strategies by which institutional public relations spokespersons are skillfully trained. Again, this collection offers us a model for how we connect with readers, how we document with accuracy, and how we become transparent. In short, this collection needs to be reading material not only for our field, but more importantly, for higher education more broadly, including its academic leaders. As readers, we have connected strongly with this collection, and look forward to unpacking its broader impact on how we navigate "uncommon times" in the future.

WORKS CITED

Albracht, Lindsey. "On Choosing." *Recollections from an Uncommon Time: 4C20 Documentarian Tales*, edited by Julie Lindquist, Bree Straayer, and Bump Halbritter, NCTE/CCCC Studies in Writing and Rhetoric 2022, ch. 7.

Craig, Collin Lamont, and Staci M. Perryman-Clark. "Troubling the Boundaries Revisited: The More Things Change the More They Still the Same." *WPA: Writing Program Administration*, vol. 39, no. 2, 2016, pp. 20–26.

---. "Troubling the Boundaries: (De)Constructing WPA Identities at the Intersections of Race and Gender." *WPA: Writing Program Administration*, vol. 34, no. 2, 2011, pp. 37–58.

Duckworth, Angela. *Grit: The Power of Passion and Perseverance*. Collins, 2016.

Kundu, Anindya. *The Power of Student Agency: Looking Beyond Grit to Close the Opportunity Gap*. Teachers College P, 2020.

Lindquist, Julie, Bree Straayer, and Bump Halbritter, editors. *Recollections from an Uncommon Time: 4C20 Documentarian Tales*. NCTE/SWR Series, 2022.

---. "Introduction." *Recollections from an Uncommon Time: 4C20 Documentarian Tales*, edited by Julie Lindquist, Bree Straayer, and Bump Halbritter, NCTE/CCCC Studies in Writing and Rhetoric, 2022.

Panton, Rachel. "'You Good, Fam'?': Mindful Journaling, Africana Leadership, and Dialogic Compassionate Rhetorical Response Pedagogy during a Pandemic." *Recollections from an Uncommon Time: 4C20 Documentarian Tales*, edited by Julie Lindquist, Bree Straayer, and Bump Halbritter, NCTE/CCCC Studies in Writing and Rhetoric 2022, ch. 21.

Perryman-Clark, Staci M., and Collin Lamont Craig, editors. *Black Perspectives in Writing Program Administration: From the Margins to the Center*. National Council of Teachers of English, 2019.

Editors

Julie Lindquist is Professor of Rhetoric and Writing and Director of First-Year Writing at Michigan State University. At MSU, she has taught courses in first-year and professional writing, and graduate courses in cultural rhetoric, research methods, and pedagogy. She is author of *A Place to Stand: Politics and Persuasion in a Working-Class Bar* (Oxford) and, with David Seitz, *Elements of Literacy* (Pearson). Her writings on rhetoric, class, literacy,  and writing pedagogy have appeared in *College Composition and Communication, College English, JAC,* and *Pedagogy*, as well as in edited collections, including *Keywords in Writing Studies*. She has coauthored several articles on literacy research, writing pedagogy, and reflective learning with Bump Halbritter, her colleague at MSU. Her article, coauthored with Bump ("Time, Lives, and Videotape: Operationalizing Discovery in Scenes of Literacy Sponsorship,"), received the Richard Ohmann Award for Outstanding Article in *College English* in 2013. Julie was elected in 2018 to serve as Assistant Chair for the Conference on College Composition and Communication, and as Program Chair for the 2020 Convention in Milwaukee, WI; she currently serves as the Immediate Past Chair of CCCC.

Bree Straayer graduated in 2020 with her PhD in Rhetoric and Writing with a Cultural Rhetorics Emphasis and a Specialization in Women and Gender. Her dissertation, *Once I Believed: Critical Thinking and the Process of Change* focuses on the intersections of religion, sexuality, and education. Bree has also conducted research on language acquisition and writing program administration. Her research on international student

experience is included in a collection which came out in January 2022 entitled *International Students' Multilingual Literacy Practices*. Bree works in the non-profit sector with English language and adult basic education learners as a Family Literacy Program Director at The Literacy Center of West Michigan.

Bump Halbritter is Associate Professor of Rhetoric and Writing and former Director of First-Year Writing (FYW) at Michigan State University. His research attends to teaching and learning in FYW and to the integration of audio-visual writing into scenes of college writing and scholarly research and production. Bump's long-term collaboration with Julie Lindquist has yielded many articles and chapters, including their 2013 article, "Time, Lives, and Videotape: Operationalizing Discovery in Scenes of Literacy Sponsorship," which received The Richard Ohmann Award for Outstanding Article in *College English*. Bump's book, *Mics, Cameras, Symbolic Action: Audio-Visual Rhetoric for Writing Teachers*, received the *Computers and Composition* Distinguished Book Award for 2013. Bump has served on the CCCC Executive Committee and many CCCC working groups.

BOOKS IN THE CCCC STUDIES IN WRITING & RHETORIC SERIES

This book was typeset in Garamond and Frutiger by Mike Palmquist. Typefaces used on the cover include Garamond and News Gothic.